NEW ORLEANS JAZZ

AL ROSE AND EDMOND SOUCHON

NEW ORLEANS JAZZ

A FAMILY ALBUM

THIRD EDITION, REVISED AND ENLARGED

LOUISIANA STATE UNIVERSITY PRESS

BATON ROUGE AND LONDON

Library of Congress Cataloging in Publication Data

Rose, Al.
New Orleans jazz.

Includes index.
1. Jazz musicians—Louisiana—New Orleans—Portraits.
I. Souchon, Edmond. II. Title.
ML3508.R67 1984   785.42'09763'35   84-5721
ISBN 0-8071-1158-9
ISBN 0-8071-1173-2 (pbk.)

Louisiana Paperback Edition, 1984
93 92   5 4 3

CONTENTS

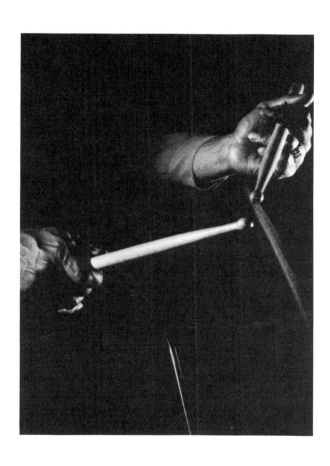

ABBREVIATIONS

acc	accordion		pc	piccolo
ah	alto horn		s	saxophone
as	alto saxophone		sb	string bass
b	string bass, tuba		sn	snare drum
bd	bass drum		sou	sousaphone
bh	baritone horn		ss	soprano saxophone
bjo	banjo		t	trumpet
c	cornet		tar	tarapatch
cl	clarinet		tb	trombone
d	drums		ts	tenor saxophone
eu	euphonium		tu	tuba
f	flute		u	ukulele
fh	french horn		v	violin
g	guitar		vo	vocal
har	harmonica		vt	valve trombone
l	leader		w	washboard
mdl	mandolin		x	xylophone
mel	mellophone, pfleugelhorn		z	zither
p	piano			

PREFACE

The authors of this work do not intend that it should be a history of New Orleans jazz, though history pops from every page. Rather do we look upon it as a kind of deluxe family album of pictures of which it has been our good fortune to be the custodians. Many of the photographs herein, approximately four-fifths we estimate, have never before been published. Others have been offered to the public in volumes so poorly produced that most of their detail succumbed to cheap paper and slipshod press work.

Unfortunately, many of the photographs were taken in early times by people not in the photographic business. Mathew Brady, so far as is known, never turned his lens to the subject. Some of the shots are mere scraps luckily rescued either by design or accident. Some are scalloped by flame, others rent in anger, water-soaked, or otherwise mutilated. For these we make no apology but, rather, acknowledge our pride in being able to bring them to you at all.

In any work of this nature, selectivity is a factor, and the basis for our choices should be made clear without going into the theoretical aspects of jazz analysis. We do not scorn theory but do feel that a picture book is no place for it. Both of the authors have long since rejected the myth of the evolution of jazz from its so-called primitive or archaic form to what contemporary critics call modern or progressive. Hence, individuals like the late Lester Young (his experience in the King Oliver orchestra notwithstanding) and the ebullient Sam Butera, we consider, without discussing their musical merit, to be outside the scope of a book on New Orleans jazz, though both were born in the Crescent City. Likewise, the authors feel that such phenomena as rock-and-roll and what

is called, in the commercial record field, rhythm and blues, while they have descended from jazz sources, at least in part, are so degenerate as to be of no interest to enthusiasts of legitimate jazz as an art form. Thus, data on many popular New Orleans personalities such as Fats Domino and the teenage idol Jimmy Clanton have no place between these covers.

Suffice it to say that the authors, disagreeing on many things between themselves, agree nevertheless that to be jazz, music must (a) be improvised, (b) be played in 2/4 or 4/4 time, and (c) retain a clearly definable melodic line. All the hundreds of musicians whose names and pictures appear in these pages have at one time or another played jazz music as we define it.

We are happy to observe that a great many of them are still among us and that a reasonable number of younger men are represented who are playing in the jazz idiom.

Foremost among our allies has been the indefatigable Bill Russell who has freely supplied rare photographs and detailed information. Such collectors as John Steiner of Chicago, Sinclair Traill of England, Hugues Panassie of France, Duncan Schiedt of Indianapolis, George Hoefer of New York, Myra Menville, Joe Mares, Harry Souchon, and Barbara Glancey Reid of New Orleans all have contributed heavily. The magazine *Eureka* has supplied gems from its own files. Allen and Sandra Jaffe, besides providing many of the splendid portraits from their Preservation Hall publicity box, also gave us a headquarters in which to interview hundreds of musicians over a period of many months. Countless jazzmen helped identify the personnels of the group photographs, but special appreciation must be acknowledged for the aid given by Dave Winstein, president of local 174, American Federation of

Musicians, Paul Barbarin, Creole George Guesnon, Papa John Joseph, Alvin Alcorn, Harry Shields, Louis Cottrell, Jr., president of Musicians Protective Union No. 496, Papa Jack Laine, Monk Hazel, Joe Capraro.

We are pleased to acknowledge the aid received from the Tulane University Jazz Archive and its research staff, especially Richard B. Allen and Paul Crawford.

The work of many superb photographers is represented herein. Unfortunately, in many cases we don't know whose picture is whose, but for the record, may we express our thanks to John Kuhlman, Ray Cresson, Jules L. Cahn, Carey J. Tate, Dan Leyrer, Mary Mitchell, George Fletcher, Grauman Marks, Florence Mars, John Reid, and Ronnie Soderberg. The files of the New Orleans Jazz Museum are well represented here.

Important and unclassifiable help was rendered by Larry Borenstein of New Orleans and by Pancho Carner of Philadelphia.

We will not attempt to establish finally who was the inventor of jazz. (Some of our best friends have claimed this distinction.) Nor will we assert that we know who were the first to play it. We feel that it was not invented at all, but that it came into being so gradually that any attempt to pin down a first time would be based on the most specious type of reasoning. Credit for the creation of jazz is due no individual man or race. If anything, it is a product, an inevitable product we think, of the avenues and alleys of a unique city—polyglot, multiracial, seething with love and conflict, a battleground of nations and cultures, a landscape of mire and magnolias.

The evidence of these photographs—their very existence—demonstrates the extent to which New Orleans was permeated with this music and, to a great extent, how it brought this music about.

Naturally, in an undertaking of this size, we have solicited the support of our talented friends who have generously helped to fill the gaps in our collections and scholarship. There are so many of these friends that we take for granted we must miss crediting some of them.

PREFACE TO THE SECOND EDITION

Not long after *A Family Album* was published in late 1967, it became apparent that a revision would be needed. My collaborator, the late Dr. Edmond Souchon, would have enjoyed sharing the task; but I am happy that he lived long enough to see the first edition in print and to sit with me on the dais when we received the Louisiana Library Association's Literary Award for that year.

In the original text, I have corrected errors, mostly dates, and a few names. Several pictures have been replaced by better or more accurate ones. Unhappily, the most numerous additions have been the obituary dates of over a hundred jazzmen who have died since the original publication of *A Family Album.* Our celebrated brass bands have been playing "Oh, Didn't He Ramble" with distressing frequency since 1967.

New text and illustrations have been added in a supplement that opens on page 305. This includes biographical notes on some few musicians who should have been included in the first edition. Also, as a result of a general revival of interest in jazz, a substantial number of musicians who have been around for many years playing for the fun of it or devoting their careers to commercial music have latterly joined the ranks of serious jazzmen. In the period since 1967 they have established themselves in the forefront of New Orleans jazz.

We have been blessed with an invasion of young foreign musicians, intensely knowledgeable and thoroughly competent, who have become, or are in the process of becoming, American citizens in order to live in New Orleans permanently and play their music. They have filled many gaps in the depleting ranks, and they have an important place in this book.

Among additional material that turned up are some great photographs. I hope they add to the enjoyment of this book, and I believe they will add interest to the music on your LPs.

To the list of helpers I am pleased to add the names of Richard B. Allen, Curator of the New Orleans Jazz Archive, Howard-Tilton Memorial Library, Tulane University, and his aides, Elizabeth S. Baur and Ralph Adamo; photographers Johnny Donnels and Justin D. Winston; Martha Bendich and Pat Wynn of the New Orleans Jazz Museum, Paul Lentz, proprietor of Heritage Hall; Lars Edegran and Orange Kellin, the Swedish jazzmen; Yoshio Toyama, the trumpet-playing archivist of Tokyo; also Joseph P. Mares and Tom Bethell of New Orleans.

AL ROSE

PREFACE TO THE THIRD EDITION

Like renaissance painting, French impressionism, and Greek tragedy, the art form we knew as jazz has vacated the stage and accepts its institutionalized role in our libraries and museums. Like other cultural peaks in human history, it becomes now the province of the scholars and researchers rather than the live object of the enthusiasm of a variety of audiences.

As we wrap up a century of jazz, it's appropriate to take some note of its status as it settles comfortably into its place in the cultural history of the world. Arriving as a stepchild in the family of the arts, it began as the music of the most benighted elements in society, scorned by the critics, derided by musicians, denounced by press and pulpit, associated in the public consciousness with whores, pimps, derelicts and, most unforgivably, poor people. It had few supporters among "decent" folks. In the thirties it took a certain courage to come forward in its defense, let alone to announce one's preference for it.

Sitting in McAllister Auditorium at Tulane University in June of 1981, watching an honorary degree of Doctor of Humane Letters being conferred on Bill Russell for his contributions to the preservation of the once lowly art form, I couldn't help reviewing what he and his colleagues went through to bring about that moment. None of us could fail to exult in that recognition.

Fifty years ago the fact that the wife of the mayor of New Orleans was a niece of Kid Ory could have lost the election. The fact that such phenomena as the William Ransom Hogan Jazz Archive, the Jazz Museum in the newly renovated Old Mint Building, Preservation Hall, and a sixteen-acre center-city park dedicated to the memory of a jazz musician now exist represents the triumph of a tiny group of people who never even played the music but just loved it. Looking back, we understand that this unique artistic phenomenon was the product of an extraordinary historical period in an extraordinary place in an extraordinary society which is gone forever.

We may, however, be confident that a century hence, thanks to phonograph records and the efforts of contemporary and future researchers, New Orleans jazz will be enjoyed and appreciated by an infinitely greater audience than it ever commanded when living musicians played it. It will share the fate and the glory of the golden ages of great art.

It's with pardonable pride and even exultation that we now present this third, enlarged, revised, and *final* edition of *New Orleans Jazz: A Family Album*. It is now as complete as I can ever make it, and I'm all too aware that the altered cultural environment in which we live guarantees that nothing of prime significance will ever clamor for admission to these pages.

We have checked and rechecked facts, dates, and spellings and are convinced of the research reliability of this book. When the late Dr. Edmond Souchon and I set out to produce it some sixteen years ago, the idea of making it into the standard reference work it has become never crossed our minds. All we intended was a delightful book of great photographs which we had originally entitled "New Orleans Jazz: A Pageant in Pictures." It became apparent as we proceeded in the work that we had to fulfill what we suddenly perceived as our obligation to the jazz world. As a result, we achieved objectives of far more value than we had planned. I am confident Doc would have been gratified at how it's all turned out.

Besides the many people who helped in the preparation of the two earlier editions, I wish to thank Joseph Neves Marcal III for sturdy copies of frail original photographs, Chet Barnett and the audiovisual department of the University of New Orleans, Curt Jerde, Bruce Raeburn, Don Messer, Alma Williams and Francis Squibb of the William Ransom Hogan Jazz Archive, Don Marquis, editor of the *Second Line*, and E. Frederick Starr of Tulane University.

AL ROSE

NEW ORLEANS JAZZ

WHO'S WHO IN
NEW ORLEANS JAZZ

I t seemed between 1900 and 1930 that every family in the city of New Orleans had produced one or more jazzmen. So many families had their own bands that the task of deciding which musicians belonged in this "Who's Who" had to be limited by certain criteria. We have tried to count only those who played professionally to a reasonable extent. Even so we find evidence for more than a thousand of these. There were also certain amateurs who were not only remarkably skilled but also widely known and acknowledged by the best of the jazzmen. It has been very satisfying to track down so many of them and to find these hundreds of photographs to accompany the biographical listings. Fortunately, many musicians who seem never to have been photographed alone appear in group shots elsewhere in this volume.

The details given here, especially the spellings of names, have been carefully checked and sometimes even tracked down to surviving kin or other primary sources. Such names as Roppolo, Duson, Coustaut, Duhé, and Staulz have been misspelled in print so frequently that their proper orthography may appear unfamiliar. Not only have the facts presented here been verified, but they have also had the advantage of being filtered through two previous editions, each of which brought forth refinements of the work we began in 1966.

We wish to repeat in this edition that the amount of space allocated to the individuals represented does not reflect our estimate of their relative importance. Rather, these matters have been determined by the requirements of book design and the quality of the available photographs as well as the body of known facts about particular musicians. In the first two editions, there was substantial concern that a large number of jazzmen would be inadvertently omitted. As it turned out, very few were, and by this time it's safe to say that there are no significant omissions. We have purposely avoided editorial comment or any attempt to evaluate any of the musicians except to take note of existing universal opinion on such apparently noncontroversial performers as Louis Armstrong, Baby Dodds, Larry Shields, Bunk Johnson, and a few others.

Abraham, Martin, Sr. See Martin, Chink.

Abraham, Martin, Jr., "Little Chink" (sb, g). b. N.O., April 13, 1908. Played in a family band during early 1930s. With Sharkey, Santo Pecora, Dukes of Dixieland during the forties and fifties. Son of Chink Martin; nephew of Willie Abraham.

Abraham, Willie (bjo, g, sb). b. N.O., ca. 1888. Played with most of the best dixieland bands from 1907 until the 1940s. Brother of Chink Martin.

Adams, Dolly (née Douroux) (p, b, d). b. N.O., Jan. 11, 1904; d. N.O., Nov. 6, 1979. Member of an important musical family that included her uncle, Manuel Manetta, and her sons, bass playing Placide and Jerry and guitarist Justin. She led bands of her own and was among the first piano players to perform at Preservation Hall.

Adams, Jerry (sb). b. N.O., April 22, 1927. Son of Dolly Adams. Played with many dance groups in the fifties and was a mainstay at Heritage Hall during the seventies.

Martin Abraham, Jr.

Placide Adams

Don Albert

Tom Albert

Alvin Alcorn

Oliver Alcorn

Adams, Justin (g). b. N.O., 1925. Identified with small groups often headed by Alvin Alcorn. Son of Dolly Adams.

Adams, Placide (sb). b. N.O., Aug., 30, 1929. Best known of Dolly Adams' sons. Frequently leads his own groups. Played with Papa Celestin's orchestras in the early 1950s. Toured Japan with George Lewis. Known for Louis Armstrong vocal imitations.

Adde, Leo (d). b. N.O., April 21, 1904; d. N.O., March, 1942. Rhythm star of the famed New Orleans Rhythm Kings. Began playing a cigar box on the streets of the city with Raymond Burke on harmonica. Already popular before the 1920s he was the choice of Norman Brownlee, Johnny Bayersdorffer, the Halfway House Orchestra, and

the Christian brothers. Dixielanders of the twenties rated him number one.

Albert, Don (t). b. N.O., 1909; d. San Antonio, Tex., 1980. Real name Albert Dominique. Nephew of Natty Dominique. Trained by Lorenzo Tio, Jr., and Milford Piron. Led swing band based in San Antonio during the thirties. Recorded on Southland Records with Louis Cottrell, Jr., Paul Barbarin. Recorded with Alamo Jazz Band in San Antonio, 1962.

Albert, Tom (t). b. near Algiers, La., Dec. 23, 1877; d. N.O., Dec. 13, 1969. A true pioneer of jazz. One of the original members of the Eureka Brass Band, he led his own band for a quarter of a century, until 1929.

Ricard Alexis

Henry Allen, Sr.

Red Allen

Alcorn, Alvin (t). b. N.O., Sept. 7, 1912. His early playing days were in the notable bands led by Sidney Desvigne, A. J. Piron, Clarence Desdunes, and Don Albert. He replaced Mutt Carey in Kid Ory's band on the West Coast and performed on Bourbon Street under the leadership of Papa Celestin and Octave Crosby. He was a member of the Young Tuxedo Brass Band and the Onward Brass Band and also served in George Williams' parade band. In 1981 he was leading his own Imperial Brass Band. He represented the city of New Orleans during the U.S. Bicentennial, when his band played in Paris for the French celebration of Louisiana Week. He has made many world tours and is widely recorded.

Alcorn, Oliver (cl, s). b. N.O., Aug. 3, 1910; d. Chicago, Ill., March 18, 1981. Brother of Alvin Alcorn, he performed with Clarence Desdunes and in groups led by George McCullum, Jr., in the twenties and thirties. He passed most of his later life in Chicago, playing with Lee Collins, Natty Dominique, Little Brother Montgomery, and Lonnie Johnson.

Alexander, Adolphe, Sr. (c, bh). b. N.O., 1874; d. N.O., 1936. Played in the Golden Rule Orchestra in 1905 and in the Superior and Imperial dance orchestras, 1909–1912. He was a member of the Excelsior Brass Band and a charter member of the Eureka Brass Band.

Alexander, Adolphe, Jr., "Tats" (s, cl, bh). b. N.O., July 15, 1898. Began his musical career with the Tuxedo Brass Band in 1921 and played the riverboats with Sidney Desvigne's orchestra, 1921–1923. He was with the huge

WPA bands during the Depression and with Papa Celestin from the mid-forties to 1954. During the war years he performed with other distinguished jazzmen in the Algiers Naval Station Band. He was also a member of the Eureka Brass Band and retired from music in 1955.

Alexander, Joe. See Allesandra, Guiseppe.

Alexis, Ricard (t, sb). b. N.O., Oct. 16, 1896; d. N.O., March 15, 1960. With Bob Lyons' Dixie Jazz Band, 1918–1925, Tuxedo Orchestra at Pelican Dance Hall under Bebé Ridgley. Recorded on trumpet with Papa Celestin in 1927. Switched to bass when his jaw was broken by racist hoodlums in the mid-thirties. From 1937 to his death he was identified with Celestin, Paul Barbarin's orchestra, Octave Crosby's group at the Paddock, and Sweet Emma Barrett.

Allen, Henry, Sr. (c). b. Algiers, La., 1877; d. Algiers, La., Jan. 11, 1952. Leader of the famous Allen Brass Band of Algiers for more than forty years. Father of renowned trumpet star, Red Allen.

Allen, Henry, Jr., "Red" (t, vo). b. Algiers, La., Jan. 7, 1908; d. New York, N.Y., April 17, 1967. He began with his father's brass band, later worked with the Excelsior and Eureka brass bands. During the twenties he performed with fellow trumpet players and bandleaders Chris Kelly, Kid Rena, and Sidney Desvigne. Allen joined the King Oliver orchestra in 1927 in New York after working on the riverboats with Fate Marable and Walter Pichon. During the thirties he made records with Luis

Giuseppe Allesandra

Frank Amacker

Russell, Fletcher Henderson, Lucky Millinder, Louis Armstrong, and Jelly Roll Morton. From 1940 on, he led his own orchestra and was usually considered, along with a host of other trumpet men, as a Louis Armstrong imitator, an appraisal not entirely adequate.

Allesandra, Guiseppe (tu). b. Italy, Nov. 21, 1865; d. N.O., 1950. Also known as **Joe Alexander**, he played in street parades with Papa Laine's Reliance Brass Band as early as 1904 and in dance orchestras led by Johnny Provenzano, Dominick and Joe Barocco. Well known as a teacher of brass instruments.

Almerico, Tony (t, vo). b. N.O., 1905; d. N.O., Dec. 5, 1961. Operated the Parisian Room on Royal Street, 1948–1960. Became nationally famous for his weekly coast-to-coast radio broadcasts from the club, featuring sidemen like young Pete Fountain, Irving Fazola, Harry Shields, and Jack Delaney. He maintained his own disc jockey jazz show for years and was an occasional jazz program TV host. In the thirties he played with Slim Lamar's Argentine Dons and organized his first band in 1936. During the forties they frequently played for dancing on the Streckfus riverboats, the *Capitol* and later the *President*.

Amacker, Frank (p, g). b. N.O., March 22, 1890; d. N.O., 1976. A veteran of the bagnios of Storyville where he was an authentic "professor," Amacker was recorded late in his life and spent his last years sitting benignly on a bench in Preservation Hall enjoying the music and conversation with patrons and friends.

Andy Anderson

Anderson, Andy (t). b. N.O., Aug. 12, 1912. Anderson was prominent in the Young Tuxedo and George Williams brass bands and frequently played dance jobs until well into the seventies.

Andrus, Merwin "Dutch" (d, t). b. N.O., Feb. 25, 1912. Popular dance band leader and played for years on the SS *President*. During the fifties he recorded on Southland Records, as well as for Sapphire. His performing career ended when he was shot in the neck by a stranger after leaving the Maple Leaf Club in Carrollton one night in 1980. The assault left him an invalid.

Angrum, Steve (cl). b. New Roads, La., July 4, 1895; d. N.O., Nov. 26, 1961. Angrum played in the Elton The-

Dutch Andrus

Johnny Collins

Louis Armstrong

odore band until 1925 and thereafter often worked with Kid Howard, Kid Clayton, and Charlie Love. In the fifties he was a regular at the Happy Landing along with Albert Jiles, Louis Keppard, and Sweet Emma Barrett.

Aquilera, Bob "One-Leg" (p, tb, g). b. N.O., *ca.* 1895; d. N.O., Feb. 27, 1945. On a wooden leg he paraded with Fischer's Brass Band, 1908–1911. Before World War I, he was part of the Happy Schilling orchestra that entertained at the Pelican Baseball Park during games. Later, he toured the Southwest as a solo piano player. In 1915 he turned down the opportunity to make the historic trip to Chicago as a pianist with Tom Brown's Band from Dixieland.

Arcenaux, Whitey (bjo). b. N.O., *ca.* 1895. A street musician in pre–World War I skiffle bands, he played with the Young Superior band in the twenties.

Armstrong, (Daniel) Louis (c, t, vo). b. N.O., July 4, 1900; d. New York, N.Y., June 6, 1971. The most famous of all jazz musicians, he served his apprenticeship under his patron, King Oliver. His career began in the Waif's Home band when he was a child. He played the drums briefly, then the bugle, and at last, the cornet. Some of his

earliest New Orleans jobs were in Kid Ory's band, and from 1919 to 1920, he worked with Fate Marable aboard the SS *Capitol*. He joined Oliver's band in Chicago in 1922 and thereafter played only one extended engagement in his hometown—in 1931 at the Suburban Gardens, leading his own band. Satchmo returned to his native city to reign as King Zulu in the 1949 Mardi Gras. In the forties, fifties, and sixties he toured the world with his All-Stars and was sponsored by the U.S. State Department as America's Good Will Ambassador. He was the most recorded of all jazz musicians, composer of many hits, including "Someday You'll Be Sorry" and, with his second wife, Lil Hardin Armstrong, "Struttin' with Some Barbecue" and "Big Butter and Egg Man." His recorded sessions with the Oliver orchestra and with the Louis Armstrong Hot Five are among the most desired discs ever made. He was featured in more than thirty movies, of which those with Bing Crosby were most widely circulated. He played Satan in "Cabin in the Sky" and turned the Baptist hymn "When the Saints Go Marchin' In" into a jazz standard.

5

Albert Artigues

Arnolia, Walter (d). b. N.O., *ca.* 1895. Usually played in bands led by Buddy Petit, Chris Kelly. Cousin of well-known bass man, Sidney Brown.

Arodin, Sidney (cl, s). b. N.O., March 29, 1901; d. N.O., Feb. 6, 1948. Came to prominence in the Half-way House Orchestra during the twenties. Also played with the New Orleans Rhythm Masters. First white musician to record in New Orleans with blacks in the historic session of the Jones-Collins Astoria Hot Eight. Composer of "Up a Lazy River." Played with Sharkey, Louis Prima, and Wingy Manone orchestras during the thirties and forties.

Artigues, Albert (c, t). b. N.O., Aug. 23, 1907; d. N.O., June 21, 1980. His informal group, the French Market Gang, was one of the best and most joyful bands in town. Owner of a prosperous marine supply store on Decatur Street, Artigues wasn't free to travel or to work full-time at music, but the best dixieland musicians were always happy to play in his band. He booked his Gang for informal functions.

Assunto, Frank (t). b. N.O., Jan. 29, 1932; d. Feb. 25, 1974. Leader of the world-famous Dukes of Dixieland, he learned music from his father, Jac. The Dukes' records were issued in floods and sold in the millions.

Assunto, Freddie (tb). b. N.O., Dec. 3, 1929; d. Las Vegas, Nev., April 21, 1966. His entire musical career was spent with his brother Frank and his father, Jac, in the Dukes of Dixieland. He was married to the Dukes' singer, Betty Owens.

Assunto, Jac (tb, bjo). b. N.O., Nov. 1, 1905. Father of Frank and Freddie. Played in dixieland bands of the twen-

Fred and Frank Assunto

ties and made his living as a music teacher and high school bandmaster. He participated in the organization of the Dukes of Dixieland in the late forties and often played with them on tour.

Atkins, Boyd (v, s). b. N.O., *ca.* 1900. Left New Orleans in 1922 after having played in pickup brass bands. He played in Fate Marable's band on the riverboats, then in 1923 formed his own band in Chicago. He was the composer of Louis Armstrong's first big hit, "Heebie Jeebies." Atkins worked in Armstrong's band and also in the big Carroll Dickerson theater orchestra and with Clifford King.

Atkins, Eddie (tb, bh). b. N.O., 1887; d. Chicago, Ill., *ca.* 1926. He played in the Olympia Orchestra in 1909 and was with Manuel Perez in Chicago, 1915–1916. In late 1916 and 1917 he was in the Tuxedo Brass Band and the Onward Brass Band. He was with King Oliver at times during the Storyville years and was drafted into the army in 1917. He settled permanently in Chicago in 1919.

Augustin, George (b, bjo). b. N.O., *ca.* 1890. He joined Wooden Joe Nicholas in 1918 and worked in the pit band

Jac Assunto

Achille Baquet

with John Robichaux's orchestra at the Lyric Theater until it burned down in 1927. Until 1928 he was with the Moonlight Serenaders, a co-op band. Into the thirties he was playing on the SS *Capitol* and on lake steamers in the bands of Walter Pichon and A. J. Piron.

Avery, Joseph "Kid" (tb). b. Waggeman, La., Oct. 3, 1892; d. Waggeman, La., Dec. 9, 1955. A pupil of the important early musician, Dave Perkins, Avery was in the Tulane Orchestra between 1915 and 1922. He spent time on tour with Evan Thomas' legendary Black Eagles and played with the Yelping Hounds in Crowley, La. He led his own band into the mid-fifties and was the regular trombone player in the Young Tuxedo Brass Band. He recorded for Southland Records in 1954. The ancient riff melody that early blues musicians knew as "Holler Blues" he made his own; it became widely, if inaccurately known as "Joe Avery's Tune" and is now performed by contemporary brass bands under the title of "The Second Line" (not to be confused with Paul Barbarin's excellent march).

Babin, Al (d). b. N.O., Sept. 10, 1927. Popular dixieland musician worked with the best bands of the mid–twentieth century including Sharkey's Kings of Dixieland and Santo Pecora's Tailgaters. Continued active into the eighties.

Bachman, Jack (t). b. N.O., May 21, 1917. Best known as trumpeter of the Crawford-Ferguson Night Owls, which played on the steamer *President* during the sixties.

Badie, Pete (cl). b. N.O., *ca.* 1900; d. N.O., *ca.* 1960. Played with Percy Humphrey's first band in 1925.

Bailey, David (d). b. N.O., *ca.* 1898. During twenties, with Chris Kelly and other authentic jazz bands. Remained active until 1965 in dance and parade bands, his last regular work with the Gibson Brass Band.

Banks, Joe (c). b. Thibodaux, La., *ca.* 1882; d. Thibodaux, La., *ca.* 1930. Played with the Youka Brass Band in the early 1900s and led his own dance orchestra in Thibodaux until the mid-twenties. The town produced many jazz stars, all of whom got their start in Banks's orchestra.

Baptiste, Albert (v). b. N.O., *ca.* 1872; d. N.O., *ca.* 1931. Leader of the historic Silver Leaf Orchestra, 1896–1912.

Baptiste, Milton (t). b. N.O.,———. Young Olympia Brass Band, Preservation Hall with Harold Dejan.

Baptiste, Quentin (b, p). b. N.O.,———. Bass with Freddie Kohlman's band at Sid Davila's Mardi Gras Lounge on Bourbon Street during the 1950s.

Baptiste, René (g). b. N.O., *ca.* 1880; d. N.O., *ca.* 1933. A brother-in-law of Big Eye Louis Nelson, he played with

George Baquet

Isidore Barbarin

Manuel Perez' Imperial Orchestra and under the highly respected leadership of Edward Clem. On a number of occasions he performed in the Buddy Bolden band.

Baptiste, Tink (p). b. N.O., 1897; d. Texas, 1960. Played during the twenties with the Foster Lewis Jazz Band and is on the famous 1927 Columbia recording session with Sam Morgan's band.

Baptiste, Willie (bjo). b. N.O., ——; d. N.O., ——. A skilled musician, he became known to jazz fans mainly through his Preservation Hall appearances in the sixties and seventies.

Baquet, Achille (cl). b. N.O., Nov. 15, 1885; d. N.O., Nov. 20, 1955. Great early clarinetist with the Reliance Brass Band and played with members of the Original Dixieland Jazz Band in New Orleans. In 1915 he was a member of the New Orleans Jazz Band in Coney Island, N.Y. (Jimmy Durante on piano), and later recorded with that band. His father was Theogene and his brother George Baquet.

Baquet, George (cl). b. N.O., 1883; d. Philadelphia, Pa., Jan. 14, 1949. One of the all-time great jazzmen. He was with the Onward Brass Band in 1900 and played with Buddy Bolden before 1905, later with Manuel Perez' Imperial Orchestra. He toured with P. T. Wright's Georgia Minstrels, 1902–1903, then came home to join John Robichaux' Orchestra. Until 1914 he was with the Magnolia, Superior, and Olympia orchestras, then joined the Original Creole Orchestra in Los Angeles in the company of other Orleanians. He made records with Jelly Roll Morton's Red Hot Peppers in 1929 and through the forties was in the pit band at the Earle Theater in Philadelphia. Son of Theogene, brother of Achille.

Baquet, Theogene V. (c). b. N.O., *ca.* 1858; d. N.O., *ca.* 1920. Cornet virtuoso and leader of the famed Excelsior Brass Band, *ca.* 1882–1904. He organized and led a symphonic group and was one of New Orleans' great music teachers. His sons Achille and George were clarinetists.

Barbarin, Isidore (mel, ah, eu, tu). b. N.O., Sept. 24, 1872; d. N.O., 1960. Onward Brass Band, 1896–1898, 1899–1927, occasionally filled in with other brass bands.

Louis Barbarin

Paul Barbarin

Recorded in 1939 with Zenith Brass Band and with Bunk's Brass Band in 1940s. Father of the great drummers, Paul and Louis, and grandfather of the celebrated guitarist and banjo man, Danny Barker.

Barbarin, Louis (d). b. N.O., Oct. 24, 1902. Began very young and was influenced by his very musical family, playing in bands led by his father, Isidore, and also absorbing a lot from his associations with the Piron Orchestra in the twenties. During the thirties, he worked on the steamboats on Lake Pontchartrain in the company of Eddie Pierson and Harold Dejan. During the forties and fifties he was regularly with Papa Celestin's Orchestra, and when Celestin died in 1954, he continued with the same group under the leadership first of Eddie Pierson and then Albert French. Remnants of the orchestra continued into the 1980s under the leadership of Clive Wilson, still with Louis on drums. He was also frequently on the stand at Preservation Hall late in 1981.

Barbarin, Paul (d). b. N.O., May 5, 1901; d. N.O., Feb. 17, 1969. One of the super drummers in jazz history, Barbarin played behind King Oliver, Louis Armstrong, A. J. Piron, and Fats Pichon. Leader of his own band for decades, he was widely recorded. A member of ASCAP, he composed many successful tunes, including "Bourbon Street Parade," "The Second Line," and "Come Back Sweet Papa." He died while playing the snare drum in a Mardi Gras parade and his funeral, in the rain, attracted a throng that included many celebrated jazz personalities.

Barker, "Blue Lu" (vo). b. N.O., ca. 1914. The much-recorded singing wife of guitarist Danny Barker strongly influenced café singers like Billie Holiday and Eartha Kitt, whose phrasing clearly follows the patterns developed by this charming and talented lady. Of a decidedly domestic disposition, she was never strongly motivated to live the show-business life and has not worked in nightclubs or on the vaudeville stage. She has limited her performance to records and occasional concerts—and then only to humor her husband or to accommodate a friend.

Barker, Danny (g, bjo, vo). b. N.O., Jan. 13, 1909. Studied clarinet with Barney Bigard and drums with his uncles Paul and Louis Barbarin. He played the ukulele on the streets of the city in his early teens and won some impressive contests on this instrument during the twenties. One of New Orleans' best known rhythm men, his early guitar skills were developed by Bernard Addison. He performed with Louis Armstrong, Jelly Roll Morton, and the De Paris brothers. During the thirties and forties, he was the mainstay of certain successful big bands including Lucky Millinder's, Benny Carter's, and—most famous of all—Cab Calloway's. His widely quoted but still unpublished autobiography reflects his exhaustive knowledge of the early days of jazz, his keen sense of history, and his mastery of Creole songs and dialects. During the sixties and seventies, through his Fairview Baptist Band and his other efforts, he brought the jazz world to the children of New Orleans and helped to develop a small but dedicated group of young jazz regulars able to hold their own with the surviving veterans. He was assistant curator of the New Orleans Jazz Museum from its founding and in the 1980s continued to perform with his own band and to serve on the Advisory Board of the William Ransom Hogan Jazz Archive at Tulane University, as well as taking an occasional turn as grand marshal in street parades.

Danny and Blue Lu Barker

Emile Barnes

Barnes, Emile (cl). b. N.O., Feb. 18, 1892; d. N.O., March 2, 1970. Brother of Polo Barnes. His active career ran from 1908 to 1966, one of the longest in jazz history. Played with Chris Kelly, 1919–1927. During the fifties he was often at the Happy Landing and Mama Lou's. After Preservation Hall opened in 1961, thousands became familiar with his classic style.

Barnes, Harrison (tb, mel, bh, c). b. Magnolia Plantation, La., Jan. 13, 1889; d. N.O., 1960. Pupil of Professor Jim Humphrey. Eclipse Brass Band, 1906; Henry Allen Brass Band, 1907. With Chris Kelly to 1918. Nola Band, 1923. Pit band led by John Robichaux in 1924. Recorded with Zenith Brass Band, 1946, and with Kid Thomas, 1951.

Barnes, Paul "Polo" (cl, s). b. N.O., Nov. 22, 1902; d. N.O., April 13, 1981. Brother of Emile Barnes. Debut with Young Tuxedo Orchestra, 1920. Joined Original Tuxedo Orchestra under Celestin and Ridgley, 1921; with Celestin until 1927, then joined tour with King Oliver until 1935. His diary of those years is an important jazz document. Worked with Kid Howard at Lavida Ballroom. In the navy during WW II, he was assigned to the Algiers

Naval Station Band. He settled for a while in New York and then worked in Johnny St. Cyr's band on the Mark Twain in Disneyland, before returning to New Orleans in his later years. He composed "My Josephine," recorded by Papa Celestin's orchestra.

Barocco, Dominick (t, mdl, bjo, g). b. N.O., Oct. 5, 1893; d. N.O., Jan. 28, 1970. Studied trumpet with Frank Christian. Started own band, with brother Joe, in 1912. Their Susquehanna Band played on the lake steamer of the same name, 1923–1924. He continued as a leader until 1966. His career included stints with Nick La Rocca, Larry Shields, Clem Camp, and Johnny Provenzano.

Barocco, Joe (sb, tu). b. N.O., Oct. 16, 1891; d. N.O., 1947. Brother of Dominick and coleader of the Susquehanna Band. Also played under Papa Laine in the Reliance Brass Band and in Johnny Fischer's Brass Band.

Barocco, Vincent (ah). b. N.O., ca. 1878. Early member of the Reliance Brass Band. Not related to the other Baroccos.

Polo Barnes

Dominick Barocco

Joe Barocco

Barrett, Emma (p, vo, l). b. N.O., March 25, 1898. Known as "Sweet Emma the Bell Gal" she was playing in Celestin's band in 1923 and worked with the city's top reading bands—Sidney Desvigne's, Robichaux's, and even A. J. Piron's—though she never learned to read music. During the fifties she was a regular weekend attraction at the Happy Landing and continued to draw crowds to Preservation Hall from the time it opened in 1961. She has toured the world a number of times as leader of her own Preservation Hall Jazz Band.

Barrois, Raymond. See Burke, Raymond.

Bart, Wilhelmina "Willa" (p). b. N.O., *ca.* 1900. During the 1920s played with Willie Pajeaud at the Alamo Dance Hall, Amos White's orchestra, and at Old Spanish Fort with the New Orleans Creole Jazz Band. Early in her career, she played with Jimmie Noone's band.

Barth, George (t, mel, s). b. N.O., *ca.* 1895. Versatile jazz man with Norman Brownlee's orchestra, Fischer's

11

Sweet Emma Barrett   *Photo by Lee Friedlander*

Jules Bauduc

Brass Band, and dixieland groups during the World War I era.

Batiste, Milton (t). b. N.O., Sept. 5, 1934. Regular member of the Olympia Brass Band and in Harold Dejan's group at Preservation Hall, usually on Sunday nights.

Bauduc, Jules (bjo). b. N.O., *ca.* 1904. Bandleader active in the 1920s. Brother of Ray Bauduc.

Bauduc, Ray (d). b. N.O., June 18, 1909. Participated in the first live broadcast of jazz from New Orleans in 1923. Left in 1926 to join Joe Venuti's band in New York after playing with Johnny Bayersdorffer and other top bands. With the Dorsey brothers in the Scranton Sirens. Played with Ben Pollack, Freddie Rich, Red Nichols through the middle and late twenties. Recorded with the Memphis Five in 1926. Gained world fame with the Bob Crosby Bobcats (1935–1942). Led own band and recorded for Capitol in the forties. With Jimmy Dorsey 1947–1950. Toured with Jack Teagarden in the fifties and joined Nappy Lamare to lead the Riverboat Ramblers in California through the sixties and early seventies. Retired to San Antonio, Texas, and continued to play occasionally.

Bayard, Eddie (t, l). b. N.O., Aug. 1, 1934. Student of Professor Manuel Manetta at sixteen. Worked with bands of George Brunies, Sharkey, Santo Pecora. His Bourbon Street Five was the staff band on the SS *Delta Queen* until the *Mississippi Queen* was commissioned in 1979 and the

band moved to the new vessel. Has appeared on the TV shows of Dinah Shore, Lawrence Welk, and Phil Donahue. Bayard was playing in the Louisiana Repertory Jazz Ensemble in 1982.

Bayersdorffer, Johnny (t). b. N.O., Sept. 4, 1899; d. N.O., Nov. 14, 1969. The city's most popular dixieland bandleader of the 1920s. His bands included the best sidemen in the area. Recorded on Okeh in March, 1924. Played for many years at the Tokyo Gardens in Spanish Fort. He was in the Triangle Jazz Band with Irwin Leclere, as well as with Happy Schilling and Tony Parenti, 1917–1921.

Bazoon, Otis (cl). b. N.O., Feb. 19, 1947. Younger generation jazzman, among the few following in the authentic mold. Played in the 1970s with a version of the Dukes of Dixieland that shared only the name of the original group. Has done excellent work, however, in the French Market Jazz Band led by Scotty Hill. Exceptional sense of harmony.

Beaulieu, Paul (p, cl). b. N.O., Oct. 20, 1888; d. N.O., 1967. In Melrose Brass Band with Joe Oliver in 1907. Joined John Robichaux in 1915. His career was divided between jazz and concert music.

Beaulieu, Rudolph "Big Rudolph" (d). b. N.O., 1900; d. N.O., March 9, 1972. Operated a popular drum shop after his playing days were over.

Bechet, Leonard V. (tb). b. N.O., April 25, 1877; d. N.O., March 9, 1952. Dentist. Was with the Young Superior Brass Band during the 1920s. Led his own Silver Bells Band as early as 1903 until World War I. Brother of the great jazz star, Sidney Bechet.

Ray Bauduc

Eddie Bayard

Bechet, Sidney (cl, ss). b. N.O., May 14, 1897; d. Paris, France, May 14, 1959. Started with his brother's Silver Bells Band in 1911 and played with the Eagle Band in 1914 under Frank Duson. Was with King Oliver at Pete Lala's in Storyville before World War I. He rode the rods to Texas with Clarence Williams in 1915 and went on to Chicago where he joined Freddie Keppard. To Europe with Will Marion Cook, 1919–1921. Worked in Russia with "Payton's Black Revue" in 1930. During the mid-thirties was with Noble Sissle's orchestra. Was the star of the first authentic jazz concert, produced by Al Rose in Philadelphia. Played seven years in France with Claude Luter and settled in Paris in the mid-fifties. Revered in Europe, Bechet was extensively recorded. Fascinating autobiography, *Treat It Gentle*.

Behrenson, "Doc" (c). b. N.O., *ca.* 1893. Pre–World War I dixielander. Worked with Johnny Stein in Chicago in 1916. Only an accident kept him from being the cornetist with the Original Dixieland Jazz Band.

Behrenson, Sidney (tb, vt). b. N.O., *ca.* 1895. Pre–World War I dixielander. Played with his brother Doc and with Johnny Bayersdorffer.

Belas, Henry "Ants" (t, l). b. N.O., *ca.* 1915. Led many small dance bands in 1936, frequently featuring star sidemen like Raymond Burke. Sometimes played in the band of the comedian and bass player Candy Candido during the thirties.

Belasco, Manuel (bh). b. N.O., *ca.* 1874. Charter member of the Reliance Brass Band. Frequently mistaken for Papa Laine, the leader, whom he closely resembled.

Bell, John (sb, tu). b. N.O., *ca*, 1910; d. N.O., July 28, 1946. With the Melon Pickers under Henry Waelde in the 1920s. Recorded on Keynote with George Hartman in the forties.

Ben, Paul (tb). b. N.O., *ca.* 1895. With Bob Lyons' Dixie Jazz Band from World War I through the early thirties. Also worked with Lawrence Marrero's Young Tuxedo Orchestra and in a band led by Bush Hall.

Benarby, Jim (tb). b. N.O., *ca.* 1904; d. *ca.* 1926. Member of Nat Towles's Creole Harmony Kings for the band's engagement in Yucatan, Mexico, 1924–1925. Uncle of trombonist, Ernest Kelly.

Beninate, Johnny (cl). b. N.O., ——. With Johnny Bayersdorffer's band before World War I.

Beninate, Nick (t). b. N.O., *ca.* 1910. Active dixielander from the mid-thirties through the sixties, often playing in bands led by Jeff Riddick.

Sidney and Leonard Bechet

Benoit, John (d). b. Pass Christian, Miss., *ca.* 1888. Played in the bands of Storyville between 1908 and 1913, especially with Peter Bocage, Lawrence Duhé, and Fred Keppard.

Benson, Hamilton "Hamp" (tb). b. N.O., 1885. Worked in the district with Andrew Kimball until 1905, then in 1906 with mandolinist Tom Brown at Tom Anderson's Annex. Later that year, he organized his own band. Left in 1915 and not heard of again until the 1940s when he surfaced on a date in Springfield, Ill., playing with Sidney Bechet.

Benton, Tom (bjo, vo). b. N.O., *ca.* 1890; d. N.O., *ca.* 1945. With the Crescent Orchestra under Jack Carey in 1914 and Papa Celestin in 1915. Played with Jimmie Noone in 1915. Was considered best popular singer in town. Left New Orleans in 1926.

Bergen, Stuart "Red Hott" (t). b. N.O., July 8, 1911. A jazzman for over fifty years, Bergen performed with the biggest stars of dixieland, including Tom Brown, Irving Fazola, Larry and Harry Shields. He led his own bands with great success but business interests kept him in New Orleans through his entire career. He was a mainstay in the early life of the New Orleans Jazz Club. Style and tone reminiscent of Louis Armstrong.

Berry, Mel (tb). b. N.O., *ca.* 1897; d. Los Angeles, 1929. Brief but brilliant life. A virtuoso who distinguished himself playing in theater pit bands and made his place in jazz history during the twenties playing in Johnny DeDroit's orchestra alongside Tony Parenti.

Bertrand, Buddy (p). b. 1897; d. N.O., March 23, 1956. Authentic "professor" of the bagnios of Storyville.

Bigard, Albany Leon "Barney" (cl). b. N.O., March 3, 1906; d. Los Angeles, Calif., June 27, 1980. Pupil of Luis Tio and Lorenzo Tio, Jr. Played with Oak Gaspard, 1921; Albert Nicholas, 1922. Joined King Oliver on tour in 1925. In Chicago with Charles Elgar, Luis Russell, Albert Wynn orchestras before fourteen-year stint with Duke Ellington. Settled in California. Worked with Freddie Slack in the forties and from 1946 through the 1950s was with the celebrated Louis Armstrong All-Stars. Toured in the sixties and seventies with Barry Martin's Legends of Jazz. He was widely recorded and his name appears on the copyright of "Mood Indigo."

Bigard, Alec (d). b. N.O., Sept. 25, 1898; d. N.O., June 27, 1978. Played with the A. J. Piron Orchestra in 1917 and was at Tom Anderson's and the Humming Bird Lounge with a quartet. With Excelsior Brass Band, 1918; Maple Leaf Orchestra, 1919–1920; Sidney Desvigne's or-

Hamp Benson

Red Hott Bergen

Barney Bigard

chestra, 1925; John Robichaux's orchestra, 1927; Kid Rena's Jazz Band, 1944. Brother of famed clarinetist Barney Bigard.

Bigard, Emile (v). b. N.O., *ca.* 1890; d. N.O., 1935. During World War I with the Magnolia Orchestra. Also worked with King Oliver, Kid Ory. Joined Maple Leaf Orchestra in 1919 and retired from music in 1924. Brother of Barney and Alec Bigard.

Bigeou, Clifford "Boy" (p, bjo). b. N.O., 1899. Through the Depression, worked with the Crescent City Serenaders. Brother of singer Esther Bigeou.

Bigeou, Esther (vo). b. N.O., *ca.* 1895; d. N.O., *ca.* 1936. "The Creole Songbird" sang and recorded with the A. J. Piron Orchestra in the thirties. Worked with Peter Bocage; toured Theater Owners' Booking Association vaudeville circuit. Cousin of Paul Barbarin.

Bisso, Louis (p). b. N.O., *ca.* 1905. Early 1920s played piano in silent movie theaters. Was head of New Orleans City Planning Board in the fifties. Appeared frequently at the New Orleans Jazz Club.

Blaise, Ed "Kit Totts" (d). b. N.O., *ca.* 1895; d. N.O., *ca.* 1944. Totts worked with the Papa Laine, Frank Christian, and Bill Gallaty bands in the pre–World War I era.

15

Esther Bigeou

"Blind" Gilbert (c, g). b. N.O., *ca.* 1900. A partially blind beggar who worked the streets of the district and the French Quarter, made unissued recordings for Columbia in the 1920s and claimed to be the true composer of "Angry" and "Where the Morning Glories Grow." Last heard from in Los Angeles, Calif. Legal name, Gilbert Meistier.

Blount, Jack (v). b. N.O., ———. With Liberty Bell Orchestra, 1919–1933.

Blunt, Carroll (tb). Gibson Brass Band.

Bocage, Charles (bjo, g, vo). b. N.O., *ca.* 1895; d. N.O., Nov. 4, 1963. With A. J. Piron after World War I. Recorded with this band for Victor, Columbia in 1923. Later mainly in bands led by his brother Peter. Continued active until the mid-fifties.

Bocage, Henry (tu, sb, t). b. N.O., *ca.* 1893. With A. J. Piron Orchestra, 1918–1919. Recorded with the group at the Victor and Columbia sessions in 1923. Cousin of Peter and Charles.

Bocage, Peter (t, tb, v). b. Algiers, La., Aug. 4, 1887; d. Algiers, La., Dec. 3, 1967. Began career in 1906. Original Superior Orchestra, 1909; Original Tuxedo Orchestra, 1910–1913; Onward Brass Band with Joe Oliver at Lala's. With Fate Marable's SS *Capitol* Orchestra, 1916. After 1918 with A. J. Piron Orchestra. Wrote "Mama's Gone Good-Bye"; introduced "Shimmy Like My Sister Kate." Creole Serenaders recorded in 1960s by Riverside.

Bodoyer, Rudolph (d). b. N.O., *ca.* 1902. Played with Young Morgan Band under Isaiah Morgan, 1922–1926. With Sam Morgan, 1926; in the thirties with Kid Rena. Seen often in early forties with Alphonse Picou.

Bolman, "Red" (c, t, l). b. N.O., *ca.* 1899. Led own band in twenties and thirties. Toured with New Orleans Rhythm Masters in early twenties.

Bolden, Charles "Buddy" (c). b. N.O., Sept. 6, 1877; d. Jackson, La., Nov. 4, 1931. Sometimes called the first jazz band leader. Undoubtedly one of the greatest New Orleans horn men. Mainly led his own band until incapacitated by mental illness in 1907.

Bolton, "Happy," "Red Happy" (d). b. N.O., *ca.* 1885; d. N.O., 1928. Bolton was the mainstay of the King Oliver band in New Orleans from 1912 to 1916. He remained in New Orleans when Oliver went to Chicago

Peter Bocage

Stirling Bose

and after World War I worked with John Robichaux at the Lyric Theater. In the early 1920s he was in a Canal Street cabaret and dance hall with Peter Lacaze's band.

Bonano, Joseph. See Sharkey.

Bonansinga, Frank (p, l). b. Jacksonville, Ill., April 8, 1900; d. N.O., June 6, 1973. With campus bands at University of Illinois, 1923. Fronted his own band in 1924. Longtime New Orleans resident. Headed New Orleans Jazz Club in 1956 and played piano with top musicians at club functions through the fifties and early sixties.

Bontemps, Willie (bjo, g). b. N.O., ca. 1893; d. N.O., 1958. Tuxedo Orchestra under Bebé Ridgley in 1917; Maple Leaf Orchestra, 1920–1921. Worked with Willie Pajeaud at Thom's Roadhouse, 1923. Did specialty comedy-music act at Lyric Theater during the twenties but was not member of the Robichaux pit band. Best known as singer and comic.

Bose, Stirling (c, t). b. Florence, Ala., Feb. 23, 1906; d. St. Petersburg, Fla., June, 1958. With Norman Brownlee in the late 1920s and later with Crescent City Jazzers centered in Mobile, Ala. Usually considered a New Orleans musician, but mainly worked with swing bands until he died.

Bouchon, Lester (cl, s, l). b. N.O., Sept. 29, 1906; d. N.O., April 13, 1962. With Domino Orchestra, Bayersdorffer's Red Devils, 1920s. Toured in name bands through swing era. During forties and fifties with Sharkey, Johnny Wiggs, Santo Pecora.

Bourgeau, Joseph "Fan" (p, bjo). b. N.O., July 29, 1891; d. N.O., Jan. 23, 1975. Frequent performer at Luthjen's in the late forties and the fifties.

Bourgeois, Wilfred S. "Bill" (cl, s). b. N.O., April 14, 1907. Mainly associated with Sharkey.

Boyd, George "Georgia Boy" (cl). b. N.O., ca. 1904; d. ca. 1931. Wild, untrained musician with Jack Carey's Crescent Orchestra, 1916, and Kid Lindsey's Jazz Band, 1917. Joined Punch Miller, 1920, and Chris Kelly when Punch left New Orleans. With Kid Rena Dixie Jazz Band, 1922–1925.

Braud, Wellman (sb, v). b. St. James Parish, La., Jan. 25, 1891; d. New York, N.Y., June 6, 1967. In string bass trio in the district, 1908–1913, at Tom Anderson's and at the Terminal Saloon. Switched to string bass in Chicago, 1917,

17

Lester Bouchon

Wellman Braud

Pud Brown

with Sugar Johnny Smith, Lawrence Duhé. Charles Elgar Orchestra, 1920–1923; Wilbur Sweatman, 1923. Toured in burlesque. With Duke Ellington, 1926–1936.

Braun, Billy (p, mel). b. N.O., 1892; d. N.O., April 2, 1974. Norman Brownlee, Johnny Fischer, Johnny Bayersdorffer.

Brazlee, Harrison (tb). b. N.O., Oct. 25, 1888; d. N.O., Nov., 1954. Began with Excelsior Brass Band (Mobile, Ala.). Toured with carnival and minstrel bands and with Ringling Brothers and other circuses. Joined Evan Thomas' band in the mid-twenties. Settled in New Orleans and at time of his death was a regular performer at Luthjen's.

Breaux, Mc Neal (sb, tu). b. N.O., 1916. Started on tuba in Henry Allen Brass Band. Played string bass with Isaiah Morgan's orchestra in the early 1930s. In the thirties and forties was active in the Moonlight Serenaders and the Dixie Syncopators. Briefly in U.S. Navy. Through late forties and fifties mainly with groups led by Papa Celestin and Paul Barbarin.

Brooks, Joe (bjo, g). Member of Alcide Frank's Golden Rule Orchestra, working at Fewclothes Cabaret in Storyville in 1905.

Broussard, Theo (sb). First bass player in Papa Celestin's Original Tuxedo Orchestra, which opened in Storyville in 1912.

18

Steve Brown

Tom Brown (strings player)

Brown, Albert "Pud" (cl, s, c, b). b. Sacramento, Calif., Jan. 22, 1917. Multi-talented, much-traveled jazzman, grew up in a family band where he learned to play all instruments. Career includes long musical association with Jack Teagarden. Regularly employed on Bourbon Street and in the show band for *One Mo' Time* in the 1980s. Skilled at restoring and reconditioning old musical instruments and master of many other crafts.

Brown, James (sb). b. N.O., *ca.* 1880; d. N.O., *ca.* 1922. Played in the Golden Rule Orchestra under Alcide Frank at Fewclothes Cabaret in 1905. Also with Manuel Perez' Imperial Orchestra, 1907.

Brown, Johnny (cl). b. N.O., *ca.* 1880; d. *ca.* 1935. Played "vaudeville" style clarinet. Used horn mainly for comic effects, but led bands of fine musicians, beginning about 1910. In early twenties worked with Wooden Joe Nicholas and later with Dan Moody's dance group from Bogalusa, La., and Mandeville, La.

Brown, Ray (tb). b. N.O., *ca.* 1892; d. *ca.* 1940. With Clarence Desdunes' Joyland Revelers in early twenties, Fats Pichon, 1927. Joined Sidney Desvigne in 1928.

Brown, Sidney (b, tu, v). b. Deer Range, La., July 19, 1894; d. N.O., 1968. Also known as **Jim Little**. Played violin in Golden Leaf Band, 1919, after service discharge. Young Morgan Band, 1922; with his uncle, Jim Robinson, he recorded on Sam Morgan discs until Depression years. In the 1930s played tuba with the Tuxedo Brass Band and from the early 1940s to 1954 was with Papa Celestin.

Brown, Steve (tu, sb). b. N.O., *ca.* 1890; d. California, Sept. 15, 1965. Original bass man with the New Orleans Rhythm Kings in the early 1920s. Played in New Orleans earlier under the leadership of his brother, Tom Brown. Worked in Chicago with Husk O'Hare organization. Later with Jean Goldkette.

Brown, Tom (g, mdl). b. N.O., *ca.* 1878; d. N.O., *ca.* 1918. Popular string trio musician of early Storyville days, 1898–1906. Played at Tom Anderson's. Brother-in-law of Willie and Papa John Joseph.

Brown, Tom (tb, sb, l). b. N.O., June 3, 1888; d. N.O., March 25, 1958. Led first dixieland group to go north, 1915. This was the first band advertised as a "jass" band. Toured and recorded with Ray Miller, Yerkes band during twenties. In later years heard frequently in New Orleans with Johnny Wiggs–led groups. Late records on GHB, Southland.

Brown, William (tu, sou). b. N.O., July 31, 1918; d. N.O., Oct. 25, 1975. Popular sousaphone player with George Williams' Brass Band for many years. In 1966 played with Eureka Brass Band.

Tom Brown (trombonist)

Brownlee, Norman (p, sb). b. Algiers, La., Feb. 7, 1896; d. Pensacola, Fla., April 10, 1967. His orchestra played in New Orleans from 1920 until 1930. Recorded on Okeh in January, 1925. Moved to Pensacola in 1932, where he became secretary-treasurer of the musicians' union.

Brue, Steve (g, bjo). b. N.O., Feb. 10, 1904; d. Netherlands, Oct. 11, 1944. Princeton Revellers, New Orleans Owls, Triangle Band.

Brundy, Walter (d). b. N.O., *ca.* 1883; d. Natchez, Miss., 1941. One of the truly great drummers of all time. Teacher and inspiration for Baby Dodds and Ernest Rogers, among others. Superior Orchestra, 1905–1914; John Robichaux orchestra, 1912. Led his own band in Baton Rouge during World War I. Killed in auto crash.

Steve Brue

Brunies, Albert "Abbie" (c). b. N.O., Jan. 19, 1900; d. Biloxi, Miss., Oct. 2, 1978. In his early years, 1917–1918, he led Papa Laine units at Bucktown and Milneburg, lakefront resorts. Led the famous Halfway House Orchestra, 1919–1926. Had best nightclub jobs in town until he went into war industry in late thirties. Moved to Biloxi, Miss., in 1945 and was still leading a band there in 1960.

Brunies, Albert "Little Abbie" (d). b. N.O., 1914; d. New York, N.Y., Feb. 12, 1955. An outstanding dixieland drummer and member of a famed jazz clan; nephew of brothers Albert, George, Henry, Merritt, Richard. He died on the bandstand of Childs Paramount in New York on an engagement with Sharkey's band just as he'd begun to receive recognition.

Brunies, George (tb). b. N.O., Feb. 6, 1902; d. Chicago, Nov. 19, 1974. Best known of the many Brunies jazzmen. Original member of the New Orleans Rhythm Kings. At age eight, he was a member of Papa Laine's ju-

George Brunies

Henry Brunies

nior band and played in family bands all his early life. Worked regularly from 1923 to 1925 in the Ted Lewis orchestra. Was identified with the Eddie Condon group in New York for twenty years. In 1964 he was leading his own group in Cincinnati.

Brunies, Henry "Henny" (tb). b. N.O., *ca.* 1882; d. N.O., *ca.* 1934–35. Reliance Brass Band; Fischer's Brass Band; recorded with Merritt Brunies' orchestra in the twenties.

Brunies, Merritt (t, tb). b. N.O., Dec. 25, 1895; d. Biloxi, Miss., Feb. 4, 1973. His was the band that replaced the New Orleans Rhythm Kings at Friars Inn in Chicago. The seven records he cut for Okeh and Autograph are among the rarest and most prized of collectors' items. Recorded for American Music in the fifties.

Brunies, Richard "Richie" (c). b. N.O., Nov. 29, 1889; d. N.O., 1960. Powerful cornetist whose tone was said to rival Buddy Bolden's. Leader of one of Papa Laine's Reliance brass bands in pre–World War I era. Played with Fischer's Brass Band, 1907–1908.

Brunious, John "Picket" (p, t). b. N.O., Oct. 17, 1920; d. May 7, 1976. A nephew of Paul Barbarin, Brunious played and recorded on trumpet in his uncle's band. During the late 1940s as pianist he drifted into modern movement, but returned in early 1950s to legitimate New Orleans jazz. In the 1960s he helped revive the Onward Brass Band.

Richard Brunies

Burbank, Albert (cl). b. N.O., March 25, 1902; d. N.O., Aug. 15, 1976. Studied with Lorenzo Tio, Jr., 1916. Played in the city and at the lakefront through the twenties. During the Depression worked with Kid Milton's band. After navy duty, he worked with Herb Morand and Albert Jiles, mainly at Little Woods. Through the fifties worked at the Paddock, mainly with Octave Crosby, Paul Barbarin. Played with the Eureka and Young Tuxedo brass bands. Last days at Preservation Hall.

Albert Burbank

Raymond Burke

Joseph Butler

Burke, Chris (cl, s). b. Islington, London, Eng., Feb. 17, 1936. Pupil of Barney Bigard. Played in British jazz bands, especially in Nottingham during the 1970s. Settled in New Orleans, 1979, to play in local bands.

Burke, Raymond (cl). b. N.O., June 6, 1904. One of the greatest creative artists jazz has produced; completely self-taught. Has worked sporadically with all top dixieland stars and is widely recorded, but is disinclined to commit himself to steady employment. Nephew of early jazzman Jules Cassard and drummer Harold Peterson. Burke kept an antique and curiosity shop on Bourbon Street. His legal name is Barrois.

Burrella, Tony (d). b. N.O., ———. With Dixola Jazz Band in late twenties and early thirties.

Butler, Joseph "Kid Twat" (sb). b. Algiers, La., Dec. 25, 1907. Kid Thomas' band for many years. First job with Robert Clark's band.

Cagnolatti, Ernie (t). b. Madisonville, La., April 2, 1911. "Cag" worked with Papa Celestin, Paul Barbarin, and the Young Tuxedo Brass Band through much of his career. Played during the 1930s with Herb Leary's large society swing band. Through the sixties, seventies, and early eighties, he worked mainly at Preservation Hall.

Calier, Manuel (t). b. N.O., *ca.* 1897. Leader of the Bulls Club band, 1921–1922.

Calliste, Lester A. (tb). b. N.O., Aug. 13, 1947. Grand nephew of Buddy Petit. In the 1970s played with Olympia Brass Band, Young Tuxedo Brass Band.

Camp, Clem (cl). b. N.O., *ca.* 1894; d. N.O., 1968. Early dixieland musician at his peak before 1914 with the Brunies brothers, Nick La Rocca, Papa Laine.

Campbell, Arthur (p, tb). b. N.O., *ca.* 1890; d. Chicago, Ill., *ca.* 1941. A Storyville "professor" between 1908 and 1917, he sometimes played piano in King Oliver's band in 1915 at Pete Lala's Cafe. He played in Piron's Or-

Murphy Campo

chestra at Spanish Fort in 1918. He played trombone in the Magnolia Brass Band before World War I and recorded in Chicago with Freddie Keppard.

Campo, Murphy (t). b. Delacroix Island, La., Dec. 30, 1935. Was house bandleader at the Famous Door through most of the 1960s and has been a fixture on Bourbon Street most of his professional life. Also worked extended national tour in band led by Big Tiny Little.

Candido, Candy (sb, vo). b. N.O., ca. 1909. During the 1930s played in bands led by Louis and Leon Prima. With Orleanian Otto Himel formed the famed music and comedy team known as "Candy and Coco" and was featured on the stage and in films with Ted Fiorito's orchestra. Candy and Coco teamed with Monk Hazel to accompany the popular singer Gene Austin on records.

Capra, Jimmy. See Capraro, Angelo.

Capraro, Angelo (g, l). b. N.O., March 22, 1910; d. Las Vegas, Nev., Dec., 1963. During the 1930s played with bands led by Leon Prima, Louis Prima, and Sharkey. On tour under the name of **Jimmy Capra**, he spent many years playing for dancing in Hot Springs, Ark. In his youth he played in his brother Joe's band at the Cotton Club in New Orleans.

Capraro, Joe (g, l). b. N.O., June 26, 1903. Worked under Sharkey and the New Orleans Rhythm Masters with Sidney Arodin, Chink Martin, and Leo Adde. He had the house band on radio station WSMB during the twenties, and during the thirties his band at the New Orleans Cotton Club and other places worked more consistently than any other in town.

Joe Capraro

Carey, Jack (tb). b. Hahnville, La., ca. 1889; d. N.O., ca. 1935. May have been first to play in tailgate style. From 1908 was among first to use French melodies for jazz. His Crescent Orchestra was one of the great early jazz bands. The celebrated tune "Tiger Rag" was previously called "Jack Carey."

Carey, Thomas "Papa Mutt" (c). b. Hahnville, La., 1891; d. San Francisco, Calif., Sept. 3, 1948. In brother Jack's Crescent Orchestra, 1910–1914. Worked in the district until 1916, mainly with Kid Ory. In 1917 went to Chicago with Johnny Dodds, replaced King Oliver orchestra at Dreamland. He was back in New Orleans in 1918 with Wade Whaley and rejoined Ory in California in 1919. In 1944 made weekly network broadcasts with Ory for Orson Welles. Played in New York during late forties, mainly with Edmond Hall.

Carr, Son (b). A member of Kid Lindsey's band at Rice's Cafe in the district, 1916–1917.

Carroll, Albert (p, tb). b. N.O., ca. 1880; d. ——. Played piano in the brothels of Basin Street until Storyville closed in 1917, then worked the best band jobs in town, notably at the Lyric Theater until 1927. He sometimes played trombone in parades.

23

Mutt Carey

Carter, Buddy (p). b. N.O., *ca.* 1870. A Storyville piano player until about 1910 who is generally spoken of by his contemporaries as "King of the Blues."

Casey, Bob (p). b. Detroit, Mich., 1921; d. N.O., 1980. Regular with the Last Straws.

Casimir, Joe (d). b. N.O., *ca.* 1902. Brother of John Casimir. Worked with him in Young Eagles Band, 1919. With Kid Milton's band in early twenties.

Casimir, John (cl). b. N.O., Oct. 16, 1898; d. N.O., Jan. 3, 1963. For many years manager and clarinetist for the Young Tuxedo Brass Band; recorded on Atlantic with this group. Started career in 1919 with Young Eagles Band of Lee Collins.

Cassard, Jules (sb, tb). b. N.O., *ca.* 1895. Early dixieland musician. Played with members of Original Dixieland Jazz Band before they left for fame in New York. Composer of jazz standard, "Angry." Uncle of Raymond Burke; brother of Leo Cassard. Living in Miami, Fla., 1982.

Castaign, Johnny (d). b. N.O., 1912; d. N.O., Oct. 30, 1972. Dixielander associated primarily with Sharkey, Tony Almerico, and Earl Dantin orchestras.

Castigliola, Angelo J. "Bubby" (tb). b. N.O., Aug. 28, 1924. Only jazzman from a noted concert-trained family. Toured with Jack Teagarden's dance band. Worked with Irving Fazola, Tony Almerico, and in WWL studio band, the Dawn Busters.

John Casimir

Cates, Sidney (bjo, g). b. N.O., *ca.* 1900; d. N.O., Sept. 6, 1968. Active musician from the 1920s. Started with Leo Dejan's Moonlight Serenaders. During mid-thirties worked in WPA music program. Was an executive of the musicians' union.

Papa Celestin

Boojie Centobie

John Chaffe

"Cato" (d). b. N.O., *ca.* 1875. Full name not known. Very popular drummer with Frank Duson's Eagle Band, 1907, after latter took over Bolden group. Also with Herb Lindsay's Primrose Orchestra, 1912, and Amos Riley's Tulane Orchestra, 1915.

Cato, Adam (p). Active dance band piano man during late 1920s and early Depression years.

"Cato, Big" (bjo). b. N.O., *ca.* 1869. Correct full name not known. Member of Amos Riley's Tulane Orchestra in 1915. Uncle of Cato the drummer. May have introduced "Careless Love."

Celestin, Oscar "Papa" (t, c). b. Napoleonville, La., Jan. 1, 1884; d. N.O., Dec. 15, 1954. Played with Algiers Brass Band in early 1900s. Founded Original Tuxedo Orchestra in 1910 and Tuxedo Brass Band in 1911. Popular bandleader in New Orleans for forty-four years. Recorded for Okeh, 1925, Columbia, 1926–1928, and many others in his last years.

Centobie, Leonard "Boojie" (cl). b. N.O., Oct. 14, 1915. Dixielander who made his reputation with Sharkey, Wingy Manone, Johnny Wiggs, beginning in the mid-thirties.

Chaffe, John (bjo, tu, mdl). b. N.O., March 29, 1938. Banjo virtuoso, co-founder of the Last Straws. Recorded with Edmond Souchon on the Banjo Bums LP. With the very popular Louisiana Repertory Jazz Ensemble, 1980–

Hippolyte Charles

Photo by George Fishman

Julius Chevez

Emile Christian

1982, attracting crowds to Carrollton's Maple Leaf Club on Wednesday nights. Was also cofounder of the Last Straws (1957). Studied with Lawrence Marrero and Edmond Souchon.

Chambers, Tig (c). b. N.O., *ca.* 1880; d. Chicago, Ill., 1950. In 1907 he joined the Eagle Band under Frank Duson. In 1910 he formed the Magnolia Sweets. Played at Fewclothes Cabaret, Pete Lala's, Abadie's. Left New Orleans permanently in 1915.

Chandler, Dede "Dee Dee" (d). b. N.O., *ca.* 1866; d. N.O., 1925. Drummer for John Robichaux before Spanish-American War. First drummer to play jazz style in dance band. Often credited with inventing the foot pedal. Excellent showman and comic. Played with the grace of a professional juggler.

Charles, Hippolyte (c). b. St. Martinville, La., April 18, 1891. With Manuel Perez, 1909; Silver Leaf Orchestra, 1911. Played with Tuxedo Brass Band before World War I. Joined Maple Leaf Orchestra, 1919, then started own band. Active until illness forced his retirement from music in 1925.

Charles, Jesse (cl, s). b. N.O., June 25, 1900; d. N.O., Aug. 4, 1975. Parade musician for many years in George Williams' Brass Band. In the forties with Abby Williams' Happy Pals Brass Band.

Chase, Samuel (bjo).

Cherie, Eddie (s, cl). b. N.O., 1889; d. Chicago, Ill., 1941. Played with Sidney Desvigne on the SS *Island Queen* (1927). Also with Manuel Perez.

Red Clark

Chevez, Julius (p). b. N.O., Aug. 16, 1908. Very popular dixieland rhythm man, much favored by Johnny Wiggs, Digger Laine, Irving Fazola, the Melon Pickers.

Christensen, Siegfried (p). b. N.O., Oct. 27, 1907; d. N.O., Dec. 19, 1980. Son of a well-known concert band leader of the Reconstruction era, he became a successful attorney. In his early years he was a ranking dixieland pianist, much favored by Johnny Wiggs, Sharkey, Bill Padron, and other prominent leaders of the 1930s.

Christian, Charles (tb). b. N.O., July 25, 1886; d. N.O., July 11, 1964. Brother of Frank and Emile. Played in the Domino Orchestra.

Christian, Emile (tb, sb, t). b. N.O., April 20, 1895; d. N.O., Dec. 31, 1973. Played in the Reliance Brass Band, later replaced Daddy Edwards in the Original Dixieland Jazz Band when the band went to England, 1919–1921. With Morgan's Euphonic Band, 1910. Trombone and string bass for top New Orleans dixieland groups like Sharkey's, Santo Pecora's, 1966.

Christian, Frank (t, cl, v, tu). b. N.O., Sept. 3, 1887; d. N.O., Nov. 27, 1973. Started about 1908 with Papa Laine's Reliance Band. Ragtime bandleader, 1910–1918, in New Orleans. Then led New Orleans Jazz Band in Chicago and New York, with Jimmy Durante on piano. Worked with Fischer's Brass Band, and in groups including his brothers Emile and Charles. Featured in vaudeville in the early twenties with Gilda Gray. Last jobs in New Orleans were with Durfee's Band.

Christian, Narcisse J. "Buddy" (p, bjo, g). b. N.O., ca. 1895; d. late 1940s. Another of the legendary Storyville "professors," Christian also played in bands with Peter Bocage at the Tuxedo, 1912–1913, and with Joe Oliver at Lala's Cafe, 1915–1916. During the twenties he recorded extensively on piano with bands led by Clarence Williams and on banjo and guitar in smaller groups.

Cinquemano, Paul (tb). b. N.O., ca. 1893. With Johnny Bayersdorffer in pre–World War I era.

Clark, Aaron Warren (bh). b. Louisville, Ky., 1858; d. N.O., Sept. 4, 1894. With Excelsior Brass Band, 1882–1890, and Onward Brass Band, 1890–1894. Father of Red Clark.

Clark, Joseph "Red" (tb, tu). b. N.O., Feb. 12, 1894; d. N.O., Nov. 30, 1960. Studied brass with Dave Perkins. Joined the Tonic Triad Band in 1928. With the Masonic Brass Band in the 1930s. Beloved manager and musician of the Eureka Brass Band, 1947–1960. A diligent collector and preserver of the music of the earlier New Orleans marching bands.

Clayton, James "Kid" (t). b. Jasper County, Miss., March 2, 1902; d. N.O., Dec. 17, 1963. An untutored musician, Clayton was mainly limited to rhythm and blues. Played with Jack Carey's band in the 1920s. Worked many jobs with saxophonist John Handy.

Clem, Edouard (c). b. St. Joseph, La., before Civil War; d. N.O., early 1920s. An almost blind, one-eyed musician, but a fast "reader." Before Spanish-American War played with Charlie Galloway's orchestra and a group led by Wallace Collins. Replaced Bolden when Frank Duson took control of Buddy's band. Led his own band, 1907–1912. Ended musical career in Johnny Brown's band about 1920. Paraded sometimes with Onward and Excelsior brass bands.

Kid Clayton

Lee Collins   *Photo by John Minter*

Kid Sheik Colar

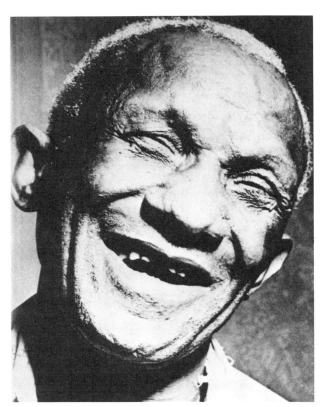

Wallace Collins

Clifton, Chris (t). b. Detroit, Mich., July 12, 1939. A protégé of both Louis Armstrong and Lil Hardin Armstrong before he settled in New Orleans in 1966. Plays and sings in the Armstrong style and, though employed full time in the plumbing business, has found ample time to perform with leading dance orchestras and brass bands besides leading his own groups.

28

Harry Connick, Jr.

Ann Cook

Colar, George "Kid Sheik" (t). b. N.O., Sept. 15, 1908. Protégé of Wooden Joe Nicholas. Led small dance groups for many years. During mid-thirties was in Kid Rena's marching band. Since 1952, with Eureka Brass Band. Regular at Preservation Hall in 1982.

Collins, Lee (t). b. N.O., Oct. 17, 1901; d. Chicago, Ill., July 3, 1960. At age fifteen was filling in with Original Tuxedo Orchestra and marching with Tuxedo Brass Band. In 1919 worked parade with Buddy Petit, Chris Kelly. Pupil of Professor Jim Humphrey. In 1920 with Young Eagles and Golden Leaf Band. In 1924 replaced Louis Armstrong in King Oliver's orchestra in Chicago. Recorded with Jelly Roll Morton same year. In the 1920s worked in New York, Chicago with Luis Russell, Dave Peyton, Zutty Singleton, Mezz Mezzrow orchestras. Cut famed 1929 discs with the Jones-Collins Astoria Hot Eight in New Orleans. Settled and worked in Chicago. Went to France in 1951 on tour with Mezzrow. Played for a while in 1954 on Bourbon Street at the Paddock with his close friend, Ricard Alexis.

Collins, Wallace (tu, bh). b. N.O., 1858; d. N.O., ca. 1944. Led own group as early as 1888. Member of Charlie Galloway orchestra in 1894. Played with Buddy Bolden.

Cómes, Count (p). b. N.O., ———. Played with the Dixola Jazz Band in the 1920s.

Connick, Harry, Jr. (p). b. N.O., Sept. 11, 1967. At age ten played TV duet with Eubie Blake. Went on to perform with leading New Orleans jazzmen, holding his own despite his youth, before he was fifteen years old. Son of New Orleans District Attorney Harry Connick and the late Judge Anita Connick.

Cook, Ann (vo). b. Franzenville, La., ca. 1888; d. N.O., Sept. 29, 1962. A popular blues singer who recorded in 1927 accompanied by Louis Dumaine's Jazzola Eight.

Cooper, Harold (cl, ts). b. N.O., July 21, 1924; d. Texas, March 23, 1978. In the 1950s with George Girard, Al Hirt, Dukes of Dixieland. In 1966 with the Alamo Jazz Band, San Antonio.

Robert Coquille

Willie Cornish

Louis Cottrell, Sr.

Copland, Thomas (sb, tu). b. N.O., ——; d. N.O., *ca.* 1945. With Magnolia Orchestra, 1910. Early member of the Sam Morgan band, 1918–1919. From 1927 was in the second Olympia Orchestra, formed by Arnold Depass. Sometimes played with Dee Dee Pierce.

Coquille, Robert (sb). b. N.O., Sept. 15, 1911; d. N.O., Aug. 15, 1982. Regular with George Girard's New Orleans Five. Played with Sharkey and with groups led by Al Hirt and Pete Fountain.

Cordilla, Charles Joseph (cl, s). b. Baton Rouge, La., May 25, 1900. Early dixielander much associated with the Brunies groups, Leon Roppolo, Emmett Hardy, Papa Laine. Worked five years at Halfway House in 1920s. Also with Stalebread Lacoume and the Shields brothers. Was with Leon Prima, Sharkey on the SS *Greater New Orleans.*

Cornish, Willie (vt). b. N.O., Aug. 1, 1875; d. N.O., Jan. 12, 1942. An early jazz pioneer. Played with Buddy Bolden. Veteran of the Spanish-American War. From 1903 played almost exclusively in brass bands. Joined Eureka Brass Band soon after it was founded.

Costa, Anthony J. "Tony" (cl, s). b. N.O., Feb. 9, 1910. Associated with Tony Almerico and Phil Zito, Dukes of Dixieland, Sharkey.

Costa, Michael A. (cl, s). b. N.O., May 4, 1915.

Cottrell, Louis, Sr. (d). b. N.O., *ca.* 1875; d. N.O., 1927. One of the greatest of New Orleans drummers. Prominent with A. J. Piron Orchestra from 1918 until his

Louis Cottrell, Jr.

Paul Crawford

death. Worked in the district, 1909–1913. In 1915 was with Manuel Perez in Chicago. Made recording sessions with Piron in the early twenties.

Cottrell, Louis, Jr. (cl, s). b. N.O., March 7, 1911; d. N.O., March 21, 1978. Studied with Lorenzo Tio, Jr., and Barney Bigard. Joined Young Tuxedo Orchestra, 1927. In 1928 worked with Golden Rule Orchestra, Bebé Ridgley, Sidney Desvigne, and Chris Kelly. Toured with Don Albert Orchestra, 1929–39. With A. J. Piron on riverboats. Returned to Desvigne in 1942. Marched with Young Tuxedo Brass Band. Played frequently with Paul Barbarin. President of local 496, American Federation of Musicians, when there was a separate black union.

Cousin Joe. See Joseph, Pleasant.

Coustaut, Manuel (c). b. N.O., before Civil War; d. N.O., ———. Early dance-band leader, 1888–1893.

Coustaut, Sylvester (c). b. N.O., before Civil War; d. N.O., ca. 1910. Founding member of the Onward Brass Band, 1886. Played in dance band led jointly by his brother, Manuel, and Daniel Desdunes, 1890.

Coycault, Ernest "Nenny" (c). b. Violet, La., ca. 1890. Left New Orleans in 1914, but between 1908 and that time worked with the Peerless Orchestra under Bab Frank, the Superior Orchestra, and the Gaspard brothers. Brother of Pill Coycault.

Coycault, Jerome "Pill" (cl). b. Violet, La., ca. 1895; d. Cleveland, Ohio, Oct. 4, 1928. Crippled. Often worked with Buddy Petit. Had jobs with the New Orleans Creole Jazz Band under Amos White and with Peter Lacaze for dance hall work. Actually played in New Orleans for only three years, 1919–1921.

Cozzens, Jimmy (d). b. N.O., ca. 1898. Dixielander active in the twenties and thirties, especially with Alfred Laine.

Crais, William J. "Bill" (tb). b. N.O., June 20, 1927. Attorney. Popular dixielander of the fifties and early sixties with Al Hirt, Pete Fountain, Sharkey. Operated Vieux Carré Record Shop, Bourbon and St. Peter streets.

Crawford, Joseph. See Petit, Buddy.

Crawford, Paul (tb, bh, sb, tu, l, arr). b. Atmore, Ala., Feb. 16, 1925. Co-leader of Crawford-Ferguson Night Owls. Began jazz career in the fifties. Made his first recording session in 1957 with Lakefront Loungers on GHB.

Octave Crosby

Joe Darensbourg   *Photo by Gene Williams*

Percy Darensburg

Periodically with Punch Miller at Preservation Hall. Helped to develop the jazz archive at Tulane University and frequently made musical arrangements for out-of-town bands. Mainly known as trombonist. Played baritone horn in the musical *One Mo' Time.*

Creger, Bill (cl, s). b. N.O., *ca.* 1900; d. N.O., July 26, 1927. Dixielander who worked with Johnny Bayers-dorffer after World War I.

Crombie, Alonzo (d, tb). b. N.O., *ca.* 1895. Dixieland-style drummer active in New Orleans in post–World War I era. Mainly identified with Norman Brownlee Orchestra and with Emmett Hardy.

Crosby, Octave (p). b. N.O., June 10, 1898; d. N.O., Oct. 1, 1971. From 1953 to 1962 a fixture at the Paddock on Bourbon Street as bandleader. Began his career with Herb Morand about 1922. Soon organized his own combination.

Crumb, Earl (d, l). b. N.O., April 30, 1899. Invincibles String Band, Six and 7/8 String Band. Leader of famous New Orleans Owls, 1920–1928.

Crump, Frank (s). b. N.O., *ca.* 1903; d. N.O., 1957. Worked with Chris Kelly in the mid-twenties. During

Depression years was in Crescent City Serenaders Orchestra led by Albert Walters. Was in ERA Orchestra in 1935.

Sid Davilla

Crusto, Manuel (cl, s, t). b. N.O., May 2, 1918. With Fats Pichon on the SS *Capitol* in the thirties and forties. Often heard at Heritage Hall, Preservation Hall.

Cuny, Frank (p). b. N.O., Dec. 14, 1890; d. N.O., 1966. Played with Tony Parenti, Johnny DeDroit, 1917–1928.

Dalmado, Tony (t). b. N.O., Oct. 25, 1918. Trumpet player on outstanding Keynote session with Irving Fazola.

Darensbourg, Joe (cl, ts). b. Baton Rouge, La., July 9, 1906. Career began in 1924 with Martel's family band of Opelousas. He then went to work traveling with a medicine show playing to attract attention to the "medicine man's" pitch. In the late twenties with Fate Marable and worked for a while on the riverboats. Through the forties and fifties he was identified with the Kid Ory band in California. Under his own name he made the record of "Yellow Dog Blues" that became the nation's overnight jukebox favorite.

Darensburg, Caffrey (bjo, g). b. N.O., *ca.* 1880; d. Texas, late 1920s. Virtuoso soloist. Sometimes with A. J. Piron, Manuel Perez.

Darensburg, Percy (bjo, g, mdl). b. N.O., *ca.* 1882. Played banjo on 1928 discs with Frenchy's String Band, a quartet that included Johnny St. Cyr, Tommy Ladnier, Lonnie Johnson.

Darensburg, Willie (t, c, v). b. N.O., *ca.* 1885.

Dave, Johnny (bjo). b. N.O., *ca.* 1898; d. N.O., *ca.* 1943. Banjo player on the historic Sam Morgan disc sessions of 1927. During the Depression with Kid Milton and in nickel-a-dance palaces with Alphonse Picou.

Davilla, Sid (cl, s). b. N.O., Sept. 9, 1915. Musician-owner of the Mardi Gras Lounge on Bourbon Street for many years. Veteran of swing band era.

Davis, George (d). b. Algiers, La., *ca.* 1875. Bass drummer with the Pacific Brass Band from 1900 to the beginning of World War I. Sometimes played with the Allen Brass Band.

Davis, Howard (s). b. N.O., *ca.* 1900. Played in dance groups during the 1920s; sometimes with Louis Dumaine's Brass Band. Was in ERA Orchestra in 1935 and WPA Brass Band in 1936, both under Dumaine's direction. In 1962 was still playing parades sponsored by the New Orleans Jazz Club of Southern California.

Davis, Sammy (p). b. N.O., *ca.* 1881. Reputed to be one of the fastest hot piano players in history. Played in the district's brothels from 1897 to 1915. Was still going strong in the mid-fifties in upstate New York nightclubs.

Davis, Stuart (sb). b. N.O., *ca.* 1927. Played with Celestin band.

Dawson, Eddie (sb). b. N.O., July 24, 1884; d. Memphis, Tenn., Aug. 12, 1972. A favorite of King Oliver, he played with him in pre–World War I years in Storyville. Jobbed

Harold Dejan

Buglin' Sam Dekemel

around town all his life. Frequently seen in the 1950s playing at Mama Lou's in Little Woods with Peter Bocage. Ended his career at Preservation Hall.

Decou, Walter (p). b. N.O., *ca.* 1890; d. N.O., Dec. 12, 1966. Band piano player in New Orleans during Storyville days. Led his own group during the twenties at cabarets. He is on the Sam Morgan records of 1927. Recorded with Bunk Johnson.

Dedroit, Johnny (t). b. N.O., Dec. 4, 1892. Leader of a popular dance band for nearly forty years.

Dedroit, Paul (d, x). b. N.O., Dec. 24, 1894; d. Los Angeles, Calif., Jan. 2, 1963. Mainly in theater pit bands with Emile Tosso and in brother Johnny's band.

Deichman, Benny (tb). b. N.O., 1893; d. N.O., Jan. 13, 1939. Dixieland pioneer worked with Papa Laine bands and with the Barocco brothers. In the twenties he was on the lake steamer *Susquehanna.*

Deichman, Charles (v, c, l). b. N.O., Oct. 12, 1894; d. N.O., Oct. 3, 1927. A major bandleader before World War I. Held many carnival ball contracts, and his Moonlight Serenaders were the house band at the Tudor. He was a concert-trained musician but pioneered with a

dixieland band in New York almost simultaneously with the Original Dixieland Jazz Band. Brother of Benny.

Dejan, Harold (s). b. N.O., Feb. 4, 1909. Usually a leader of small rhythm-and-blues type groups. Played in his brother Leo's Moonlight Serenaders as a teenager about 1918. In the 1930s he led a band on the lake steamers, and during the fifties, he was frequently in the Young Tuxedo Brass Band. Leader of the Olympia Brass Band.

Dejan, Leo (t). b. N.O., May 4, 1911. At fifteen he led his own band, the Moonlight Serenaders. Later in the twenties led a group he called the Black Diamond Orchestra.

Dekemel, Matthew Antoine Desire (bugle, vo). b. N.O., *ca.* 1900; d. N.O., Jan. 6, 1967. Known as "Buglin' Sam, the Waffle Man." Dekemel's bizarre specialty was playing jazz tunes on a regulation army bugle. He was featured for years in Tony Almerico's Parisian Room broadcasts and has been adequately recorded.

De La Houssaye, Frank (p). b. N.O., ——. The Last Straws.

Delandry, Frank (g). b. N.O., *ca.* 1888. A virtuoso who worked in the brothels of Storyville where music was desired but no piano was available, about 1900.

Delaney, Jack (tb). b. N.O., Aug. 27, 1930; d. N.O., 1976. With Tony Almerico and Sharkey in the 1950s. Played with Leon Kellner's orchestra in the Roosevelt Hotel during the 1960s. Then with Pete Fountain.

Jack Delaney

Delay, Mike (t). b. N.O., Sept. 29, 1909; d. Los Angeles, Calif., Jan. 28, 1980. Dance band leader of the thirties with the Hollywood Orchestra of New Orleans. Member of Johnny St. Cyr's band, Disneyland, 1966.

Delisle, Baptiste (tb). b. N.O., *ca.* 1868; d. N.O., *ca.* 1920. Joined the Onward Brass Band about 1890; John Robichaux in 1894. Delisle and the entire Onward Brass Band enlisted for Spanish-American War. Rejoined Robichaux in 1905 after long illness.

Delisle, Louis Nelson. See Nelson, "Big Eye Louis."

Delrose, Harold (s). b. N.O., ———. Played in Pop Hamilton's orchestra in the early Depression years.

Delrose, Henry (cl).

Demond, Frank (tb, bjo). b. Los Angeles, Calif., April 3, 1933. Preservation Hall Jazz Band. One of few younger musicians able to play correctly in the Kid Ory–Jim Robinson tradition.

Dent, Lawrence (cl). b. N.O., ———. With Gibson Brass Band. Nephew of Johnny and Baby Dodds.

Depass, Arnold (d). b. N.O., *ca.* 1900; d. N.O., *ca.* 1945. Led small combinations in the district before World War I. After coming out of the service, he played with Jack Carey, Chris Kelly, Buddy Petit, and Kid Rena. Mainly played with Punch Miller, 1920–1927. Until the Depression, he led his own group, the Olympia Orchestra, 1927–1932. Gave up music about 1934.

Arnold Depass

Depass, Dave (cl). b. N.O., *ca.* 1888. Older brother of Arnold Depass, the drummer. Played in the Magnolia Orchestra in 1910.

Derbigny, Arthur (t, s). b. N.O., *ca.* 1906; d. N.O., Oct. 20, 1962. With Young Superior Band, mid-1920s, on trumpet; and with Bebé Ridgley's Original Tuxedo Orchestra on saxophone, 1925.

Desdunes, Clarence (v, bjo, l). b. N.O., 1896; d. Arizona, *ca.* 1934. Concert-trained bandleader. With help of A. J. Piron, formed the Joyland Revelers, a successful big band employing many prominent jazzmen during the twenties, mainly touring the South. Active during late twenties, early thirties. Well known throughout the Midwest, especially in Omaha, Neb.

Desvigne, Sidney (t). b. N.O., Sept. 11, 1893; d. Los Angeles, Calif., Dec. 2, 1959. Although he was leader of a large swing orchestra of the 1930s, Desvigne was an excellent jazz musician. Began at Rice Cafe and 101 Ranch in the district, 1917; later with Maple Leaf Orchestra and Excelsior Brass Band. With Fate Marable on the SS *Capitol*, 1922. Through most of the 1920s, led his own band on the *Island Queen*, New Orleans–Cincinnati. Moved to California in 1946.

35

Horace Diaz

Johnny Dodds

36

Baby Dodds

Natty Dominique

Diaz, Horace (p). b. N.O., *ca.* 1906. Played with Leon Prima, Jules Bauduc. Became music director for Holiday Inns.

Dientrans, Pete (t). b. N.O., *ca.* 1882. Pre–World War I dixieland musician. Worked with Papa Laine, Frank Christian, Bill Gallaty, Sr.

Dimes, Bill (cl). b. N.O., *ca.* 1895. Played for and managed the Liberty Bell Orchestra, 1919–1920.

Dinkel, Wilbur (p). b. N.O., *ca.* 1880; d. April, 1940. Early dixielander with Tony Parenti. Also in pit band at Dauphine Theater.

Dodds, Johnny (cl). b. N.O., April 12, 1892; d. Chicago, Ill., Aug. 8, 1940. Widely considered the greatest of New Orleans clarinetists. Pupil of Lorenzo Tio, Jr. Began his professional career about 1910 with Frank Duson's Eagle Band. Worked with Ory. Left New Orleans in 1918 with Billy Mack vaudeville troupe. Joined King Oliver in Chicago. Led his own group, 1924–1930. Member of Louis Armstrong's Hot Five recording group. Accurate biography of Dodds in "Kings of Jazz" paperback series, A. S. Barnes & Co.

Dodds, Warren "Baby" (d). b. N.O., Dec. 24, 1896; d. Chicago, Ill., Feb. 14, 1959. King of New Orleans drummers. Brother of Johnny. Musically trained by Walter Brundy, Dave Perkins, Manuel Manetta. From 1913 to 1918 worked with Papa Celestin, Jack Carey, Willie Hightower, Big Eye Louis Nelson. On steamers *Sidney*, *St. Paul*, and *Capitol* under Fate Marable. Joined King Oliver on tour in California, 1921, and jobbed around Chicago for the next fifteen years. Widely recorded, mainly with Jelly Roll Morton, Louis Armstrong. Joined Bunk Johnson band in 1944. Worked in New York through 1949, mainly at Jimmy Ryan's, with weekend concerts at Stuyvesant Casino, the Central Plaza, and the Philadelphia Academy of Music, in Al Rose's "Journeys into Jazz." Made series of demonstration drum recordings for students. Excellent autobiography, Contemporary Press, Los Angeles.

Lawrence Duhé

Louis Dumaine

Dolliole, Milford (d). b. N.O., Oct. 23, 1903. Member of the Young Tuxedo Orchestra in the early 1920s. Retired from music about 1950 after having played for many years in lakefront resorts. Sometimes at Preservation Hall in the seventies.

Dominguez, Paul, Sr. (sb). b. N.O., *ca.* 1865. A classical musician who frequently played jobs with jazzmen. Did not pluck, but bowed the string bass. Frequently seen with John Robichaux in the early 1900s.

Dominguez, Paul, Jr. (v, g). b. N.O., *ca.* 1887. Concert musician, but played jazz in the Storyville cabarets. Was with Armstrong in 1923 at Anderson's on Rampart Street. In California in 1965.

Dominique, Albert. See Albert, Don.

Dominique, Anatie "Natty" (t). b. N.O., Aug. 2, 1896. Career mainly tied to the Dodds brothers in Chicago. Played a little in New Orleans before his family moved north. In 1925 was with Johnny Dodds at Kelly's Stables. Played a concert in 1965. Uncle of Don Albert.

Don, Wesley (t). b. N.O., *ca.* 1892; d. Baton Rouge, La., 1934. Leader of the Liberty Bell Orchestra, 1919–1920. Excellent trumpet man whose career was cut short by an auto accident.

Doria, Al (d). b. N.O., Dec. 24, 1899; d. N.O., May 26, 1977. Dixieland drummer who worked with most of top musicians in the field of jazz from 1920. Worked in band instrument department at Werlein's music store in New Orleans.

Douroux Family. A large family of musicians that has been supplying jazz, dance, and concert music in the New Orleans area for a century. Its distinguished membership includes Dolly Adams and her sons Placide and Jerry. The Manettas, too, are part of this clan.

Duconge, Albert (t). b. N.O., *ca.* 1895. Member of great early jazz family. Played with Fate Marable on the SS *Capitol*, 1925, and briefly with Sidney Desvigne on the *Island Queen*.

Duconge, Oscar (c). b. Napoleonville, La., *ca.* 1870; d. N.O., *ca.* 1924. Early member of the Onward Brass Band, 1890, he enlisted with the rest of the band at the time of the Spanish-American War. Later led dance band in which Alphonse Picou played.

Maurice Durand

Frank Duson

Honoré Dutrey

Duconge, Pete (cl). b. N.O., *ca.* 1900. Played on Streck-fus steamers in early 1920s.

Dugie, "Red" (p). With New Orleans Creole Jazz Band under Amos White in the mid-twenties, playing at Spanish Fort.

Duhé, Lawrence (cl). b. LaPlace, La., April 30, 1887; d. Lafayette, La., 1959. Made jazz debut in New Orleans in 1913, coming from hometown with friend, Kid Ory. Became leader same year at 101 Ranch and studied with Lorenzo Tio, Jr. Left for Chicago in 1917; led a band at the Deluxe Cafe, 1917–1919. After brief tour in vaudeville returned to Louisiana. Played in small towns with Evan Thomas' band. Retired from music in 1944.

Duke, Charlie (d). b. N.O., Aug. 23, 1913; d. N.O., Nov. 4, 1973. Dixielander usually associated with Basin Street Six, George Girard in the 1950s.

Dumaine, Louis (c, t). b. N.O., *ca.* 1890; d. N.O., *ca.* 1949. From 1922 to his death, usually worked as a leader. Played in the Tuxedo Brass Band in the early and mid-twenties. Also had his own marching band. Led WPA Band in 1935, ERA Orchestra in 1936, and during the Depression years was partner of Fats Houston in a dance band. His Jazzola Eight made some early jazz discs.

Dupont, Charles (t, sb). b. N.O., Oct. 20, 1907. Active dixielander; was business agent of American Federation of Musicians local 174 during the 1950s. Played Fairhope, Ala., with Von Gammon, 1965.

Durand, Maurice (t). b. N.O., July 4, 1893; d. Calif., Nov. 23, 1961. Played in Onward and Tuxedo brass bands in the 1920s. Also led own dance band through this period. Known to have been an exceptional technician. Resided in California.

Duson, Frank (vt). b. Algiers, La., 1881; d. N.O., April 1, 1936. Early 1900s with Buddy Bolden. Took over the band in 1907 when Bolden was committed to mental institution. Active musically until the mid-thirties. On SS *Capitol* and with own band at cabarets and Thom's Roadhouse. In mid-Depression was in the ERA Orchestra. Worked irregularly with Louis Dumaine.

Sam Dutrey, Jr.

Lars Edegran

Dutrey, Honoré (tb). b. N.O., 1894; d. Chicago, Ill., July 21, 1937. Started with Melrose Brass Band at seventeen. Worked with his brother Sam in Silver Leaf Orchestra; with Noone-Petit Orchestra, 1913. Lungs injured in accident during World War I. Joined King Oliver in Chicago, 1919–1924. Also worked through the late 1920s with Carroll Dickerson, Johnny Dodds, and Louis Armstrong (1927).

Dutrey, Sam, Sr. (cl, s). b. N.O., 1888; d. N.O., 1941. Silver Leaf Orchestra, 1907; Tulane Orchestra, 1915; Papa Celestin, 1916; SS *Capitol* orchestra, 1920. With Eddie Jackson's dance band in early 1920s and with John Robichaux at the Lyric Theater in 1925. Brother of Honore.

Dutrey, Sam, Jr. (cl). b. N.O., *ca.* 1915; d. N.O., Aug. 26, 1971. Occasionally played parade jobs and dances. Recorded on Southland records. Worked with Joe Robichaux in the 1930s.

Early, Tom (sb). b. N.O., *ca.* 1880; d. N.O., Sept. 8, 1958. Dixieland man, worked irregularly. Led Harmony Band.

Eastwood, Bill (bjo, g, s). b. N.O., Aug. 31, 1899; d. N.O., *ca.* 1960. With Norman Brownlee in the early 1920s. Also in the 1920s with Halfway House Orchestra. In later years was business agent for the American Guild of Variety Artists.

Ebbert, Tom (tb). b. Pittsburgh, Pa., Sept. 9, 1919. Composer. Identified with Connie Jones's band and as a charter member of the Louisiana Repertory Jazz Ensemble.

Daddy Edwards

Edegran, Lars Ivar (p, g, cl, s, l). b. Stockholm, Sweden, 1944. Moved to New Orleans in 1966. Leader, New Orleans Ragtime Orchestra; International Jazz Band. Played with Sharkey, Alvin Alcorn, New Orleans Joymakers. Recorded with Kid Thomas, George Lewis, Jim Robinson, Dee Dee Pierce.

Charles Elgar

Alex Esposito

Homer Eugene

Edwards, Eddie "Daddy" (v, tb). b. N.O., May 22, 1891; d. New York, N.Y., April 9, 1963. About 1910 was playing violin for silent movie theaters. Began trombone in 1914 in parades. With Ernest Giardina orchestra, 1914. Played in the Reliance Brass Band with Nick La Rocca. The two founded the Original Dixieland Jazz Band, 1916. Edwards quit music about 1925 but played with this group when it was revived in the thirties. Recorded with his own band for Commodore in the forties.

Edwards, Johnny (d). b. N.O., 1922; d. Lorman, Miss., Dec. 21, 1973. Basin Street Six, Dukes of Dixieland, Al Hirt, Pete Fountain.

Edwards, Paul (d). b. Aug. 6, 1916. Dixieland rhythm man with George Girard, Sharkey, Santo Pecora through the 1950s. With Pete Fountain group. Well-known drum teacher.

Edwards, Willie (c). d. ——. With A. J. Piron Orchestra in 1920.

Eiermann, Edward "Lefty" (sb, tu). b. N.O., ca. 1894; d. N.O., May 27, 1971. Worked with Happy Schilling from 1915 through World War I and remained active until the early forties. Security guard at Pan-American Insurance Company.

Elgar, Charles (v). b. N.O., June 13, 1879. Classically trained musician who played only occasionally with jazzmen. Worked at the Tuxedo Dance Hall in pre–World War I days and emigrated to Chicago in 1913. Began to book bands and later became active in the union movement.

Ellerbusch, Joe (tb). b. N.O., ——. Pre–World War I dixielander.

Esposito, Alex (g, mdl). b. N.O., ca. 1880; d. N.O., ca. 1951. Played in the Regal ragtime band in 1904.

Eugene, Homer (tb, bjo, s). b. N.O., June 16, 1914. Brother of Wendell. Frequently seen in bands led by Peter Bocage and with the Young Tuxedo Brass Band.

Wendell Eugene

Irving Fazola

Leonard Ferguson

Eugene, Wendell (tb) b. N.O., Oct. 12, 1923. Nephew of Albert Burbank and Paul Barbarin. First job with Kid Howard, 1938. With Papa Celestin, George Lewis. Toured with the Lucky Millinder and Buddy Johnson orchestras.

Evans, Roy (d). b. Lafayette, La., *ca.* 1890; d. *ca.* 1943. Played drums on famed second session of Sam Morgan band in fall of 1927. With Earl Humphrey, 1920; Buddy Petit, 1920; Red Allen, 1927.

Fazola, Irving "Faz" (cl). b. N.O., Dec. 10, 1912; d. N.O., Feb. 20, 1949. Legally named Irving Prestopnik. In 1920s at Fern Cafe No. 2. With Armand Hug, Julian Laine; played in New Orleans with Louis Prima, Candy Candido. Later toured with Ben Pollack, Gus Arnheim, Glenn Miller, Bob Crosby, Muggsy Spanier, Tiny Thornhill. Recorded with Sharkey, Billie Holiday, and under his own name. Well known for records with the Bobcats. "There's only one 'Faz,'" said Glenn Miller.

Federico, Frank (g, vo). b. N.O., *ca.* 1908. With many top dixieland stars during professional life. Especially identified with Leon Prima, 1920s; Louis Prima, 1930s; and through the 1950s with Tony Almerico. Also worked with regular dance bands.

Ferbos, Lionel (t). b. N.O., July 17, 1911. New Orleans Ragtime Orchestra; *One Mo' Time* orchestra.

Ferguson, Leonard (d, l). b. Harriman, Tenn., May 2, 1923. Coleader of the Crawford-Ferguson Night Owls, the band with the widest repertoire of jazz classics in New Orleans. On steamer *President*, Saturday nights, 1965–1966.

Ferrer, Edward Harry "Mose" (p, v) b. Biloxi, Miss., Feb. 12, 1894. One of the Invincibles. Founding member of the New Orleans Owls. Left New Orleans in 1915 to

George Filhe

Chinee Foster

join Tom Brown's band in Chicago. Musical career only from 1914 to 1925.

Ferrer, Frank William (p, g, v, uk). b. N.O., July 17, 1896. Veteran of the Invincibles and the New Orleans Owls. Active only from 1919 to 1923. Successful Lake Charles, La., banker. Brother of Mose Ferrer.

Fields, Frank (sb, tu). b. Plaquemine, La., May 2, 1914. Began with Claiborne Williams band in Donaldsonville, La. Worked with Papa Celestin and in the navy band. In 1965 with Albert French's band. With New Camelia Band in the 1980s.

Fields, Mercedes Garman (p). b. N.O., ——. d. N.O., Nov. 14, 1967. With Papa Celestin in the thirties and forties.

Filhe, George (tb). b. N.O., Nov. 13, 1872; d. Chicago, Ill., 1954. Started with Coustaut-Desdunes Orchestra, 1892. Played eighteen years with the Onward Brass Band, 1893–1911. Peerless Orchestra, about 1903–1904; Imperial Orchestra, 1905. Went to Chicago in 1913 after several years in Storyville. During the early twenties, he worked with King Oliver, Manuel Perez, Sidney Bechet, Lawrence Duhé. In the late twenties, he worked in the pit at Grand Theater in Chicago. Dave Peyton's Orchestra. Retired from music at the beginning of Depression.

Finola, George (t). b. Chicago, Oct. 5, 1945. Student of Johnny Wiggs. Regular on Bourbon Street.

Fischer, Johnny (cl, l). b. N.O., May 28, 1877; d. N.O., Oct. 9, 1948. Legal name John Henry Phillips, Sr. One of the prominent turn-of-the-century brass band and dance band leaders. Also worked at times with the Brunieses, Anton Lada, and Five Southern Jazzers. Original New Orleans Jazz Band in 1916. Along with Papa Laine and Happy Schilling, he dominated the dixieland scene for fifteen years.

Ford, Henry (sb). b. N.O., *ca.* 1878; d. N.O., *ca.* 1919. String band musician of the turn-of-the-century era. Big Eye Louis Nelson started with Ford's group in 1903. Ford played in a dance band with Alphonse Picou and Bouboul Valentin in the early 1900s. Later led own band on Delacroix Island, La., 1908–1912.

Foster, Abbey "Chinee" (d, vo). b. N.O., 1900; d. N.O., Sept. 8, 1962. Chinee is ranked with the all-time great Crescent City drummers. Started his career in Storyville, playing for Bebé Ridgley's Tuxedo Orchestra. Associated with Buddy Petit from 1915 (in the Eagle Band) through 1931. Recorded with Papa Celestin, 1927. He was reactivated by Allen and Sandra Jaffe and had reached a new success at Preservation Hall at the time of his death.

43

Pops Foster

Willie Foster

Foster, "Dude" (t). b. N.O., *ca.* 1890; d. N.O., *ca.* 1958. Young Tuxedo Orchestra, 1916; Foster Lewis Jazz Band, 1922; Kid Avery Orchestra, 1946.

Foster, Earl (d). b. N.O., *ca.* 1902. Busy jazz band leader of the 1920s. Played in groups led by Percy and Willie Humphrey during the Depression.

Foster, George "Pops" (sb, tu). b. McCall, La., May 19, 1892; d. San Francisco, Calif., Oct. 29, 1969. Joined string trio in 1906; Magnolia Orchestra in 1908. Till World War I worked in Olympia Brass Band, the Eagle Band, and with Kid Ory. In 1919 joined Fate Marable on SS *Capitol.* With Charlie Creath, 1921. With Ory in California in the twenties. Worked with big bands through the late twenties and thirties, especially with Louis Armstrong's. During the forties was featured on Mutual Radio Network in *This Is Jazz.* Probably the most recorded of all bass players. In the forties and early fifties he played many concerts in New York and at Al Rose's *Journeys into Jazz* concerts at the Philadelphia Academy of Music. About 1953 he moved to California to play in Earl Hines—led jazz band. In 1966 toured Europe.

Foster, Willie (bjo, v, g). b. McCall, La., Dec. 27, 1888. Brother of the famed bass player Pops Foster. Willie frequently worked with his brother in New Orleans; from 1910 to 1913 they were in the cabarets of the district with King Oliver. During the twenties he worked the riverboats under both Sidney Desvigne and Fate Marable, recording with the latter's band for Okeh in 1924.

Fouché, Earl (s, cl). b. N.O., Feb. 5, 1903. With Young Morgan Band, 1925; Sam Morgan Band, 1926. With Ridgley's Tuxedo Orchestra during the early Depression years. With Don Albert's big band, 1937, 1938. Migrated to California after World War I. Nephew of Kaiser and Papa John Joseph.

Fougerat, Tony (c, t). b. N.O., April 25, 1900; d. N.O., Feb. 2, 1979. A popular dixieland bandleader from the early 1920s to 1966.

Fountain, Pete (cl, s). b. N.O., July 3, 1930. Once a member of the Dukes of Dixieland and a star of the Basin Street Six during the 1950s. Fountain became world renowned through the success deriving from his appear-

Pete Fountain

Cié Frazier

ances on the Lawrence Welk TV show during the late fifties. Owned the French Quarter club in the sixties and seventies. At New Orleans Hilton in 1982.

Francis, Albert (d). b. N.O., March 24, 1894. Played with Louis Armstrong at Anderson's Restaurant on North Rampart Street in 1920. In later years played at Mama Lou's and the Happy Landing. Appeared in the 1960s at Preservation Hall. In 1981 a member of the Louis Armstrong Park Committee.

Francis, Edna. See Mitchell, Edna.

Frank, Alcide (v). b. N.O., *ca.* 1875; d. N.O., 1942. Leader of the Golden Rule Orchestra in 1905 at Few-clothes Cabaret in the district. Brother of piccolo player, Bab Frank.

Frank, Gilbert "Bab" (pc, f). b. N.O., *ca.* 1870; d. St. Louis, Mo., June, 1933. Leader of the Peerless Orchestra in the early 1900s. Made solo appearances with John Robichaux. Migrated to Chicago in 1919 and worked briefly at the Deluxe Cafe with Lawrence Duhé.

Franklin, Henry "Careful" (cl). b. N.O., 1903; d. N.O., Aug. 12, 1969. A part-time musician of excellent ability. Late teens with King Oliver, Louis Armstrong. Played in early 1920s with Yank Johnson. With Gibson Brass Band in early 1960s.

Franks, "Bunny" (sb). b. N.O., Sept. 17, 1914. Manager and bass player for the Basin Street Six during the 1950s.

Franzella, Sal (cl). b. N.O., Apr. 25, 1915; d. N.O., Nov. 8, 1968. First professional job in Saenger Theater pit band, 1930. Spent six years working with local dance bands, then on tour with Benny Meroff, 1936; Isham Jones, 1937; Paul Whiteman, 1938. Later was involved with concert and studio work, mainly in Hollywood.

Frazier, Josiah "Cié" (d). b. N.O., Feb. 23, 1904. Veteran of the best-known dance bands of the city. Played with A. J. Piron, Sidney Desvigne, John Robichaux, Papa Celestin. Made his first records with Celestin in 1927. Started professionally about 1921 with Lawrence Marrero. Was in the Young Tuxedo band in 1923. Worked in the ERA and WPA bands in the mid-thirties and with all the leading brass bands of his time. In recent years associated with Emma Barrett, the Humphrey brothers, and Billie and Dee Dee Pierce, with whom he made frequent tours.

French, Albert (bjo). b. N.O., Nov.·16, 1910; d. N.O., Sept. 28, 1977. Outstanding banjo rhythm man always identified with Papa Celestin groups during his career.

French, Behrman (bjo). b. N.O., *ca.* 1900. With Norman Brownlee's band in the early 1920s. Played with Emmett Hardy.

Albert French

Bill Gallaty, Sr.

French, Maurice (tb). b. LaPlace, La., *ca.* 1890. One of the great pre–World War I virtuosos, he played with Kid Rena in the early 1920s, Lyons Brass Band, 1928–1930.

Frisco, Johnny (d). b. N.O., June 23, 1895; d. N.O., July 15, 1969. Played in school with Larry Shields, Clem Camp. By 1915 was Happy Schilling's regular drummer and assistant manager of the band. Associated with Schilling for thirty years.

Froeba, Frank, Jr. (p). b. N.O., *ca.* 1904. Son of a "legitimate" musician, Froeba was a boy wonder of the keyboard, much in demand for theater work. He played some jobs in the 1920s with Johnny Wiggs and John Tobin but hit the road to reemerge as pianist with the Benny Goodman band of 1935. Has worked in recent years at the Gold Coast nightclub in Hollywood Beach, Fla., and is widely recorded as a soloist. Also played with Johnny DeDroit.

Gabriel, Albert (cl). b. Algiers, La., *ca.* 1875; d. ———. Trained musician. With Tom Albert, 1910; Pacific Brass Band, 1910–1912. Worked with some ragtime bands to 1912. Last jobs in band led by Manuel Manetta.

Gabriel, Clarence (g, bjo, p). b. N.O., June 3, 1905; d. N.O., 1973. With Louis Dumaine in late 1920s. Toured with Sam Morgan. With Mike Delay at Lavida. Spent Depression days working in nickel-a-dance places.

Gabriel, Martin Manuel, Sr. (cl). b. N.O., 1876; d. N.O., Nov. 11, 1932.

Gabriel, Martin Manuel, Jr., "Manny" (cl). b. N.O., *ca.* 1897. Musical career around Detroit, Mich.

Gagliardi, Nick (tb). b. New York, N.Y., June 22, 1921. Regular with the Last Straws.

Gallaty, Bill, Sr. (vt). b. N.O., Nov. 9, 1880; d. N.O., Sept. 29, 1943. Standout star of Reliance Brass Band. Said by Papa Laine to have been greatest of all trombone players. Led his own band before World War I.

Gallaty, Bill, Jr. (t). b. N.O., Oct. 23, 1910. Son of Papa Laine's legendary trombonist. Became active dixielander, notably with Santo Pecora. Worked in swing bands of the 1930s with Charlie Bourgeois, Joe Petrie.

Gallaud, Louis (p). b. N.O., Feb. 27, 1897. Frequently at Milneburg in the 1920s. Luthjen's with Big Eye Louis Nelson in the 1940s. Often with Kid Howard, Albert Burbank.

Gallé, Jules (cl). b. N.O., *ca.* 1903. With Brunies brothers band in Biloxi-Gulfport area during the 1950s.

Louis Gallaud

Von Gammon

Montudie Garland

Galloway, Charlie "Sweet Lovin'" (g). b. N.O., during Civil War; d. N.O., *ca.* 1916. Paralyzed by polio, Galloway was playing on the street for tips in the mid-1880s. Became extraordinarily skilled instrumentalist. Led ragtime band in the 1890s. Played frequently with Buddy Bolden.

Gammon, William A. "Von" (d, vib). b. N.O., July 12, 1905; d. Fairhope, Ala., March 25, 1974. Johnny Wiggs, Sharkey, Santo Pecora, Hal Jordy bands. With a combo at the Grand Hotel, Fairhope.

Garland, Ed "Montudie" (sb, tu, bd). b. N.O., Jan. 9, 1895; d. Los Angeles, Calif., Jan. 22, 1980. Already an active parade drummer at thirteen, he worked with Frank Duson's Eagle Band, 1910, on bass drum; and with Excelsior Brass Band on tuba. In 1911 he was with Perez' Imperial Orchestra on string bass. Also played regularly in the same year in Joseph Petit's Security Brass Band. Left town in 1913 and worked with Lawrence Duhé at the Deluxe Cafe, then with Freddie Keppard, Manuel Perez. Joined King Oliver in 1916 for a five-year hitch that took him to California. During the early Depression years, he led a band of his own, the One-Eleven Jazz Band. In the early forties he participated in the Kid Ory–led revival.

René Gelpi

George Girard

Tony Giardina

Gaspard, Ed (d). b. N.O., *ca.* 1877. Sometimes played bass drum for Onward Brass Band and Excelsior Brass Band prior to the Spanish-American War. Best known to early musicians as a teacher. Younger brother of Oak and Vic Gaspard.

Gaspard, Nelson Octave "Oak" (sb). b. N.O., *ca.* 1870; d. Dallas, Tex., ——. Mainly a concert musician. Played with Peerless Orchestra, 1903–1913. Earlier was in Piron-Gaspard Orchestra led by his father and A. J. Piron's father. Between 1913 and 1917 with John Robichaux. In 1920, with his brother Vic, he organized the Ma-

ple Leaf Orchestra, which operated until Oak emigrated to Texas early in the Depression.

Gaspard, Vic (tb, bh). b. N.O., April 14, 1875; d. N.O., Aug. 27, 1957. Worked in the Onward Brass Band until 1910, and in the Peerless Orchestra. Sometimes marched with Excelsior Brass Band. With John Robichaux, 1913–1917, 1926–1930. From 1917 to 1926 worked with his brother Oak as coleader of the Maple Leaf Orchestra. Retired from music at the start of Depression.

Gelpi, René (g, 5-string bjo). b. N.O., March 18, 1904. First with Invincibles String Band; later with New Orleans Owls. Became a prominent architect.

Gerbrecht, "Pinky" (t, l). b. N.O., 1901; d. N.O., Nov. 29, 1963. Pioneer dixielander. Recorded early with Naylor's Seven Aces. Participated in first live music broadcast from New Orleans in 1923.

Gerosa, Joe (g). b. N.O., ——. Pre–World War I dixielander.

Giardina, Ernest (v, vo). b. N.O., *ca.* 1870. Leader of early ragtime band. Played in Christian Ragtime Band.

Giardina, Tony (cl). b. N.O., 1897; d. N.O., *ca.* 1956. Jazz pioneer played with Reliance Brass Band before World War I. Frequently played in groups led by the Brunies brothers and with members of the Original Dixieland Jazz Band. Also with Christian Ragtime Band.

Gibson, Jim (bjo).

Gilbert, Vernon (t). b. N.O., ——. Member of the Young Tuxedo Brass Band in the 1940s.

Booker T. Glass

Albert Glenny

Gillen, Bill (t). b. N.O., *ca.* 1903. With New Orleans Swing Kings in 1920s; with Sidney Arodin, Charles Cordilla, Joe Capraro, 1930s.

Gillin, Mike (d). b. N.O., *ca.* 1868; d. ——. Founding member of the Onward Brass Band and its first bass drummer, 1889.

Gilmore, Eddie (sb). b. N.O., *ca.* 1897. With the Liberty Bell Orchestra, 1920; with New Orleans Creole Jazz Band under Amos White, 1923. Played briefly with John Robichaux.

Girard, George (t). b. Jefferson Parish, La., Oct. 7, 1930; d. N.O., Jan. 18, 1957. Pupil of Johnny Wiggs. Toured with Jimmy Archer Orchestra, 1946, at age sixteen. Featured along with Pete Fountain in Basin Street Six, 1950–1954. Organized his own band for the Famous Door, 1954. His New Orleans Five played opposite the Dukes of Dixieland. Had a weekly CBS broadcast. Recorded with Phil Zito, the Basin Street Six, and his own band. Was featured at Los Angeles Jazz Jubilee, 1955, with Raymond Burke, Johnny St. Cyr.

Glapion, Raymond (g). b. N.O., *ca.* 1895. A "reading" musician usually employed during World War I at the lakefront resorts, mainly with the Gaspards or with Paul and Emile Barnes. Was in Polo Barnes's big traveling dance orchestra in 1932.

Glass, Booker T. (d). b. N.O., Aug. 10, 1888; d. N.O., June 25, 1981. One of the great brass band bass drummers. Pupil of Ed Gaspard. Began with "Holcamp's Greater Shows" in 1908. With Camelia Brass Band, 1918; Wooden Joe Nicholas, 1918–1919; Johnny Predonce's dance orchestra, 1920. With Eureka Brass Band, 1960s.

Glass, Nowell (d). b. N.O., May 18, 1927. Played with George Williams, Theo Riley brass bands. Eureka Brass Band, 1966. Son of Booker T. Glass.

Glenny, Albert (acc, bd, tu, sb). b. N.O., March 25, 1870; d. N.O., June 11, 1958. For seventy-five years an active jazzman. Played bass drum in Bolden's marching band in 1901. Played with virtually all the great names of New Orleans jazz. During the Depression was with WPA and ERA bands. Considered by musicians among the greatest of all bass players.

Goldston, Christopher "Black Happy" (d). b. N.O., Nov. 27, 1894; d. March 17, 1968. Started before World War I in the Tulane Orchestra; with the Crescent Orchestra, 1917; Golden Leaf Band, 1920–1921; Onward Brass Band, 1922; WPA Brass Band, mid-thirties. With Papa Celestin after World War II. Later, to 1955, at the Paddock with Bill Matthews and Octave Crosby.

Happy Goldston

Israel Gorman

Gonsoulin, Tommy (t). b. Opelousas, La., Feb. 12, 1910. Worked mainly in traveling swing bands.

Goodson, Sadie (p). b. Pensacola, Fla., *ca.* 1900. Well known in the 1920s as the pianist for Buddy Petit's band, especially during its run on the SS *Madison*. Also in the band was her husband, Chinee Foster. Played cabaret jobs during the thirties with Kid Rena. Also for dances with Alec Bigard. Sister of Billie Pierce.

Gordet, Allen "Hunter" (ts). b. N.O., *ca.* 1905; d. N.O., 1954. Played trumpet with Joe Gable during the mid-twenties, reeds with ERA Orchestra during the Depression days. Brother-in-law of Wilbert Tillman.

Gorman, Israel (cl). b. Oakville, La., March 4, 1895; d. N.O., Sept. 21, 1965. Worked in the district before 1917 with Henry Peyton, 1913; Tom Brown's trio at Anderson's, 1914; Camelia Orchestra and Brass Band, 1917–1922. During the mid-twenties with Chris Kelly, Louis Dumaine, Buddy Petit, Lee Collins, Kid Rena. During the Depression, worked with the Dumaine-Houston Orchestra, WPA Brass Band, and ERA Orchestra. During the fifties, his own band played in Little Woods resorts and on other dance jobs. Recorded with Kid Howard.

Goudie, Frank "Big Boy" (cl, c). b. Royville, La., 1898; d. Calif., *ca.* 1964. Pupil of Bunk Johnson, 1915. Played with Magnolia Orchestra; in 1920 played with Yank Johnson. Left New Orleans in 1924, toured Mexico, Central America; lived and worked in Europe from 1925 to World War II then went to Brazil. During early thirties, switched to clarinet. Became very popular in South America. After the war, he recorded in Europe with Sidney Bechet, Bill Coleman, Django Reinhardt. Returned to the U.S., 1957. Played concert in San Francisco with Amos White in 1960.

Greene, Jerry (sb, tu). b. N.O., June 23, 1910. Primarily a dance musician with such bands as William Houston's; in jazz bands of the fifties and sixties with Sweet Emma Barrett. Tuba with brass bands.

Gregson, Harry. b. N.O., *ca.* 1885; d. N.O., Feb. 19, 1963. A member of Stalebread Lacoume's spasm band before 1900, playing homemade instruments and singing. During World War I years was police captain of the Storyville district.

Guarino, Felix (d). b. N.O., *ca.* 1898. Drummer in Crescent City Jazzers and Arcadian Serenaders during the 1920s.

50

Emile Guerin

Creole George Guesnon

Guerin, Emile (p). b. N.O., Jan. 3, 1911. Dixieland musician often with Digger Laine, Sharkey, Leon Prima. Worked on steamer *J.S.* in 1930 with the Earl Dantin orchestra.

Guesnon, George "Creole George" (bjo, g). b. N.O., May 25, 1907; d. May 5, 1968. Outstanding musician and musicologist; began to work in cabarets just before the Depression. Was on the road with Sam Morgan in the early thirties; later recorded for Decca in New York. Returned to New Orleans in 1946. Worked with George Lewis in the mid-fifties. Exceptional student of jazz history; preserved gombo French dialect songs.

Guiffre, Joe (g). b. N.O., ——. Pre–World War I dixielander.

Guiffre, John (sb, tu). b. N.O., ——. Pre–World War I dixielander.

Guitar, Willie (sb). b. N.O., *ca.* 1894; d. N.O., *ca.* 1945. Early dixielander dating back to Papa Laine bands. Later with Tony Fougerat. In early days, about 1912, was in Bill Gallaty's band. With Frank Christian until after World War I.

Guma, Paul (cl, g). b. N.O., June 30, 1919. Dixielander.

Gutierrez, Sal (d). b. N.O., 1905; d. Aug. 10, 1974. Dixielander who played with top New Orleans names.

Hall, Andrew (d). b. Chesterfield, Eng., Oct. 5, 1944. Played in the Society Jazz Band with Tony Fougerat and with Mike Casimir's band in England.

Hall, Clarence (cl, s). b. Reserve, La., *ca.* 1900. Worked with Papa Celestin's Original Tuxedo Orchestra from about 1924 to 1931, recording with the group in 1927. Brother of Edmond, Herb, and Robert. Started in Reserve in 1915 in a band composed of his own family led by Kid Thomas, the only outsider.

Hall, Edmond (cl). b. Reserve, La., May 15, 1901; d. New York, Feb. 11, 1967. One of the most famous New Orleans jazzmen. Began in Kid Thomas' orchestra in Reserve, La., in 1915. With Buddy Petit, 1920, and briefly with Bud Roussel, Lee Collins, Jack Carey, and Chris Kelly. Went to Pensacola in the early twenties. Played with Mack Thomas' orchestra. In the big bands of New York during the thirties—Claude Hopkins, Lucky Millinder. During the late forties and the fifties, with Louis Armstrong's All-Stars. Played mainly in New York in the sixties.

Edmond Hall

Hall, Edward (c). b. Reserve, La., *ca.* 1875. Father of the family of great reed musicians. Played cornet in the Onward Brass Band in Reserve during the early 1900s.

Hall, Fred "Tubby" (d). b. Sellers, La., Oct. 12, 1895; d. Chicago, Ill., May 13, 1946. At eighteen, played in Jack Carey's Crescent Orchestra. Joined Eagle Band, 1915; Silver Leaf Orchestra, 1916. Left for Chicago in 1917 to join other New Orleans exiles, Lawrence Duhé, Sugar Johnny Smith. In the twenties was with King Oliver at Lincoln Gardens and with Louis Armstrong at Sunset Cafe. Worked with Jimmie Noone, Carroll Dickerson, Boyd Atkins during the mid-twenties. Through the Depression, mostly with Louis Armstrong, Half-Pint Jaxon, Johnny Dodds.

Hall, Herb (cl, s). b. Reserve, La., *ca.* 1904. Member of the family from Reserve, La. Active in New York in the 1960s. Toured with Bob Greene's "Jelly Roll Morton Revisited" concert series in the late seventies, early eighties.

Hall, Minor "Ram" (d). b. Sellers, La., March 2, 1897; d. Los Angeles, Calif., 1963. Started in 1914 substituting on jobs for his brother, Tubby Hall. Went to Chicago in 1916 and to California with King Oliver in 1921. Joined Kid Ory in 1922; was in the successful Ory revival band of the mid-forties.

Hall, René (bjo, g). b. N.O., *ca.* 1905. One of the city's most dexterous technicians and fastest "readers." Played with the Jones-Collins Astoria Ballroom Orchestra, 1929, and worked with Sidney Desvigne's big band in the 1930s.

Hall, Robert (cl, s). b. Reserve, La., *ca.* 1912. Another member of the famous Reserve clan. Played with Hippo-

Ram Hall   *Photo by Jazz Man Shop*

lyte Charles orchestra, 1920–1925, and afterwards was associated with the Original Tuxedo Orchestra under Bebé Ridgley's leadership in 1926. Recorded in the spring, 1927, session of the Original Tuxedo Orchestra under Papa Celestin.

Hall, Sam "Bush" (t). b. N.O., *ca.* 1904; d. N.O., *ca.* 1934. With Lawrence Marrero's Young Tuxedo Orchestra in 1920; through the twenties and thirties, led a small band of his own with constantly shifting personnel on minor jobs.

Hamilton, Bill (g). Led a band in the mid-twenties called the Oriental Orchestra.

Hamilton, Charlie (p, bjo). b. Ama, La., April 28, 1904. First jobs with Evan Thomas' Black Eagles band (1927). Played mainly with big dance bands, such as Herb Leary's in the twenties and thirties. During the sixties, he reverted to traditional jazz. Toured the Orient with George Lewis. Frequently at Preservation Hall.

Hamilton, George "Pop" (t, b, ah). b. New Iberia, La., Oct. 9, 1888. Led the Lyons Brass Band in 1928. In 1930 he organized his own dance orchestra, which lasted almost a year before being killed off by the Depression. In

Charlie Hamilton   *Photo by Grauman Marks*

George Hartman

1919 he was with Chris Kelly, and he played frequently with Sam Morgan in the twenties. Also was in early bands with Bunk Johnson, Lawrence Duhé, Evan Thomas, and he worked in Gus Fortinet's Banner Band about 1909. Father of Lumas Hamilton.

Hamilton, Lumas (t, c, fh). b. N.O., Feb. 12, 1912. With Lyons Brass Band under his father's leadership, 1928. With Pop Hamilton's orchestra, 1930.

Handy, John "Captain John" (as, cl). b. Pass Christian, Miss., June 24, 1900; d. N.O., Jan. 12, 1971. Started a band called the Louisiana Shakers in 1930. Often seen at Preservation Hall.

Handy, Sylvester (sb). b. Pass Christian, Miss., June 24, 1900; d. N.O., Oct. 12, 1972. Brother of John Handy. Worked riverboats in the 1930s.

Hardin, Henry (cl, t, l). b. N.O., *ca.* 1905; d. N.O., *ca.* 1955. With the Joe Robichaux, John Handy, and Kid Rena bands. Led his own dance group during the Depression days and worked in the ERA Orchestra.

Hardy, Charles J. (uk). b. N.O., 1895; d. Chicago, Ill., Sept. 22, 1966. Original member of the Six and 7/8 String Band.

Hardy, Emmett (c). b. Gretna, La., June 12, 1903; d. Gretna, La., June 16, 1925. Boy prodigy of the dixieland world. When he died at twenty-two, he had already toured the Orpheum circuit with Tony Catalano's band, played in Chicago with the New Orleans Rhythm Kings and in Carlisle Evans' band in Davenport, Iowa, where he is said to have influenced the young Bix Beiderbecke. In New Orleans he played mainly in the Norman Brownlee orchestra and was replaced by Johnny Wiggs.

Harris, Dennis (s). Golden Rule Orchestra, 1920.

Harris, Joe (tb). Bandleader of the 1920s. Joe Harris Dixieland Band.

Harris, Kid (t). b. N.O., *ca.* 1906; d. N.O., *ca.* 1951. Active in the twenties and thirties. Was in ERA Orchestra.

Harris, Tim (sn). b. N.O., *ca.* 1882. Drummer for Papa Laine's Reliance Brass Band in the early 1900s.

Harris, Tom (sb, sou, tu). Played with the Kid Avery jazz band after World War I.

Hartman, George (t, sb). b. N.O., 1910; d. N.O., Feb. 13, 1966. Played for many years in a trio at Pete Herman's cabaret in the Vieux Carré. Made Keynote recording session in the forties.

Charles Hartmann

Hartmann, Charles (tb). b. N.O., July 1, 1898. With Johnny Bayersdorffer, Tony Parenti's Liberty Syncopators, and Johnny Hyman's Bayou Stompers. Was secretary of local 174 for many years and a prominent jazzman for over thirty years.

Harvey, Charles "Buzz" (sb). b. N.O., *ca.* 1885. Played with the King Watzke orchestra and on jobs with members of the Shields family.

Hays, "Blind Charlie" (g, bjo, v, vo). b. N.O., *ca.* 1885; d. N.O., Feb., 1949. Played with Bunk Johnson and with Louis Dumaine. In 1948 he was in Peter Bocage's band.

Hazel, Arthur "Monk" (d, c, mel). b. Harvey, La., Aug. 15, 1903; d. N.O., Mar. 5, 1968. Kingpin of dixieland-style drummers. Began his career with Emmett Hardy in 1919. Played in New Orleans through the 1920s with Happy Schilling, Bill Creger, Jules Bauduc, and with Abbie Brunies at the Halfway House. He recorded first in 1927 with Johnny Hyman's Bayou Stompers; in the twenties, too, with the New Orleans Rhythm Kings, Tony Parenti's orchestra, and Jack Petit's Pets. Was on network radio in 1934 behind singer Gene Austin. Widely recorded. From the forties through the late sixties, he was associated closely with Sharkey's Kings of Dixieland and had short intervals of work with Santo Pecora and George Girard.

Monk Hazel

Henderson, George (d). b. N.O., Sept. 17, 1900. Led Black Diamonds, 1919–1922. Entire career in pickup jobs. Worked at Luthjen's in the 1950s. Recorded with Kid Thomas in 1951.

Henderson, Tommy (d). b. Grenta, La., *ca.* 1905. Played with Elton Theodore band in early 1920s. Mainly in Algiers, La.

Henry, Charles "Sunny" (tb). b. Magnolia Plantation, Nov. 17, 1885; d. N.O., Jan. 7, 1960. Began at age seventeen with Eclipse Brass Band under Jim Humphrey, 1902. Began in New Orleans in 1913; to 1920 played in Excelsior Brass Band and with Hippolyte Charles dance orchestra. Worked with Amos White during the early 1920s and with John Robichaux at the Lyric Theater to 1927. For years worked in a taxi dance hall at Carondelet and Canal streets. Henry was lead trombone under Louis Dumaine in the WPA band during the thirties. In the forties he worked with the young Tuxedo Brass Band until 1947, then switched to the Eureka Brass Band for which he played until his death.

Henry, Oscar "Chicken" (tb, p). b. N.O., June 8, 1888. Began his career as a bordello "professor," playing piano at Hattie Rogers' sporting house in 1906. Studied

Sunny Henry

Chicken Henry

music at Straight University. His hand was severely burned in an accident and in 1931 he switched to trombone because of this. During the Depression he worked in the WPA Brass Band, in the ERA Orchestra, and sometimes in a group led by Kid Howard. Became a fixture in the Eureka Brass Band about 1959. Played sometimes at Preservation Hall in the 1960s.

Henry, Son (d).

Henry, "Trigger Sam" (p). b. N.O., *ca.* 1875. One of the best of the Storyville piano players. Much admired by Jelly Roll Morton. Played in the district from 1898 to 1914.

Hessemer, Al (b, bjo, g, v). b. Jackson, Mich., Jan. 21, 1909. Mainly with leading dance bands in the 1930s. Charlie Bourgeois, Joe Petrie. Frequently heard on the riverboats *President* and *Capitol* with the best dixieland leaders. At times with Crawford-Ferguson Night Owls. One of busiest musicians in town in the sixties. Still playing in 1982.

Al Hirt

Fats Houston

Hightower, Willie (c, t). b. Nashville, Tenn., Oct. 1889; d. Chicago, Ill. Leader of the American Stars orchestra. Played dance jobs in St. Katherine's Hall in 1913. By 1917 the group was more or less regularly at the Cadillac. Moved to Chicago in 1921 where he worked in Lottie Hightower's band and in other big bands until 1927, when he again became a leader. Band lasted until the Depression. Made one recording, under his own name, in 1924.

Hill, Scott (tb). b. N.O., Oct. 7, 1947. Leader of the French Market Jazz Band.

Himel, Otto "Coco" (g). b. N.O., *ca.* 1904. Dixieland rhythm man associated, in his New Orleans days, with Frank Clancy groups in Jefferson parish. Played jobs with Raymond Burke in the late twenties and early thirties. Later, joined singer Gene Austin as comedy-accompanist, where he worked with fellow Orleanian Candy Candido. Monk Hazel also was in this group, but after Candy had left.

Hirt, Al (t). b. N.O., Nov. 7, 1922. Internationally famous. Symphonically trained, he has little traditional jazz background. Physically powerful, energetic, he has captured popular fancy. His success is based mainly on extraordinary virtuosity.

Hirt, Gerald "Slick" (tb). b. N.O. Trombone-playing brother of trumpeter Al Hirt. Long active in the New Orleans police department band. In the 1960s with his brother's combo.

Holloway, "Kildee" (t, arr). b. N.O.; d. N.O., 1953. Kildee worked for Papa Celestin through the Depression and with Joe Robichaux in the late thirties. Though he was an excellent trumpet player, he was best known for his easy-to-play arrangements for the Celestin band.

Hooker, George (c, bh). b. Algiers, La., 1882. A brass band musician who worked almost exclusively with the Pacific Brass Band about 1900, the Tuxedo Brass Band in the mid-twenties. Until the Depression he worked regularly with the Allen Brass Band of Algiers, La., and occasionally with the Excelsior Brass Band during this period.

Hountha, John Philip. See Stein, Johnny.

Houston, Matthew "Fats" (d). b. N.O., July 22, 1910; d. Feb. 25, 1981. Well known as the grand marshal of the Eureka Brass Band, Houston shared leadership of a dance band with Louis Dumaine during the Depression days.

Howard, Avery "Kid" (c, t, d). b. N.O., April 22, 1908; d. N.O., March 28, 1966. During the Depression became prominent on cornet. Played drums with Chris Kelly and Isaiah Morgan. Sometimes played with the Young Tuxedo Brass Band, but mainly led a brass band of his own and organized small combinations for dances. During the fifties, he played in the George Lewis band as regular trumpet. Was widely recorded in the fifties and sixties.

56

Kid Howard   *Photo by Grauman Marks*

Howard, Joe (c, tu). b. Waggeman, La., *ca.* 1870; d. N.O., 1946. Started in New Orleans during the Storyville days. With Papa Celestin in the Original Tuxedo Orchestra after having played in brass bands at home and in Algiers with the Allen Brass Band, 1909–1911. During World War I, he led his own group both in the district and at the lake resorts; later, he worked on riverboats. In 1920 with Louis Dumaine's Jazzola Eight. Made the celebrated discs in 1927. Through the twenties and thirties, he was a mainstay of the Tuxedo Brass Band. Recorded with the Zenith Brass Band, 1946.

Hug, Armand (p). b. N.O., Dec. 6, 1910; d. N.O., Mar. 19, 1977. Considered finest piano soloist in New Orleans. First professional job at fifteen. In Fern Cafe, 1926. Self-taught; played with all the dixieland stars; was world renowned for his records. For years was cocktail lounge performer, but played an enormous repertoire in wide variety of styles, from Joplin rags to low-down blues and pop tunes. Was an avid student of jazz history.

Humphrey, Earl (tb, sb). b. N.O., 1902; d. N.O., June 26, 1971. Learned trumpet from his celebrated grandfather, Jim Humphrey. At age fifteen was working jobs at lakefront resorts. At seventeen toured with his father for Al G. Barnes Circus. Spent more time on road than most New Orleans musicians, but appeared irregularly in town to play with his brothers or Buddy Petit, Chris Kelly, Louis Dumaine. Moved to Charlottesville, Va., but returned to N.O. in 1960s.

Humphrey, James B. "Professor Jim" (t). b. N.O., Nov. 25, 1859; d. N.O., 1937. One of the greatest of the music teachers, Humphrey taught the Eclipse Brass Band of the Magnolia Plantation. Among his protégés are his

Armand Hug

own son and daughters and grandchildren, one of the most celebrated families in jazz. Also Sam, Isaiah, Al, and Andrew Morgan, Chris Kelly, Harrison Barnes, and Sunny Henry.

Humphrey, Percy (t, d). b. N.O., Jan. 13, 1905. Leader, from 1947, of Eureka Brass Band. Youngest of the Humphrey brothers and a protégé of his grandfather, Professor Jim Humphrey. During the late forties, he played with the George Lewis band, but in later years acted as leader himself or with Emma Barrett at Preservation Hall.

Humphrey, Willie Eli (cl). b. N.O., May 24, 1880; d. N.O., Jan. 8, 1964. Father of the famed Humphrey brothers. He, too, learned from Professor Jim Humphrey, his father, and played in the Magnolia Plantation's Eclipse Brass Band, 1900–1910. He was in the Crescent Orchestra in 1913 and was frequently seen with Tig Chambers.

Percy Humphrey

Willie James Humphrey

Humphrey, Willie James (cl). b. N.O., Dec. 29, 1900. Eldest of the Humphrey brothers. Began professionally with George McCullum, Sr., in the Excelsior Brass Band, 1919. Made short trip to St. Louis and Chicago to play with George Filhe. Veteran of the riverboats. Worked at Anderson's restaurant on Rampart Street; led band of his own with Maurice Durand; with Lee Collins at Spanish Fort. Seen in the 1940s in Young Tuxedo and Eureka brass bands. Frequently in his brother Percy's band, with Paul Barbarin, or with Emma Barrett. Much recorded.

Humphries, Bill (bjo, g). b. Allendale, S.C., March 19, 1927. With Crawford-Ferguson Night Owls in the 1960s.

Huntington, Billy (g, b, s, bjo). b. N.O., Oct. 2, 1937. As a youth was closely associated with members of the George Lewis band, especially Lawrence Marrero, and was jobbing around in his teens with such old masters as Charlie Love, Steve Angrum, Emile Barnes, and Albert Jiles. At age fifteen, he recorded on banjo with British bandleader Ken Colyer. Gave up authentic jazz in the mid-fifties.

Hyman, John Wigginton "Johnny." See Wiggs, Johnny.

Ice, Bob (bjo). b. N.O., ca. 1914. Not related to Bob Ice of the Last Straws. Regular with the Crawford-Ferguson Night Owls.

Ice, Bob (sb, tu, l). b. Fairmont, W.Va., Jan. 3, 1931. Leader of the popular Last Straws dixieland band of the 1960s.

Jackson, Albert "Loochie" (tb). b. N.O., March 13, 1898; d. N.O., March 3, 1978. Began his musical career in 1918 with the Elton Theodore Orchestra of Algiers, La. Sometimes played in the Tuxedo Brass Band in 1920 and was with the Young Tuxedo Brass Band from 1932 until his retirement from music in the early fifties.

Jackson, Eddie (tu, sb). b. N.O., ca. 1867; d. N.O., 1938. For forty years among the finest New Orleans bassists. Began with Edward Clem about 1907. Was a veteran of the advertising wagons and the "jitney" dance halls. With the Onward Brass Band, 1910–1912. During the late twenties, he led his own dance band and played with the Tuxedo Brass Band. During the late thirties, he played in the Young Tuxedo Brass Band.

Jackson, Frank (c, tu, bd). b. N.O., ca. 1866; d. N.O., ca. 1912. Played with the Onward, Oriental, and Excelsior brass bands from 1899 to 1912. Sometimes played bass drum with Buddy Bolden's marching band about 1900.

Jackson, "New Orleans Willie" (vo). b. N.O., ca. 1895. A popular entertainer of the 1920s whose fourteen recorded sides had distinguished accompanists—specifically, Steve Lewis, Clarence Williams, Buddy Christian. Drew big crowds to Brown's Ice Cream Parlor.

Preston Jackson

Tony Jackson

Jackson, "Pickles" (d). d. N.O., 1972.

Jackson, Preston (tb). b. N.O., 1903. Never played in New Orleans in his early years but gained considerable fame playing in the Crescent City tradition. His family moved to Chicago in 1917. During the 1920s he worked with the big bands of Dave Peyton, Erskine Tate, Carroll Dickerson; also with the Dodds brothers, Jimmie Noone, Natty Dominique. Recorded with Richard M. Jones, Punch Miller, Noone, and others. Returned to New Orleans in the seventies. Often at Preservation Hall in the eighties.

Jackson, Skeeter (g, sb). b. N.O., ——. Played with Tom Albert's orchestra in 1910; later with Sam Ross.

Jackson, Tony (p). b. N.O., June 5, 1876; d. Chicago, Ill., April 20, 1921. Unrivaled king of Storyville "professors," a rare musical genius. Jackson worked the brothels from the age of fifteen until 1904. In New Orleans he played

mainly at Gipsy Shaefer's, Hilma Burt's, Lulu White's, and Countess Willie Piazza's. He returned to New Orleans and worked in (Frank) Early's, 1911–1912. Composed hundreds of popular songs and sold them for five or ten dollars each. Somehow retained copyright ownership of some numbers, including "Some Sweet Day," "Pretty Baby."

Jaeger, Alfred L. (d). b. N.O., 1869. d. N.O., Jan. 6, 1953. Veteran of early vaudeville, circus bands. Left New Orleans in the 1880s. Worked in original Paul Whiteman group. Was with Jefferson marching bands in the New Orleans area under Frank Clancy. Was last seen in the early fifties in a Tony Almerico Parisian Room jam session.

Jaffe, Allen (tu). b. Pottsville, Pa., April 24, 1935. Young proprietor of Preservation Hall. Sometimes sits in with the bands there. Played in the Zulu parade, 1965 Mardi Gras, with the Olympia Brass Band. Regular in this group through 1982.

Louis James

James, Joe (p). b. Algiers, La., 1901; d. N.O., 1964. Long-time piano player for the Kid Thomas orchestra.

James, Kid (d). b. N.O., *ca.* 1907. Played some jobs with Bunk Johnson, but chiefly known as member of the Louis Keppard–Wooden Joe Nicholas band.

James, Louis (cl, s, sb). b. Thibodaux, La., April 9, 1890; d. N.O., Oct. 26, 1967. In 1905 he played in family band in hometown. Came to New Orleans in 1917; worked with Jack Carey, Frank Duson, the Tulane Orchestra with Joe Howard at Villa Cabaret. Played again at home with his family. Recorded with Dumaine on famed Jazzola Eight session, 1927; with Dumaine off and on until 1949. In the fifties he played bass for Percy Humphrey; was seen occasionally at Preservation Hall in 1965.

Jean, Nelson (t). b. N.O., Dec. 28, 1902. Polished musician, related to the Joseph family. He worked on riverboats and lake steamers through the 1930s.

Jean, Ulysses (t). b. N.O., *ca.* 1905. A nephew of Nelson Jean and Papa John Joseph, he was on the road in the early 1930s with Polo Barnes and, during the forties, sometimes had jobs with George Lewis, Lawrence Marrero, Eddie Summers.

Jefferson, Andrew (d, vo). b. N.O., Nov. 24, 1912. Older brother of popular trumpet player Thomas Jefferson; he played for a long time at the lake resorts, mainly with Peter Bocage at Mama Lou's in the 1950s. Frequently with Young Tuxedo Brass Band.

Andrew Jefferson

Jefferson, Thomas (t, vo). b. N.O., about 1923. Oriented to Louis Armstrong style. Worked in Lafon Brass Band in the late 1930s. Seen mainly at the Paddock during the late forties and through the fifties, under Octave Crosby. Frequently with Young Tuxedo Brass Band. On Bourbon Street in the eighties.

Jerde, Curtis (sb, tu). b. Sisseton, S.D., Nov. 29, 1939. Broad experience in dance bands. During the 1970s at the Fairmont-Roosevelt Hotel with the Dick Stabile Orchestra. Cofounder in 1980 of the Louisiana Repertory Jazz Ensemble. Curator of the William Ransom Hogan Archive of New Orleans Jazz at Tulane University.

Jiles, Albert, Sr. (d). b. Thibodaux, La., *ca.* 1878; d. N.O., *ca.* 1922. Son of a Civil War drummer boy, Jiles played in turn-of-the-century brass bands; Youka Brass Band, 1904.

Curt Jerde

Dink Johnson

Jiles, Albert, Jr. (d). b. Thibodaux, La., Nov. 7, 1905; d. N.O., Sept. 3, 1964. Nephew of great bass drummer Clay Jiles. First job in 1922 with Chris Kelly. In 1923 began long run with Lawrence Toca. Worked during the Depression with Kid Howard's band and with Isaiah Morgan's Young Morgan Band. In the early forties, he played with Papa Celestin or Kid Clayton. Recorded with Wooden Joe Nicholas for American Music in 1949. Worked in the fifties at Happy Landing.

Jiles, Clay (d). b. Thibodaux, La., *ca.* 1880; d. June 15, 1927. Played in Excelsior Brass Band in the early 1900s; sometimes worked with Onward or Allen brass bands.

Johnson, Alphonse (ah). b. N.O., *ca.* 1900. Founding member of the Eureka Brass Band, 1920.

Johnson, Arthur "Yank" (tb). b. N.O., *ca.* 1878; d. N.O., 1938. Younger brother of Buddy Johnson. Worked with Imperial Orchestra, 1906; later with Superior Orchestra, 1910. In 1920 he was in a band with Big Boy Goudie and Chinee Foster. After World War I, he worked mostly

with Sam Morgan band to 1925, then for a while with Chris Kelly and in the Magnolia Orchestra under Willie Pajeaud. Worked with Pajeaud and others in dance halls till about 1938.

Johnson, "Buddy" (tb). b. Algiers, La., *ca.* 1870; d. N.O., 1927. Allen Brass Band, Pacific Brass Band, about 1900; Onward Brass Band, about 1910. Imperial Orchestra under Manuel Perez, about 1905; Superior Orchestra with Bunk Johnson, Big Eye Louis Nelson, 1910. During the mid-twenties, with Perez' dance orchestra. Older brother of Yank Johnson.

Johnson, "Chick" (s, cl). b. N.O., ——. d. N.O., March 25, 1977. Dixielander of the twenties and thirties with Dixola Jazz Band. His only record—Goofus Tin Roofers, with Blind Gilbert, Ray Burke, 1927—was never released by Columbia. In 1960s with Dominick Barocco.

Johnson, Dave Ernest (d). b. N.O., *ca.* 1890; d. N.O., *ca.* 1932. With Chris Kelly band, 1919–1925.

Johnson, "Dink" (cl, p, vo, d). b. Biloxi, Miss., Oct. 28, 1892; d. Portland, Ore., Nov. 29, 1954. With Original Creole Orchestra in California as drummer. Also with Freddie Keppard, George Baquet, Jelly Roll Morton. Later was nightclub entertainer in California, playing piano and singing blues. Recorded for American Music. Dink was a brother-in-law of Jelly Roll Morton.

Noon Johnson

Johnson, "Duck Ernest" (b). b. N.O., *ca.* 1888; d. N.O., *ca.* 1931. With Chris Kelly band, 1919–1925. Led his own band at Beverly Gardens in the mid-twenties.

Johnson, Jimmy (sb, tu). b. N.O., *ca.* 1876; d. *ca.* 1937. Buddy Bolden band. Played in Silver Leaf Orchestra, 1911. Toured with Don Albert's orchestra out of San Antonio, Tex., in the late twenties, early thirties.

Johnson, Joe (c). b. N.O., *ca.* 1890; d. N.O., *ca.* 1928. Played in the district with Herb Lindsay's Primrose Orchestra, 1912, and in the Eagle Band.

Johnson, Lonnie (g). b. N.O., Feb. 8, 1889; d. Philadelphia, Pa., June 18, 1970. Played solo guitar in Storyville bordellos, 1910–1917. Went to London with a show, 1917, as intermission entertainer. Played on riverboat SS *St. Paul* with Charlie Creath and on SS *Capitol* with Fate Marable. One of the most recorded of jazzmen, he made his first cuts with Creath in 1927. Never returned to New Orleans, but spent his whole life on tour. Was in Philadelphia, 1966.

Johnson, Noon (tu, bazooka, g). b. N.O., Aug. 24, 1903; d. N.O., Sept. 18, 1969. Led "skiffle" trio. Paraded with Young Tuxedo Brass Band. As a youth, played in the streets of Storyville for coins.

Johnson, Steve (vt). b. N.O., *ca.* 1865. In 1889 a founding member of the Onward Brass Band.

Johnson, William Manuel "Bill" (sb, g, ah, tu, bjo). b. N.O., Aug. 10, 1872; d. Mexico, 1975. Began his career playing guitar in district bagnios in 1890. Played bass with a trio in Tom Anderson's Basin Street Cafe, 1900–1909. During the day, he worked with the Excelsior, Uptown, Eagle, and Peerless brass bands. Organized the Original Creole Orchestra and toured the U.S. on the Orpheum circuit until 1918. Johnson originally got the job at the Royal Garden and invited King Oliver to front the band, bringing world fame to Oliver. Johnson stayed busy with the best jazz and dance bands for another twenty years, building the longest active musical career of any major jazzman.

Johnson, Willie "Bunk" (c, t). b. N.O., Dec. 27, 1879; d. New Iberia, La., July 7, 1949. A giant of New Orleans jazz from his first job in 1894 with Adam Olivier's orchestra through twenty busy years. From 1914 on, he played outside of New Orleans, mainly in Mandeville and Baton Rouge, La., and in the western part of the state. Toured with tent shows in the early 1920s. Was rediscovered mainly through the efforts of Bill Russell and

Bunk Johnson   *photo by Nick Alexakis*

Chester Jones   *Photo by Grauman Marks*

Roger Johnston

went on to several years of concerts and extensive recording. Was largely responsible for the jazz revival of the forties.

Johnston, Roger (d). b. N.O., March 12, 1918; d. N.O., Oct. 9, 1958. Began his professional dixieland career at age thirteen. Worked with Santo Pecora, Leon Prima, Sharkey, Roy Liberto, Dukes of Dixieland. Spent many years at the Famous Door.

Jones, Bris (cl). b. N.O., July 12, 1926. Regular with the Last Straws.

Jones, Chester (d). b. N.O., March 3, 1913. Worked with George Lewis, Eureka Brass Band, and many dance groups. Still active in 1982.

Jones, Clifford "Snags" (d). b. N.O., *ca.* 1900; d. Chicago, Ill., Jan. 31, 1947. In his teens worked with high-school buddy, Lee Collins; also with Jack Carey, Buddy Petit. Sometimes substituted in Celestin's Original Tuxedo Orchestra in 1918 and 1919. Joined King Oliver up north in 1924; then worked in Milwaukee with Art Sims's and Bernie Young's orchestras. He was back in Chicago in the thirties, with Charlie Elgar and worked steadily thereafter. He appeared at a Chicago concert with Bunk Johnson in 1946.

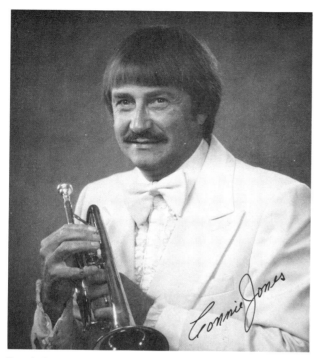

Connie Jones

Richard M. Jones

Jones, Conrad "Connie" (t, s). b. N.O., March 22, 1934. Replaced George Girard in the Basin Street Six in 1954. Worked with Santo Pecora's band, 1958–1960. Toured with Jack Teagarden's Orchestra. Spent seven years with Pete Fountain. House bandleader at the Blue Angel on Bourbon Street into 1982.

Jones, David (d, mel, s). b. Lutcher, La., *ca.* 1888; d. Los Angeles, Calif., 1953. In 1910 began his career in the Holmes Brass Band of Lutcher. Worked jobs in the district, then joined Fate Marable in 1918 for three years on the SS *Capitol.* Joined King Oliver in Chicago in 1921. In the mid-twenties, he was leader at Pelican Dance Hall; worked for a short while with Bebé Ridgley's Tuxedo Orchestra. In 1929, with Lee Collins, he recorded four sides, under the name of the Jones-Collins Astoria Hot Eight, that made jazz history.

Jones, John L. (g). b. N.O., Dec. 12, 1910.

Jones, Leroy (t). b. N.O., Feb. 20, 1958. A product of Danny Barker's "youth movement." Founder-leader of the young Hurricanes Brass Band, which recorded in 1978, he became a regular in the Louisiana Repertory Jazz Ensemble in 1981. Began trumpet at age eleven. Featured as "Little Louis Armstrong" at Superbowl VI, 1972.

Jones, Richard Myknee (p). b. Donaldsonville, La., June 13, 1889; d. Chicago, Ill., Dec. 9, 1945. Primarily a solo pianist, Jones worked the higher class Basin Street bordellos before he was twenty years old. From a musical family; knew many instruments. At thirteen he was playing alto horn in a brass band. Led his own groups at Abadie's, the Poodle Dog, and Fewclothes in the district, 1910–1912. King Oliver worked regularly in his band. In 1919 he joined the Clarence Williams Publishing Company in an administrative capacity. In 1925 became Chicago "race" recording director for Okeh. During the late thirties he worked for Decca. From about 1940 was mainly active as an arranger. His composition credits include "Trouble in Mind," "Riverside Blues," and "Jazzin' Babies Blues."

Joseph, Edgar "Sambo" (t). b. N.O., Nov. 6, 1906; d. N.O., Feb. 27, 1977. Mainly a brass band musician. With Young Tuxedo Brass Band till late 1960s.

Joseph, John "Papa John" (sb, cl, g, s). b. St. James Parish, La., Nov. 27, 1877; d. N.O., Jan. 22, 1965. Came to New Orleans in 1906. Led his own group in the district until 1917. Played brass band jobs with Claiborne Williams' band in East Baton Rouge Parish. Sometimes worked with the Original Tuxedo Orchestra. Retired to follow his profession of barbering in the twenties, but played frequently in the sixties in Preservation Hall.

Papa John Joseph

Kaiser Joseph

J. J. Joyce

Joseph toured the Orient as late as 1963 with the George Lewis band. Brother of Willie Joseph.

Joseph, Pleasant (g, p, vo). b. Wallace, La., Dec. 21, 1907. Popular entertainer, made several successful records, notably on Decca, under the pseudonym **Cousin Joe** during the 1940s. In New Orleans known as **Smilin' Joe**.

Joseph, Waldren "Frog" (tb). b. N.O., *ca.* 1918. A popular New Orleans trombone player with exceptional facility. Was in Joe Robichaux's band in the 1930s. Played with most of the Bourbon Street bands, including Octave Crosby's and Papa Celestin's. Worked in the sixties in bands led by Albert French, Paul Barbarin. In the eighties with New Camelia Jazz Band.

Joseph, Willie "Kaiser" (cl). b. St. James Parish, *ca.* 1892; d. N.O., 1951. Jobbed around in the district until it closed, 1917, frequently in Bebé Ridgley's segment of the Tuxedo Orchestra. He is on the recordings of the Louis Dumaine Jazzola Eight. During the Depression he was frequently with Willie Pajeaud. Younger brother of Papa John Joseph.

Joyce, John "J. J." (d). b. N.O., April 17, 1939. Worked with George Kramer Jazz Band in Biloxi, Miss., 1955. Joined the Last Straws in 1958. He graduated from the Juilliard School of Music in 1963 and has taught courses in jazz history at Tulane University for many years. Founding member of the Louisiana Repertory Jazz Ensemble in 1980.

Marcus Kahn

Orange Kellin

Kahn, Marcus (p, tb, bh). b. N.O., *ca.* 1890; d. N.O., *ca.* 1946. Early dixieland pianist who played frequently with members of Original Dixieland Jazz Band, Ernest Giardina band, and with the Brunies and Fischer bands.

Kay, Armin (t). Dixielander with Santo Pecora.

Keelin, Frank (t). Eagle Band.

Kellin, Orange (cl). b. Sweden, 1944. Moved to New Orleans, 1966. Associated with Lars Edegran. Leader of the New Orleans Joymakers on European tours. New Orleans Ragtime Orchestra. Frequently at the Famous Door, Maison Bourbon.

Kelly, Chris (c). b. Deer Range, La., 1891; d. April 19, 1929. Joined the Eclipse Brass Band in 1916. A protégé of Professor Jim Humphrey. Drafted in 1917. Joined the Magnolia Orchestra, replacing retiring Edward Clem in 1919. During the twenties led his own band, and was considered by many to be the best cornet man in the city. The band frequently traveled to Biloxi and Mobile and was challenged for popularity only by Buddy Petit. Never recorded.

Kelly, Ernest (tb). b. N.O., *ca.* 1886; d. N.O., *ca.* 1927. Trombonist of the pre-1920 era. Was in Tig Chambers' Magnolia Sweets, 1910, and with Bob Lyons' Dixie Jazz Band in 1918. Played many jobs with Chinee Foster. Played in first band organized by George Lewis, 1923.

Kelly, Guy (t). b. Scotland, La., Nov. 22, 1906; d. Chicago, Ill., Feb. 24, 1940. Began playing in Baton Rouge with Toots Johnson. Moved to Houston in 1927 and came to New Orleans late the same year. Worked at the Humming Bird Lounge with John Handy, then joined Papa Celestin, with whom he recorded. Went to Chicago, 1929. Worked with Dave Peyton and with Orleanians Jimmie Noone, Louis Armstrong, Boyd Atkins.

Keppard, Freddie (c, v, mdl). b. N.O., Feb. 15, 1889; d. Chicago, Ill., July 15, 1933. First job at Spanish Fort with Johnny Brown's band, 1901. Pupil Adolphe Alexander, Sr. Organized first Olympia Orchestra, 1906, with Alphonse Picou on clarinet. Sometimes played with the Eagle Brass Band about 1910. Played at Lala's, Groshell's Dance Hall in the district, 1910–1912. Toured with the Original Creole Orchestra on Orpheum circuit, 1913–1918. Worked in Chicago with Doc Cooke's Dreamland Orchestra, John Wycliffe's orchestra; with Erskine Tate, Jimmie Noone, and Lil's Hot Shots. Used many "hokum" effects and was known to be very powerful. A prime favorite of Jelly Roll Morton.

Guy Kelly

Freddie Keppard

Keppard, Louis (g, tu, ah). b. N.O., Feb. 2, 1888. Began playing professionally about 1906, mainly as a guitarist, and was in the Magnolia Orchestra with the Depass boys, Joe Oliver, and Frank Goudie. He also worked at times with his brother Freddie's Olympia Orchestra, mainly in the district. He sometimes played in the lake resorts in the forties and fifties and was still seen in street parades with the Gibson Brass Band in the sixties.

Kimball, Andrew (c). b. N.O., ca. 1880; d. Pascagoula, Miss., ca. 1929. With Peerless Orchestra, 1905–1912, under both Bab Frank and A. J. Piron. Worked with John Robichaux from 1913 until 1925; in the interim played daytime jobs with the Onward Brass Band.

Kimball, Henry (sb). b. N.O., 1878; d. N.O., 1931. With John Robichaux, 1894–1919. During the early twenties, toured in Jelly Roll Morton band and worked with Manuel Perez. Played in New Orleans in the late twenties with Fats Pichon and occasionally in Papa Celestin's band. Frequently on riverboats. Father of Narvin Kimball.

Kimball, Jeannette (née Salvant) (p). b. N.O., Dec. 18, 1908. Virtually all her musical life has been with the Papa Celestin organization. She played with Celestin's band on his 1926 disc session and on the Southland recordings of 1954. Was still working with Celestin musicians under Albert French's direction in 1965, and with the New Camelia Jazz Band in 1982.

Kimball, Margaret (p). b. N.O., ca. 1896. Wife of Andrew Kimball, she, too, played with the John Robichaux Lyric Theater pit band of the early 1920s.

Jeannette Kimball

Narvin Kimball

Kimball, Narvin (bjo, sb). b. N.O., March 2, 1909. Identified with the Papa Celestin Original Tuxedo Orchestra from the late twenties, when he recorded with the band, through the Depression. On Bourbon Street frequently in the sixties as a bandleader in Dixieland Hall. Son of Henry Kimball, he is often incorrectly listed as Henry Kimball, Jr.

King, Freddie (d). b. Springfield, Conn., 1917. Active in New Orleans during the 1950s, he was an early president of the New Orleans Jazz Club. Frequently a member of the Johnny Wiggs band, with whom he recorded. Also made discs with Santo Pecora on Capitol.

King, Wiley "Pep" (sb, tu). b. N.O., *ca.* 1885. Played in the Crescent Orchestra in 1913 and in parades with the Jack Carey band.

Kirsch, Charlie (tb). b. N.O., ———. Pre–World War I dixielander.

Kirsch, Martin (cl). b. N.O., *ca.* 1889. Member of the Reliance Brass Band.

Klein, Buster (d). b. N.O., *ca.* 1895; d. N.O., *ca.* 1946. A dixieland drummer who played in the early Johnny Bayersdorffer bands.

Kleppinger, Bill (mdl). b. N.O., *ca.* 1897; d. N.O., May 27, 1982. A mainstay of the Six and 7/8 String Band and the Invincibles, dating back to 1912. Jazz career of more than half a century. Brother-in-law of Paul Mares, leader of the New Orleans Rhythm Kings.

Kmen, Henry "Hank" (cl, s, vo). b. Saratoga Springs, N.Y., Nov. 3, 1915; d. N.O., Sept. 22, 1978. Professor at Tulane University who had wide experience in both jazz and big band work before coming to New Orleans. During the 1960s, he played with the Crawford-Ferguson Night Owls.

Knecht, Henry (c, tb). b. N.O., 1898; d. N.O., July 21, 1968. Noted brass virtuoso said to be the fastest "reader" in the city. Worked with dance bands; Happy Schilling's brass band; worked in Heineman's Ball Park ragtime band.

Knox, Emile (bd). b. N.O., May 2, 1902; d. N.O., Aug. 20, 1976. Longtime parade drummer; with the Young Tuxedo Brass Band in the 1950s.

Bill Kleppinger

Stalebread Lacoume

Tommy Ladnier

Kohlman, Freddie (d). b. N.O., Aug. 25, 1915. With Joe Robichaux in the 1930s. Bandleader at Sid Davilla's Mardi Gras lounge during the fifties. Frequently played snare drums with the Young Tuxedo Brass Band. Regular drummer at Jazz Ltd., Chicago, in the mid-sixties.

Kuhl, Charlie (p). b. N.O., *ca.* 1897; d. N.O., *ca.* 1947. With the Alfred Laine Orchestra.

Lacaze, Peter (t). b. St. Bernard Parish, La., July 14, 1893. Popular dance hall musician of the 1920s. In the late twenties he organized his popular NOLA Band.

Lacey, "Li'l Mack" (d). b. N.O., ———. Crescent Orchestra before World War I. With Kid Punch Miller in the 1920s. Long vaudeville career.

Lacoume, Emile "Stalebread" (z, g, p, bjo, vo, l). b. N.O., 1885; d. N.O., 1946. Led Razzy Dazzy Spasm Band (considered by many to be the first jazz band) in the Storyville streets as early as 1897, playing homemade instruments. In early 1900s, though blind, performed actively at lakefront resorts. Member of Halfway House Orchestra. Later, in the twenties and early thirties, at Lavida Ballroom in the Charlie Fishbein orchestra.

Ogden Lafaye

Papa Laine

Digger Laine

Lada, Anton (d, x). b. N.O., *ca.* 1893; d. Chicago, Ill., 1967. Played around New Orleans in his early teens. Led a small group called Five Southern Jazzers. Went north almost simultaneously with the Original Dixieland Jazz Band and made Columbia records in the same era, competing with the Nick La Rocca group under the name of the Louisiana Five. This group included Yellow Nunez.

Ladnier, Tommy (c, t). b. Florenceville, La., May 28, 1900; d. New York, N.Y., June 4, 1939. At fourteen Ladnier was under the tutelage of Bunk Johnson, and he played for several years in bands that Bunk organized. He never actually played in New Orleans but was much influenced by Johnson and Buddy Petit. He was in Chicago in 1920; and from 1922 to 1927 worked with Jimmie Noone, King Oliver, Fletcher Henderson, and recorded with Lovie Austin. A year before his death he made records with Sidney Bechet and with Mezz Mezzrow.

Lafaye, Ogden (p). b. N.O., *ca.* 1896. Popular pianist, much associated with Irving Fazola's New Orleans career. Recorded and broadcast daily with Faz over WTPS. Later went into the landscaping business. Father of film star, John Carroll.

Mike Lala

Nappy Lamare

Laine, Alfred "Baby," "Pantsy" (c, ah, d). b. N.O., July 12, 1895; d. N.O., March 1, 1957. Son of Papa Laine. Started playing with Papa's Reliance Brass Band in 1908 and worked mainly with Reliance groups or led his own dance band until early Depression years.

Laine, Jack "Papa" (d, ah, l). b. N.O., Sept. 21, 1873; d. N.O., June 1, 1966. Earliest dixieland bandleader. His seven dance groups, all named Reliance, worked simultaneously in New Orleans. His brass band was celebrated throughout the Gulf Coast. Withdrew from music at start of World War I before the Original Dixieland Jazz Band won its success. Never played on records, but made tapes at Tulane University under Johnny Wiggs's leadership in early 1960s.

Laine, Julian "Digger" (tb) b. N.O., 1907; d. N.O., Sept. 10, 1957. Began his career at the old Fern Cafe No. 2, a dime-a-dance place. Through most of his career, he was mainly identified with Johnny Wiggs, Irving Fazola, Sharkey. Worked for a while in Chicago with Muggsy Spanier's band. Not related to Papa Laine.

Lala, Joe (c). b. N.O., ———. Pre–World War I dixielander.

Lala, Johnny (c). b. N.O., 1893; d. N.O., Oct. 3, 1966. Pre–World War I dixielander. Worked with Happy Schilling, Reliance, Johnny Fischer.

Lala, Mike (t). b. N.O., Oct. 24, 1908; d. N.O., Oct. 8, 1976. A leading dixieland and dance band leader for forty years. Featured through two decades in such leading French Quarter locations as La Lune, Famous Door. Earlier played in bands led by Joe Capraro, Oscar Marcour, Jules Bauduc.

Lamar, Elbert "Slim" (sb, l). b. N.O., *ca.* 1900. Leader of Argentine Dons, big vaudeville and recording band that featured many well-known dixieland stars.

Billy Lambert

Nick La Rocca

Lamare, Hilton Napoleon "Nappy" (bjo, g, vo). b. N.O., June 14, 1907. Nappy got his first banjo while a student at Warren Easton High School in New Orleans and was a professional by 1925, working in bands led by Johnny Wiggs, Bill Lustig, Johnny Bayersdorffer, Sharkey, and Monk Hazel. He made his recording debut with Johnny Hyman's Bayou Stompers in 1927. His fame, however, is based on the success with the public he achieved while working with the Bob Crosby Bob Cats in the middle thirties to the early forties. Moved to North Hollywood, Calif. With drummer Ray Bauduc, he led a band called the Riverboat Dandies, touring the nation's best night spots in the 1960s. Played occasionally in 1982.

Lambert, Adam (p, b, vt). b. N.O., ca. 1886. Versatile early jazzman first played valve trombone, then string bass for the Silver Leaf Orchestra; and in 1932 was touring with Polo Barnes's dance orchestra as regular pianist.

Lambert, Billy (d). b. N.O., ca. 1893; d. N.O., May 30, 1969. Early dixielander; as a member of the original Tom Brown's Band from Dixieland, he made the historic trip to Chicago's Lamb's Cafe in 1915.

Landry, Alcide (t). b. N.O., ca. 1880; d. N.O., 1949. During the twenties played with Tuxedo Brass Band, Lyons Brass Band. Leader of the Eureka Brass Band during the thirties. He played in the WPA Brass Band during the mid-thirties, and in the forties worked at Luthjen's, sometimes at Happy Landing, and with the Tulane Brass Band.

Irwin Leclere

Landry, Tom (vt, tu, sb). b. N.O., *ca.* 1870. Occasionally with the Onward Brass Band before the Spanish-American War. Before 1900 he was playing along with Alphonse Picou and Edward Clem in bands led by Oscar Duconge. As early as 1894, he was in Charlie Galloway's band.

Langlois, Isidore (g). b. N.O., *ca.* 1910. Left the U.S. in the early 1930s. Recorded with Big Boy Goudie in 1939.

Lanoix, August (tu, sb). b. N.O., Aug. 13, 1902. First job with Martin Gabriel. Early jobs with Leo Dejan.

Laporte, Johnny (d, l). b. N.O., ——. Dance band leader of the twenties and thirties.

La Rocca, Dominick J. "Nick" (c, l). b. N.O., April 11, 1889; d. N.O., Feb. 22, 1961. Leader of Original Dixieland Jazz Band. Made first jazz disc. Credited as composer of many standard tunes. Authorized biography in *The Story of the Original Dixieland Jazz Band.*

Larsen, Morten Gunnar (p). b. Norway, Oct. 1, 1955. One of the great ragtime virtuosos of the world. Came to New Orleans in the late 1970s. Performs solo and with various jazz bands. Played with the New Orleans Ragtime Orchestra, led the band in one of the touring companies of *One Mo' Time,* and played with the Louisiana Repertory Jazz Ensemble.

Laudeman, Pete (p). b. N.O., 1908; d. N.O., May 13, 1963. Dixielander with most of the top bands.

Leblanc, Dan (sb, tu). b. N.O., 1902; d. N.O., April 19, 1962. Princeton Revellers, the Little Owls, Mike Lala's band, Murphy Campo's outfit, Saenger Theater pit orchestra, Sharkey, the New Orleans Owls, Grunewald Hotel.

Leclere, Irwin (p, vo). b. N.O., *ca.* 1893; d. N.O., 1981. Well known as composer and house pianist at the Triangle Theater up to World War I. Traveled with popular vaudeville act, the Fuzzy Wuzzy Twins. Tunes include "Triangle Jazz Blues," "Cookie."

Lee, Bill (ss, cl). b. N.O., Dec. 19, 1926. Regular member of the Last Straws.

Leglise, Vic (d). b. N.O., *ca.* 1900. Dixieland drummer with the Princeton Revellers about 1920. With Bill Padron, Pinky Vidacovich.

Legnon, Albert "Red" (s). b. N.O., *ca.* 1898. In the 1920s worked with Alfred Laine's band.

Legnon, Roscoe (sb). b. N.O., *ca.* 1895; d. N.O., *ca.* 1963. With Bayersdorffer's Jazzola Six before World War I. In later years often with the Barocco brothers.

Lenares, Zeb (cl). b. N.O., *ca.* 1885; d. N.O., *ca.* 1928. Fine clarinetist who played in many of the district combinations between 1909–1917. With the Magnolia Sweets in 1910. During the early twenties he was heard with the Foster Lewis Jazz Band and with Kid Rena.

Lewis, "Dandy" (d, sb). b. N.O., *ca.* 1888; d. *ca.* 1932. Played string bass for and managed the Eagle Band, 1911–1916. During the same period was regular bass drummer with the Onward Brass Band.

Lewis, "Father Al" (bjo, g, vo). b. N.O., Aug. 8, 1903. Preservation Hall; New Orleans Joymakers.

Lewis, Foster (tb). Bandleader of the early 1920s.

George Lewis

Son Fewclothes Lewis

Lewis, Frank (cl). b. N.O., *ca.* 1870; d. Bogalusa, La., 1924. Charter member of the Buddy Bolden band. Left New Orleans in 1917 to play in Louisiana country towns. Played with Dan Moody orchestra until 1924.

Lewis, George (cl). b. N.O., July 13, 1900; d. N.O., Dec. 31, 1968. Most celebrated of the pure traditionalists. Played his first jobs in Mandeville, La., with Black Eagles Band, 1917. During the twenties, he marched with Chris Kelly's band, Eureka Brass Band, Buddy Petit, Kid Rena's brass band. With Bunk Johnson, 1945 and 1946. Had a band on tour in Japan in 1963, 1964, and 1965. A biography of Lewis by Jay Alison Stuart has been published in England. One by Tom Bethell in the U.S.

Lewis, Robert "Son Fewclothes" (bd). b. N.O., March 10, 1900; d. N.O., June 24, 1965. One of the great bass drummers of the New Orleans marching bands. Started with Tulane Brass Band in 1925, played with Chris Kelly for parades in the mid-twenties, and with Kid Rena in the thirties. From 1939 to 1963 was the backbone of the Eureka Brass Band. Incapacitated by a stroke in 1963.

Lewis, Steve (p). b. N.O., March 19, 1896; d. N.O., 1939. Just established as a top Basin Street "professor" when the district closed down. Left for vaudeville tour with Billy Mack's troupe, along with Johnny Dodds, Mutt Carey. In 1918 joined A. J. Piron at Tranchina's, Spanish Fort; played with Piron on the SS *Capitol* and operated the ship's calliope. Composed many great tunes including A. J. Piron's theme, "Purple Rose of Cairo," "Kiss Me, Sweet," and "Sud Bustin' Blues." Recorded with the Piron orchestra, and made a piano roll of "Mama's Gone Goodbye." Also backed New Orleans Willie Jackson on Columbia Records in 1926.

Lewis, Walter (p, b). b. N.O., Sept. 2, 1918. With Louis Cottrell, Alvin Alcorn.

Liberto, Roy (t, l). b. N.O., March 11, 1928. Leader of novelty dixieland band similar in style to Dukes of Dixieland. Usually on tour.

74

Steve Lewis

Lindsay, Herb (v). b. N.O., *ca.* 1888. Played in the district from about 1909. Was at Hanan's saloon, Liberty and Iberville, in a band that included Freddie Keppard, 1910–1911. In 1912 he was with the Primrose Orchestra. Left for Chicago in 1917 where he sometimes played in the Lawrence Duhé band.

Lindsay, John (sb, tu, tb). b. Algiers, La., Aug. 23, 1894; d. Chicago, Ill., July 3, 1950. One of the true New Orleans giants of jazz. Started in the red-light district in 1910. Through the twenties he worked with John Robichaux, A. J. Piron, Papa Celestin. Left in 1924; played in Chicago with King Oliver, Willie Hightower, Carroll Dickerson. Recorded on bass or trombone with A. J. Piron, Jelly Roll Morton, Jimmie Noone, Richard M. Jones. Toured with Louis Armstrong.

Lindsey, Joseph "Little Joe," "Seefus," "Kid" (d). b. N.O., Sept. 7, 1899; d. N.O. First bandleader to employ Louis Armstrong, 1916. After World War I, he played with the Dixie Jazz Band, Bob Lyons, and on pickup jobs with Kid Rena through the 1920s. Worked occasionally in dance halls.

John Lindsay

Little, Jim. See Brown, Sidney.

Lizana, Florin J. "Curly" (cl). b. N.O., July 31, 1895; d. July 31, 1967. Early dixielander, much admired by Larry Shields.

Llambias, Joe (bjo). With Leon Prima.

Freddie Lonzo

Lobre, Al (bjo, sb). b. N.O., *ca*, 1915. Dixielander who played with top names for more than forty years. Regular with the Last Straws in the 1970s.

Long, Glynn Lea "Red" (p). b. Houston, Tex., 1895; d. Oct. 13, 1945. Rhythm man of the Halfway House Orchestra.

Lonzo, Freddie (tb). b. N.O., Aug. 20, 1950. Latter-generation stalwart in the Ory tradition. Attracted attention as trombonist in Alvin Alcorn Imperial Brass Band after playing with pickup bands and modern groups. In 1981 became regular trombonist in Louisiana Repertory Jazz Ensemble. Has made several European tours. Worked in Doc Paulin's Band, 1966–1968; Olympia Brass Band, 1968–1969; Original Storyville Jazz Band, 1971–1976.

Lopez, Ray (c). b. N.O., Nov. 28, 1889; d. Los Angeles, Calif., April 27, 1970. Member of Tom Brown's Band from Dixieland who went to Chicago in 1915. Toured vaudeville with the Five Rubes. Became movie studio musician.

Loposer, Avery (tb). b. Mobile, Ala., *ca.* 1898. Member of Crescent City Jazzers, Arcadian Serenaders recording groups.

Ray Lopez

Charlie Love

Deacon Loyacano

Love, Charlie (c). b. Plaquemines Parish, La., 1885; d. N.O., Aug. 7, 1963. Love did not play regularly in New Orleans until 1925, when he went into the Lyric Theater pit band led by John Robichaux. Since about 1900, however, he'd been in and out of New Orleans, working mainly in his hometown, and with the Caddo Jazz Band in Shreveport. Worked in dance halls through the Depression. In the late forties and the fifties he was often at the Happy Landing. He recorded for American Music in 1949. Toward the end of his life he was busy preserving the Robichaux band's book of rags, and rehearsing a ragtime band, which was recorded on Riverside in 1960. Throughout his lifetime, he took time to play in the parade bands of the city and was frequently seen in the Tuxedo Brass Band.

Lovett, Samuel "Baby" (d). b. Alexandria, La., ca. 1900. Long-time resident of Kansas City where he played at one time with Bunk Johnson at the Yellow Front Cafe.

Loyacano, Arnold "Deacon" (p, sb, tu, g, d). b. N.O., 1889; d. N.O., Oct. 5, 1962. Brother of Hook, Bud. Child prodigy played at Milneburg and the French Opera House at age eleven. Also with Papa Laine's Reliance Brass Band and Dance Orchestra as early as 1900. Went to Chicago

with Tom Brown's band in 1915. Was with the New Orleans Rhythm Kings, the New Orleans Jazz Band led by Jimmy Durante, and Sig Meyer's Druids Orchestra. Joined the music staff of NBC in the early years of radio. In New Orleans in later years, he played with Johnny Wiggs, Sharkey, Leon Prima, George Hartman, the Dukes of Dixieland, George Girard, and Tony Almerico.

Loyacano, Freddie (g, bjo). b. N.O., ca, 1905. Dixieland man frequently seen with the Sharkey, Leon Prima, Irving Fazola groups; also with Ellis Stratakos. Brother of Steve, Joe.

Loyacano, Joe (b). b. 1906; d. N.O., March 19, 1969. Played in Halfway House Orchestra. Brother of Steve, Freddie; not related to Hook Loyacano.

Loyacano, Joe "Hook" (tb, sb, tu). b. N.O., 1893; d. N.O., Nov. 30, 1967. Recorded saxophone with the Halfway House Orchestra. Worked with leading New Orleans dixielanders, steadily with Tony Almerico in the 1950s. Brother of Deacon, Bud.

Hook Loyacano

Loyacano, John "Bud" (sb, tu). b. N.O., Nov. 14, 1879; d. N.O., Feb. 25, 1960. Dixieland rhythm man with Dan Hughes, Reliance Brass Band and Dance Orchestra, Sal Magiotta. Played with his left hand a bass strung for right-handed musician. Brother of Deacon, Hook.

Loyacano, Steve (g, bjo, v). b. N.O., Dec. 19, 1903. Started in a band led by Pinky Gerbrecht. Went to Johnny Bayersdorffer in time for celebrated record date in the 1920s. In 1925 worked with the New Orleans edition of the New Orleans Rhythm Kings. Led the band at the Saenger Theater and had his own club, the Chez Paree, in 1935. Brother of Freddie, Joe.

Lyons, Bob (sb, tu, g, bjo). b. N.O., *ca.* 1868; d. N.O., *ca.* 1949. Started playing for pay about 1885 in "skiffle" bands, working the streets for coins. With Charlie Galloway in the mid-nineties, and at the turn of the century played in the Oscar Duconge band. In 1901 and 1902 he sometimes played with Buddy Bolden; between 1907 and 1910, with Frank Duson. Was with Kid Ory in 1914. Organized his Dixie Jazz Band in 1918.

McCay, Percy (all string and wind instruments). b. N.O., Dec. 13, 1896. Talented amateur played with the all-string bands of New Orleans—Invincibles, Six and 7/8, others.

Bud Loyacano

McCay, Thompson (g, sb, mdl, v, tb, tu). b. N.O., Sept. 4, 1901; d. N.O., July 4, 1963. Brother of Percy McCay and well known for his work in all-string bands in the early days of New Orleans jazz.

McClean, Richard (sb, bjo, g). b. N.O., Jan. 25, 1898; d. N.O., 1968. Played with Papa Celestin, Octave Crosby bands. Was long a fixture on Bourbon Street.

McClennon, Rube (bjo). During the 1920s McClennon was closely associated with Buddy Petit, though for a short time, during an illness of Buddy's, he worked with Dejan's Black Diamond Orchestra. When Petit died in

Bob Lyons

Percy McCay

1931, Rube took the leadership of the band and worked with it on the SS *Madison*.

McCloskey, John. See Rogers, Emmett.

McCullum, George, Sr. (c). b. N.O., July 27, 1865; d. N.O., Nov. 14, 1920. Marched in first parade at age fifteen. In 1909 joined Barnum & Bailey Circus band. Led regular brass band for the Jefferson City Buzzards. Played with Robichaux, Piron dance bands. Both Manuel Manetta and Sweet Emma Barrett played piano in his dance bands.

McCullum, George, Jr. (t). b. N.O., June 19, 1898; d. N.O., 1938. Studied with his father and succeeded George, Sr., in the Robichaux orchestra in 1920. During the twenties, marched with the Excelsior and Tuxedo brass bands and worked dance hall jobs under Eddie Jackson's leadership. In mid-Depression days was the solo trumpet in the WPA Brass Band led by Pinchback Touro.

Thompson McCay

George McCullum, Sr.

McCurdy, Charles (cl, s). b. N.O., *ca.* 1865; d. N.O., Oct. 4, 1933. A leading musician for over fifty years, Mc-Curdy was a charter member of the Robichaux orchestra in 1894. In 1905 he was coleader, with Bab Frank, of the Peerless Orchestra and marched with the Excelsior Brass Band before World War I. Again with Robichaux in 1913. Later worked with Piron in the Olympia Orchestra and played with Fate Marable on the SS *Capitol* after the war. Rejoined Robichaux in the Lyric Theater, 1925–1927, then in 1928 was in Peter Lacaze's NOLA Band. Until about 1934, he was on the road working in tent show and circus bands, especially the show *Silas Green from New Orleans.*

Mackie, Frank "Red" (sb, tu, g, bjo, p). b. N.O., April 16, 1904; d. N.O., Aug. 11, 1969. Began playing at about age twelve. One of original Invincibles and New Orleans Owls. Played and appeared with the Six and 7/8 String Band. Made all the discs with this group. Brother of Dick Mackie.

Mackie, Richard H. "Dick" (c). b. N.O., Nov. 26, 1906. One of founders of the New Orleans Owls. Later led his own band. Went on tour with big commercial bands, Hal Kemp, Kay Kayser. Sometimes plays informally and coaches young musicians. Brother of Red.

Red Mackie

MacMurray, John (d). b. N.O., *ca.* 1878; d. N.O., *ca.* 1920. A great New Orleans drummer who exerted much influence on the music of the big names who blossomed later. During the early 1900s he was often with Buddy Bolden, and was picked by Manuel Perez for the Imperial Orchestra. Ernest Rogers, Baby Dodds, and Louis Cottrell, Sr., all showed signs of his style. He built his own drums, and mainly used homemade equipment through his professional career.

McNeal, Richard (bjo). A member of Kid Rena Dixie Jazz Band, 1922.

MacNeil, James (c, p). b. N.O., about 1870; d. Chicago, 1945. Charter member of the John Robichaux orchestra in 1894, he also played in the Onward Brass Band and enlisted in the army with that group for the Spanish-American War. Up to Depression times he was a popular music teacher in New Orleans. Moved to Chicago in 1938. Brother of Wendell.

Kid Shots Madison

Manuel Manetta

MacNeil, Wendell (v). b. N.O., ca. 1872. A member of the John Robichaux orchestra from its inception in 1894 to the leader's death in 1939, at which time MacNeil moved to Detroit. Brother of James MacNeil.

Madison, Louis "Kid Shots" (t). b. N.O., Feb. 19, 1899; d. N.O., Sept., 1948. Fellow inmate, with Louis Armstrong and Kid Rena, of the Waif's Home in New Orleans. Studied with David Jones, Joe Howard, and Louis Dumaine. Played with Papa Celestin at Beverly Gardens and worked with Frank Duson—all before World War I. Recorded with the Original Tuxedo Orchestra in 1925. Veteran of the Eureka Brass Band, the Young Tuxedo Brass Band, and the WPA Brass Band. He played out his last days at the P & L Club on Lake Ponchartrain. Recorded with George Lewis and Bunk Johnson (American Music).

Maestri, "Katz" (d). b. N.O., ca. 1906. Frequently with Albert Artigues. Earlier, about 1925, with Norman Brownlee. Toured in thirties with Gus Fortmeier band.

Magiotta, Sal (cl). b. N.O., ca. 1896; d. N.O., June 29, 1970. Police band. Played with all old-time dixieland stars. Led Triangle Band in the 1920s.

Mahier, Louis (d). b. N.O., ca. 1902. Member of Nat Towles's Creole Harmony Kings in the early 1920s.

Manaday, Buddy (bjo). Played with the Buddy Petit band in the early 1920s.

Manetta, Manuel (all instruments). b. Algiers, La., Oct. 3, 1889; d. Algiers, La., Oct. 10, 1969. Began 1906 with Tom Albert. Member of notable musical family, Manetta spent more than fifty years as a music teacher. Played with Buddy Bolden, Frank Duson, Edward Clem before 1910. Solo pianist in Willie Piazza's Basin Street brothel about 1908. Was with Tom Albert and the Original Tuxedo Orchestra until 1913. He then tried his luck in Chicago but soon returned to New Orleans. During World War I days he was with Papa Celestin and Joe Howard, at the Villa Cabaret. In 1919 he worked in California with Kid Ory. During the twenties he was on saxophone with Manuel Perez. Widely known for his ability to play trombone and trumpet simultaneously and in harmony.

Mangiapane, Sherwood (sb, tu, d, t, vo). b. N.O., Oct. 1, 1912. One of the all-time great New Orleans bassists, began playing fifty-cent jobs at lawn parties before he was twelve. Closely identified musically with Johnny Wiggs, Raymond Burke, and Edmond Souchon, with whom he has made many LPs. Known not only for superb musicianship but also for his singing and whistling. Preservation Hall regular. Also with Louisiana Repertory Jazz Ensemble in 1982.

Sherwood Mangiapane

Mickey Marcour

Wingy Manone

Joseph P. Mares

Manone, Joseph "Wingy" (t). b. N.O., Feb. 13, 1900; d. Las Vegas, Nev., July 9, 1982. Wingy lost his right arm while hitching a trolly ride when he was nine years old. At the age of twelve he was playing kazoo in spasm bands on the streets of Storyville. Played very little trumpet in New Orleans but was well known at the Gulf Coast resorts. Recorded for Okeh with the Arcadian Serenaders, a Mobile, Ala., band. Has appeared in several motion pictures and is widely recorded. His autobiography *Trumpet on the Wing* (New York: Doubleday) has enjoyed an excellent sale.

Mansion, Henry (tb, bh). b. N.O., *ca.* 1898; d. N.O., Jan. 13, 1968. Best known as a brass band musician.

Paul Mares

Lawrence Marrero

Marcour, Mickey (p). b. N.O., ——. d. N.O., March 19, 1961. During the 1920s, he was an active dixieland pianist. Played with the Halfway House Orchestra and in a quartet with Abbie Brunies, Buck Rogers, and Stalebread Lacoume at Bucktown Tavern.

Marcour, Oscar (v, l). b. N.O., July 1, 1895; d. N.O., Sept. 11, 1956. A formally trained violinist, brother of Mickey Marcour,, who frequently worked in bands with top jazzmen.

Mares, Joseph P. (cl). b. N.O., Aug. 20, 1908. Younger brother of famed New Orleans Rhythm Kings leader Paul Mares, Joe had the opportunity to play with those stars in his youth. During the fifties, he recorded and issued a sustained program of authentic jazz on his Southland Records, showcasing the greatest stars of New Orleans jazz, some for the first time. Blessed with an excellent ear and a thorough structural understanding of the nature of jazz, he was able to make recordings of high musical quality. For many jazzmen, their best records were issued under his direction. He furthered many successful musical careers by his efforts to send promising musicians to major musical events around the country, thereby introducing them to the jazz public. He also conducted a regular radio show and did much to publicize the music of New Orleans during the revival period.

Mares, Paul (c, t). b. N.O., June 15, 1900; d. Chicago, Ill., Aug. 18, 1949. Played dance jobs around New Orleans as a youth. Learned to play on his father's horn. (**Joseph P. Mares, Sr.**, played in Tosso's Military Band at West End.) In 1920 was playing in Tom Brown's band. Led the New Orleans Rhythm Kings in Chicago and became a national sensation. Co-composer of "Tin Roof Blues," "Farewell Blues," "Milneburg Joys," and other jazz standards. Retired from music in the early thirties, but began to fill concert dates in New York and Philadelphia during the late forties.

Marrero, Billy (sb). b. N.O., *ca.* 1874; d. N.O., ——. Superior Orchestra, 1910–1913; Olympia Orchestra, 1913; Camelia Orchestra, 1918. Father of Eddie, John, Lawrence, Simon.

Marrero, Eddie (sb). b. N.O., Aug. 4, 1902. Son of Billy Marrero. Started his professional career in his brother Lawrence's Young Tuxedo Orchestra, 1920. In the mid-twenties, he was playing with the Chris Kelly's band.

Chink Martin

Marrero, John (bjo). b. N.O., *ca.* 1895; d. N.O., *ca.* 1945. Began after World War I with Kid Rena. Son of Billy, brother of Lawrence, Simon, Eddie Marrero. During the early 1920s, he worked with Piron, Original Tuxedo Orchestra, Bebé Ridgley. Recorded with Original Tuxedo Orchestra in 1926.

Marrero, Lawrence (bjo). b. N.O., Oct. 24, 1900; d. N.O., June 6, 1959. Started after World War I, with Wooden Joe Nicholas, Kid Rena, Chris Kelly. Formed his own Young Tuxedo Orchestra in 1920. Sometimes played bass drum in parade bands, notably with George Lewis. Became famous as the rhythm keystone of the George Lewis Ragtime Jazz Band through the forties and fifties at the height of Lewis' success.

Marrero, Simon (sb). b. N.O., *ca.* 1897. Another of Billy's busy sons. Worked in Kid Rena's band in the early 1920s and with Papa Celestin's Original Tuxedo Orchestra, with which he recorded in 1927. Joined King Oliver briefly in early Depression years and moved to New York where he finished his playing days.

Martin, Abraham (bjo). A regular member of Evan Thomas' Black Eagles band in the 1920s.

Martin, Albert (d). A member of the band that made the famous 1929 session under the name Jones-Collins Astoria Hot Eight.

Martin, Chink (g, bjo, sb, tu). b. N.O., June 10, 1886; d. N.O., July 7, 1981. Real name Martin Abraham, Sr. The grand master of jazz tuba. With Reliance Brass and Dance bands in 1910. Johnny Bayersdorffer orchestra, New Orleans Rhythm Kings (1922), Sharkey's Kings of Dixieland, Johnny Wiggs groups. In 1966 with the Crawford-Ferguson Night Owls. Played regularly at Preservation Hall as late as 1980.

Elery Maser

Martin, "Coochie" (g, p). b. N.O., *ca.* 1887; d. N.O., *ca.* 1928. In the pre–World War I period, he played first with John Robichaux, 1911–1912, then with the Peerless Orchestra under Bab Frank in 1906, and later (1910) under A. J. Piron. In 1913 he organized his own combination, with himself on piano, and got the job at the 101 Ranch.

Martin, "Fats" (d). b. N.O., *ca.* 1900. Began his career in the first George Lewis band in the early 1920s, but in later years moved into swing and then into modern deviations.

Martin, Henry (d, g). b. N.O., *ca.* 1895; d. *ca.* 1932. Before World War I, he was the idol of many of the younger drummers. Played in the district with Kid Ory and with King Oliver's band. Also was bass drummer with the Onward Brass Band about 1916. In 1917 he was leading his own small group. In the twenties, he played in Peter Bocage's Creole Serenaders.

Martin, Milton (tb). b. Algiers, La., Nov. 24, 1896; d. N.O., 1977. Played for several years with Sam Ross Orchestra in Cut Off, La. He retired from music in 1913 at the age of seventeen to play pro baseball.

Maser, Elery (cl, s). b. N.O., May 12, 1904; d. N.O., Dec. 8, 1972. Played in bands of Happy Schilling, Johnny Bayersdorffer. Recorded with Johnny Hyman's Bayou Stompers, 1927. Later with Pinky Vidacovich, Pinky Gerbrecht, Leon Prima, Sharkey, Jules Bauduc.

Masinter, Louis (sb, tu). b. N.O., Aug. 19, 1908. Frequently with the Primas in the 1930s.

Massicot, Percy "Butz" (d). b. N.O., May 11, 1910. Dixieland drummer very popular with musicians. Spent many years in Roosevelt Hotel (now Fairmont) dance orchestra.

Matthews, Lewis "Chif" (c). b. LaPlace, La., *ca.* 1885; d. ——. Brother of Stonewall Matthews. Began his career with Kid Ory about 1903 and stayed with him through 1908 when the band came to New Orleans. Lawrence Duhé left Ory to take the leader job at the 101 Ranch in 1909, and Matthews went along.

Matthews, Nathaniel "Bebé" (d). b. Algiers, La., *ca.* 1890; d. N.O., May 27, 1961. Pre–World War I drummer with Allen Brass Band, Onward Brass Band. Also played with Bebé Ridgley's orchestra. Brother of Bill and Ramos Matthews.

Matthews, Ramos (d). b. Algiers, La., *ca.* 1886; d. N.O., Oct. 20, 1958. Popular parade drummer. Worked in Allen Brass Band from about 1912 to 1926. He also played in marching groups organized by Louis Dumaine. Brother of Bill and Bebé Matthews.

Matthews, Stonewall (bjo, g). b. LaPlace, La., *ca.* 1889. Another charter member of the band Kid Ory brought to New Orleans in 1908. Brother of Chif Matthews.

Matthews, William "Bill" (d, tb). b. Algiers, La., May 9, 1899; d. N.O., June 3, 1964. Youngest of the three Matthews drummers, Bill made his debut in 1917 with the Excelsior Brass Band and in the dance orchestra of Jack Williams. Worked with Desvigne in the district just before it closed, then odd jobs with Frank Duson, Sam Morgan, Joe Howard. Took up trombone in the early 1920s; studied with Vic Gaspard and went west with Nat Towles's orchestra in 1926. Toured with Jelly Roll Morton and went back to Desvigne on the steamship *Island Queen*. In 1927, again in New Orleans, he played with

Bill Matthews

Bebé Ridgley's section of the Original Tuxedo Orchestra and recorded with Papa Celestin. From 1945 to 1963, he kept quite busy at the Paddock on Bourbon Street, usually with Celestin, up to 1952.

Meistier, Gilbert. See "Blind" Gilbert.

Mello, Leonce (tb). b. N.O., *ca.* 1888; d. N.O., *ca.* 1941. One of the great trombones of early New Orleans. An occasional dance band musician, but best known for his performance with Papa Laine's Reliance Brass Band in the pre–World War I days. Also played in 1907 with Fischer's Brass Band. With Barocco brothers' band in 1919.

Mello, Manuel John (c). b. N.O., June 18, 1886; d. N.O., Oct. 31, 1961. Made his parade debut about 1903 with a five-piece marching band, the Big Five, that included his brother Leonce on trombone. Never recorded, he was an admirer of Manuel Perez' sound and strove to duplicate it. Was a mainstay of Papa Laine's ragtime bands from about 1908 and always a member of the No. 1 unit of the Reliance Brass Band.

Mello, Samford (tb, d). b. N.O., *ca.* 1901. Played in Alfred Laine's band in the 1920s. Brother of Leonce, Manuel.

Mendelson, Stanley (p). b. N.O., June 23, 1923. Played with the Dukes of Dixieland, Sharkey, Phil Zito. Accompanied Lizzie Miles, Buglin' Sam Dekemel. In the 1960s he soloed in a cocktail lounge at the Sheraton-Charles Hotel. Recorded with Tom Brown and Johnny Wiggs.

Metoyer, Arnold (c, t). b. N.O., *ca.* 1876; d. N.O., 1935. A "legitimate" musician who spent most of his prime years playing in traveling tent shows and was out of town much of the time. He was much respected by contemporaries for his technique. In 1921 was with Luis Russell at Anderson's Restaurant, and sometimes played dance jobs with jazzmen.

Lizzie Miles

Miles, Lizzie (vo). b. N.O., March 31, 1895; d. N.O., March 17, 1963. Popular New Orleans singer who recorded in the twenties and experienced a revival during the fifties under the guidance of Joe Mares. Worked mainly at Davilla's Mardi Gras lounge and was in Los Angeles with Bob Scobey. Especially known in later years for renditions of a number of tunes in gombo French.

Miller, Charlie K. (tb). b. N.O., March 11, 1915; d. Thibodaux, La., Dec. 23, 1962. Worked in bands led by Irving Fazola, Augie Schellang, Leon Prima, Sharkey, and George Hartman. Member of WWL staff orchestra, the Dawn Busters.

Miller, Eddie (cl, s). b. N.O., June 23, 1911. In 1924 was a member of the New Orleans *Item* newsboy band. Joined the New Orleans Owls in that band's latter days. Left town for New York as tenor sax with Ben Pollack's orchestra at the beginning of the Depression. A founding member of the Bob Crosby orchestra, active from 1935 to 1943, he became leader when Crosby began his film career. He settled in North Hollywood, Calif., and played a daily TV show during the fifties. Still visits New Orleans occasionally, and during the early sixties, played with a trio in Pete Fountain's club on Bourbon Street while Pete was on tour. Widely recorded on tenor sax, but his clarinet work with the Mount City Blue Blowers may have been his artistic peak.

Eddie Miller

Miller, Ernest "Kid Punch" (t). b. Raceland, La., June 10, 1894; d. N.O., Dec. 3, 1971. Debuted in 1919 in New Orleans after discharge as military band bugle corporal. First worked in band of Duck Ernest Johnson, then with Jack Carey, whom he left after two years to form his own band. He moved to Chicago in 1927, to a job with François' Louisianians (François Mosley of New Orleans), then barnstormed with circus and carnival bands all over the U.S. Was in New Orleans through the early sixties leading his own band.

Miller, James E. "Sing" (p, bjo, vo). b. N.O., June 17, 1913. Veteran big band musician. Has worked in later years with George Lewis, Paul Barbarin, Earl Foster, Kid Thomas.

Miller, Johnny (p). b. N.O., *ca.* 1897. With Johnny Bayersdorffer's most successful band, made collector's item record with his own Johnny Miller's Frolickers.

Milton, Ernest "Kid" (t, d). b. N.O., June 14, 1905. An average trumpeter, with talent for finding jobs for a band. Always busy with his own dance groups from about 1918, he employed many well-known New Orleans musicians during his active musical life.

Kid Punch Miller

Sing Miller

Minor, Anderson (tu). b. N.O., Sept. 20, 1901; d. N.O., Nov. 22, 1973. Young Tuxedo Brass Band, Young Olympia Brass Band. A familiar figure as a grand marshal in street parades.

Minor, Donald (cl). b. N.O., May 5, 1935. With Harold Dejan's Young Olympia Brass Band. Son of H. E. Minor.

Minor, Fred "H. E." (bjo, g). b. N.O., Dec. 8, 1913. An active musician since early Depression days in the Sidney Desvigne orchestra. During the fifties and early sixties, he was frequently seen with Paul Barbarin's band. In the mid-sixties he was part of the Noon Johnson bazooka trio.

Minor, George (g). Guitar in Kid Sheik Colar Band.

Minyard, Frank (t). b. N.O., Aug. 30, 1930. Physician, coroner of Orleans Parish. When time permitted, he played with the French Market Jazz Band and on occasion with Pete Fountain. His annual "Jazz Roots" concerts draw large crowds and provide funds for a broad spectrum of New Orleans charities.

Miranda, Jack (cl). b. N.O., ca. 1908; d. N.O., ca. 1959. Dixielander who reached his peak working with Abbie Brunies in the 1940s.

Mitchell, Arthur (sb, bjo). A member of George Lewis' first band in 1923. As early as 1902 worked in a Buddy Bolden group, and in 1903 was in the district with Johnny Gould's string band playing guitar and banjo.

Mitchell, Edna (p, vo). b. N.O., ———. A gifted soloist who entertained in the cabarets as a piano-playing balladeer. She worked with Louis Armstrong at Anderson's Restaurant on Rampart Street in the early twenties. Wife of drummer Albert Francis.

Mitchell, Leonard (bjo). Member of Louis Dumaine's Jazzola Eight who made the 1927 record session.

Mix, Wes (t, g, bjo). b. N.O., Oct. 9, 1946. Versatile jazzman has played all over the U.S. Familiar French Quarter performer. With French Market Jazz Band, Louisiana Repertory Jazz Ensemble, Freddie Kohlman's All-Stars (1974), Knights of Joy Jazz Band (1981). In Denver, 1975–1978, with the Queen City Jazz Band. In New York, 1964–1973, at Your Father's Mustache.

Moliere, Ernest "Kid" (cl). b. N.O., ca. 1902. In the early 1920s a member of Nat Towles's Creole Harmony Kings touring the Southwest.

Moliere, Frank "Li'l Papa" (p). b. N.O., Oct. 4, 1914. Reactivated as a jazzman in the late 1960s. Often heard at the kitty halls (where admission was by contribution) and Maison Bourbon.

Montegue, Sidney (d). b. N.O., Sept. 13, 1908; d. N.O., Jan. 31, 1969. Played on lake steamers with Leo Dejan.

Herb Morand

Montgomery, Eurreal "Little Brother" (p, vo). b. Kentwood, La., *ca.* 1907. Played very little in New Orleans but toured Louisiana with Clarence Desdunes' Joyland Revelers. Has long been a popular favorite in Chicago clubs. Recorded solo and with Lee Collins. Led his own band in Jackson, Miss., 1931–1938, with Creole George Guesnon on banjo.

Moody, Dan (tb). b. Mandeville, La., *ca.* 1890; d. N.O., June, 1959. A popular bandleader in the small resort towns on the shore of Lake Ponchartrain opposite New Orleans in post–World War I days.

Moore, Charlie (g, bjo). b. N.O., ——; d. N.O., Jan., 1961. A charter member of Jack Carey's Crescent Orchestra before World War I. Sometimes worked at Tom Anderson's.

Moore, Robert "Buster" (tb). b. N.O., *ca.* 1898; d. Oct. 24, 1966. In the early 1920s, a member of Johnny Brown's band. Moore was little known until his comeback in the early sixties at Preservation Hall and with the Gibson Brass Band.

Moore, Sidney (cl). With Reliance Brass Band about 1914.

Morand, Herb (t, vo). b. N.O., 1905; d. N.O., Feb. 22, 1952. Self-taught musician, half brother of Lizzie Miles. First with Nat Towles's Creole Harmony Kings touring the Southwest, 1923. That same year, he made a pioneer New Orleans jazz radio broadcast. In 1924 he was a sensation playing at a carnival in Mérida, Yucatan, Mexico. In the mid-twenties, he played with Cliff Jackson in New York; returned to New Orleans and played for Chris Kelly. Went to Chicago in time for the crash and recorded with the brothers Dodds and with Frank Melrose

George Moret

and the Harlem Hamfats. In 1941 he returned to New Orleans, where he worked with George Lewis and played for several years in the lakefront resorts.

Morand, Morris (d). b. N.O., *ca.* 1903. Brother of Herb Morand. Played with Tommy Ladnier, Sidney Bechet.

Moret, George (c). b. N.O., *ca.* 1860; d. N.O., 1924. Leader of the Excelsior Brass Band, 1905–1922. A "legitimate" musician who sometimes filled in on a job with real jazzmen where reading was required.

Morgan, Al (sb, sou). b. N.O., Aug. 19, 1908; d. Los Angeles, Calif., April, 1974. Famed bass player; member of Morgan clan; seldom played in New Orleans. Spent most of his musical career on tour with Lee Collins in Florida, and with Fate Marable and Sidney Desvigne on the riverboats through the mid-twenties. Bass on the Jones-Collins Astoria Hot Eight record session. After leaving New Orleans in 1928, he jobbed in New York and California with top-name bands.

Al Morgan

Andrew Morgan

Morgan, Andrew (cl, s). b. Pensacola, Fla., March 19, 1903; d. Algiers, La., Sept. 19, 1972. Professional career began in 1924 in the Young Superior Band with Leonard Bechet. In 1925 joined the Young Morgan Band led by his brother Isaiah. With same group under his brother Sam in 1926 and made the famed record sessions. Worked through the thirties with Mike Delay, Kid Thomas, WPA Brass Band, ERA Orchestra; in the forties with Kid Rena at the Brown Derby; much work in Little Woods in late forties, early fifties. Played in the Young Tuxedo Brass Band and at Preservation Hall.

Morgan, Isaiah (c, t). b. Bertrandville, La., April 7, 1897; d. N.O., May 16, 1966. Started his own Young Morgan Band in 1922. Studied with his brother Sam. Played lead on the great recordings of the Sam Morgan jazz band, 1927. After Sam was incapacitated by a stroke, Isaiah held his brother's band together and kept it on tour, mainly through the Gulf Coast area. He settled in Biloxi, Miss., for many years. Returned to New Orleans in the fifties.

Morgan, Sam (t). b. Bertrandville, La., 1895; d. N.O., Feb. 25, 1936. Eldest of the many brothers, Sam was a prime mover of jazz in New Orleans. His recordings are typical of Crescent City music of the mid-twenties. His career as a leader was interrupted by a stroke in 1925, but he made a comeback a year later. During the 1930s the strain of being on the road was too much for him, and he died on Mardi Gras, 1936. The Tulane Brass Band and Kid Howard Brass Band played for his funeral.

Morin, Eugene (d). b. Abita Springs, La., *ca.* 1880; d. *ca.* 1950. One of the earliest dixieland musicians. Played with the Abita Springs Serenaders Jazz Band, 1912–1914.

Morris, Eddie (tb). b. Algiers, La., July 19, 1896; d. N.O., *ca.* 1962. With Kid Punch Miller through the early 1920s, to 1927; with Kid Rena, 1927–1928; with Buddy Petit until Petit's death in 1931. In mid-Depression, he played for the ERA Orchestra and the WPA Brass Band. Led his own dance band and marched with the Gibson Brass Band.

Morris, Joe (sb). b. N.O., *ca.* 1905; d. N.O., Jan. 13, 1961. Jobbed around with many bands, Kid Sheik's among them. Was in the big ERA Orchestra of the mid-thirties.

Jelly Roll Morton

Edgar Mosley

Morton, Ferdinand Joseph Le Menthe "Jelly Roll" (p). b. N.O., Sept. 20, 1885; d. Los Angeles, Calif., July 10, 1941. Most famous of Storyville "professors." Left town permanently in 1915. One of the few great men of jazz. Composed classics, including "Wolverine Blues," "King Porter Stomp," "Grandpa's Spells." Made a set of twelve LPs on jazz history for the Library of Congress. Autobiography, aided by Alan Lomax, *Mr. Jelly Roll.* Jelly Roll worked only in his own groups. His many records remain as testimony to his creative genius. In selecting the most important single figure in jazz, Louis Armstrong could be considered his main rival.

Mosley, Baptiste "Bat" (d). b. Algiers, La., Dec. 22, 1893; d. N.O., Aug. 28, 1965. Began to play professionally in early 1920s with Joe Harris' dixieland band. Was with the Kid Howard Brass Band irregularly; through the thirties worked with Kid Rena's brass band. Brother of Edgar.

Mosley, Edgar (d). b. Algiers, La., Nov. 12, 1895; d. Los Angeles, Calif., 1962. During the twenties and thirties, he was a leading bass drummer in the marching bands. Worked with the Kid Rena, Chris Kelly, George Lewis brass bands and recorded with Lewis' dance band in 1943. In 1962 he was in a parade sponsored by the New Orleans Jazz Club of Southern California.

Mueller, Gustave "Gussie" (cl, s). b. N.O., Apr. 17, 1890; d. North Hollywood, Calif., Dec. 16, 1965. Important early dixieland star. Composed "Wang Wang Blues" while with Paul Whiteman. As a youngster played with Papa Laine's Reliance Brass Band No. 1, the prime unit in the Reliance organization, 1903. Joined Tom Brown in Chicago in 1915. With Baron Long, 1918–1920.

Mukes, Daniel (sn). b. N.O., *ca.* 1901; d. N.O., March 17, 1956. Snare drummer for Eureka Brass Band.

Gussie Mueller

Leslie Muscutt

Big Eye Louis Nelson

Muscutt, Leslie (bjo, g). b. Barrows-in-Furness, Eng., Jan. 30, 1941. By 1980, he had become one of the best band banjo players in authentic jazz. Played with the French Market Jazz Band and recorded under his own name. Much influence on his contemporaries and even on older, more established musicians.

Mutz, Frank (p). b. *ca.* 1900. Participated in the first live jazz broadcast from New Orleans with Ellis Stratakos, Ray Bauduc.

Naquin, Bill (t). b. N.O., *ca.* 1900. Member of the Melon Pickers in the 1930s.

Nash, Lemon (u, bjo, g, vo). b. Lakeland, La., April 22, 1898; d. N.O., Dec. 27, 1969. Started on banjo with Pete Williams' band. Worked with Noon Johnson trio. Mainly a solo entertainer and sometime teacher of strings at Morris Music Company.

Naundorf, Frank (tb). b. Dresden, Ger., 1940. Society Jazz Band.

Ned, Louis (tu, l). b. N.O., *ca.* 1858; d. N.O., *ca.* 1895. Early bandleader of the late 1870s who, along with Wallace Collins, was playing "skiffle" music in the streets of the city as early as 1869.

Neely, May (p). Pianist with John Robichaux orchestra at the Lyric Theater in 1925.

Nelson, "Big Eye Louis" (cl, sb, bjo, acc). b. N.O., Jan. 28, 1885; d. N.O., Aug. 20, 1949. Real name Louis Nelson Delisle. One of the all-time great jazzmen. Studied with the Tios. Worked in Storyville from age fifteen. Led his own Ninth Ward Band. Joined Imperial Orchestra, 1907; Superior Orchestra, 1910. In 1916 replaced

Mumford, Jeff "Brock" (g). b. N.O., *ca.* 1870; d. N.O., ca. 1914. Reportedly one of the great jazz rhythm men of all time. Played duets in the streets with Charlie Galloway as early as 1885. Played in Buddy Bolden's first band; from 1907 to 1914 with Frank Duson's Eagle Band.

Murray, Francis (s, cl, bjo). b. N.O., 1915; d. N.O., Jan. 21, 1963. Active dixielander, played under leadership of Johnny Wiggs, Dutch Andrus, Stuart Bergen, Abbie Brunies, Pete Fountain, Jack Delaney, and the Loyacano brothers. Also worked with Nick La Rocca, Tony Parenti, and Willie Guitar on various jobs. Was in the New Orleans police band and in Clancy's Marching Band in Harahan, La. Was at times in the Leonard Ferguson Viscounts.

Louis Nelson

Freddie Neuroth

George Baquet to tour U.S. with the Original Creole Orchestra. Recorded well past his prime, 1940 and 1949. Played spot jobs and "jitney" joints through the thirties and forties.

Nelson, Davidson C. (p, t, arr). b. Donaldsonville, La., *ca.* 1906; d. April 7, 1946. Nephew of King Oliver. Accompanied Ma Rainey on discs. Toured with Jelly Roll Morton, Richard M. Jones. Led his own combo in Chicago, 1927; appeared with Jimmie Noone at Apex Club. In 1929 went to New York, worked with Luis Russell, King Oliver. Organized original Mills Blue Rhythm Band. Recorded on Victor as Dave Nelson and the King's Men. In 1930 toured with Mae West show, *The Constant Sinner*.

Nelson, George (s). b. N.O., *ca.* 1905. Brother of trombone player Louis Nelson. Played mainly on the lake steamers through the early thirties.

Nelson, Louis (tb). b. N.O., Sept. 17, 1902. Started with Joe Gable's band in Thibodaux. In the early twenties and thirties was with Original Tuxedo Orchestra, Kid Rena's band, and then for the next fifteen years with the Sidney Desvigne orchestra. During the Depression he was in the WPA music program and joined Kid Thomas about 1944. Regularly at Preservation Hall, especially with Percy Humphrey or Kid Punch Miller during the sixties.

Netto, Frank (sb, tu, tb). Dixielander, played with late version of the New Orleans Owls, 1925–1927.

Neumann, Freddie (p). b. N.O., July 20, 1904; d. N.O., Oct. 22, 1978. Dixielander of the 1920s, played with most of top bands. Also with dance bands of Joe Capraro and Jimmy Capra (Angelo Capraro).

Neuroth, Freddie (c). b. N.O., *ca.* 1892; d. Chicago, Ill., *ca.* 1923. Active with Papa Laine's Reliance Brass Band about 1910–1912. With Morgan's Euphonic Syncopators in Chicago during pre–World War I days.

Newman, Dwight (p). b. N.O., 1902; d. N.O., *ca.* 1942. In the early 1920s with the Young Tuxedo Orchestra. Later played dance hall jobs with Eddie Jackson. Joined the A. J. Piron Orchestra in 1928. Played with Peter Bocage's Creole Serenaders through the thirties. Occasionally worked with George Lewis.

Newton, Willie (sb). b. N.O., *ca.* 1885; d. N.O., *ca.* 1921. With Tig Chambers about 1905. Later with Kid Milton.

Nicholas, Albert (cl). b. N.O., May 27, 1900; d. Paris, France, Oct. 2, 1973. Pupil of Lorenzo, Tio, Jr., 1910. Nephew of Wooden Joe Nicholas. At fourteen, he worked with Buddy Petit, the Marreros, Arnold Depass. November, 1916, joined the U.S. Navy; spent the war in the band on the USS *Olympia*. He joined the Maple Leaf Orchestra in 1919 and went into the Cadillac Cabaret with Depass in 1921. In 1922 he worked at Oasis Cabaret

Albert Nicholas

Wooden Joe Nicholas

with Manuel Perez. Took his own band into Tom Anderson's on Rampart Street for a year, 1923–1924. Joined King Oliver in Chicago in 1924; stayed until 1926 then went to Shanghai's Plaza Hotel band. In 1927 he barnstormed home through the East Indies, Java, and the Middle East, spending a year in Cairo. Back in New York, 1928, with Luis Russell, then Louis Armstrong and Jelly Roll Morton. During the late thirties and the forties, he played only with small groups in New York jazz spots and concerts in New York and Philadelphia. Made his home in Europe and recorded extensively in Paris.

Nicholas, Joseph "Wooden Joe" (c, t, cl). b. N.O., Sept. 23, 1883; d. N.O., Nov. 17, 1957. One of best known bandsmen of the red-light district until 1917, as a clarinetist. Practiced on King Oliver's cornet on the bandstand during Oliver's frequent "coffee breaks." Organized his Camelia Dance Band and Camelia Brass Band

in 1918. Usually Buddy Petit played second cornet in the brass band. Remained musically active into the 1940s and was recorded on both clarinet and trumpet by American Music. Also on wax with Johnny St. Cyr and Raymond Burke. He was an uncle of Albert Nicholas.

Nickerson, Philip (g, bjo). b. N.O., ca. 1886. A son of the celebrated music teacher, Professor William J. Nickerson. Played regularly in the early 1900s with the Silver Leaf Orchestra.

Nolan, Poree (p). Storyville "professor," 1905–1913.

Nolan, Walter (d). With Jimmie Noone in 1915.

Jimmie Noone

King Oliver

Noone, Jimmie (cl). b. Cut Off, La., April 23, 1895; d. Los Angeles, Calif., April 19, 1944. Studied with Sidney Bechet, Lorenzo Tio, Jr. First real job with Freddie Keppard in 1912 in Storyville. Led a band jointly with Buddy Petit until 1917. Worked irregularly with Kid Ory, Papa Celestin in the district until it closed permanently. Vaudeville tour with Original Creole Orchestra. Migrated to Chicago; played with Joe Oliver, Doc Cook, Zutty Singleton; led his own band at the Apex Club. Recorded for Decca, Capitol just before his death. Was a brother-in-law of Paul Barbarin, Freddie Keppard.

Nunez, Alcide "Yellow" (cl). b. N.O., *ca.* 1892; d. N.O., *ca.* 1933. Pioneer dixieland star with Reliance Brass Band 1912 to 1916. Went to Chicago with what became the Original Dixieland Jazz Band, though he missed out on the chance to make the historic first jazz records. Joined Anton Lada in the Louisiana Five, then returned to New Orleans. After 1927, he played with the New Orleans police band.

Ogden, Dave (d). b. N.O., *ca.* 1888; d. N.O., Mar. 18, 1963. Played with Maple Leaf Orchestra. Onetime leader of this group. Also the ERA bands.

Ogle, Arthur (d). b. N.O., *ca.* 1895; d. N.O., April 7, 1959. Respected drummer in the Eureka Brass Band. Earlier was in the Camelia Brass Band. His career as a jazz drummer dates back to about 1918. In 1920 he was with Lee Collins in the Golden Leaf Orchestra. Plays on the rare Pax record of the Eureka Brass Band.

Kid Ory

Willie Pajeaud

Oliver, Joseph "King" (c). b. Abent, La., Dec. 19, 1885; d. Savannah, Ga., April 8, 1938. Began about 1904 as a substitute with the Onward Brass Band. To about 1910 was with Allen Brass Band, the original Superior Orchestra, the Eagle Band, and the Magnolia Orchestra, usually filling in for famed hornmen Manuel Perez, Bunk Johnson. After 1910, he worked regularly with Richard M. Jones's Four Hot Hounds at Abadie's, and then as leader at Pete Lala's. Left for Chicago and world renown in 1918, where his band at the Lincoln Gardens became the sensation of the early twenties. Louis Armstrong made his debut outside New Orleans with this band. A poor businessman, Oliver failed to capitalize on his reputation, and his career declined steadily until he was near starvation during the days just before his death. Oliver's story may be read in *King Joe Oliver*, by Brian Rust and Walter C. Allen; and in *King Oliver*, by Martin Williams. There is a chapter on him in *Jazzmen*, by Frederic Ramsey and Charles E. Smith.

Olivier, Adam (c). b. N.O., *ca.* 1865; d. before World War I. Full-time barber and part-time bandleader of the 1890s until about 1910; he was first to employ both Bunk Johnson and Tony Jackson.

"Ollie Papa" (sb). b. N.O., *ca.* 1900. An always active job musician, he played with most New Orleans jazz stars, notably with Kid Howard, Burnell Santiago, Joe Robichaux. Legal name, Charles Thomas.

Ory, Edward "Kid" (tb). b. LaPlace, La., Dec. 25, 1886; d. Jan. 23, 1973. Led a hometown band, the Woodland Band, in his teens and brought it into New Orleans about 1908, where it promptly split up. From 1913 to 1919, Ory was one of the most prominent "hot" bandleaders in town, working mainly in the district at Pete Lala's. Left for Los Angeles in 1919. In Chicago in the mid-twenties he made discs with Louis Armstrong's Hot Five and with King Oliver. Perhaps the most important influence on jazz trombone playing. In the forefront of the jazz revival of the forties, he produced some of the period's finest recordings. As late as 1963 he was seen on a telecast from Disneyland with Johnny St. Cyr and again in 1965 with Ed Sullivan. Among his composition credits are the evergreen "Muskrat Ramble" and "Ory's Creole Trombone." He appeared in New Orleans in 1971.

Ouilliber, Emile (tb). b. N.O., 1921; d. N.O., Sept. 13, 1964. Dixielander who played with most of the best-known musicians of his period.

Oxley, Dave (d, vo). b. N.O., May 1, 1910; d. N.O., July 20, 1974. Regular with George Lewis' band. Played with Papa Celestin, Joe Robichaux, Kid Howard, Henry Hardin. Toured with Bessie Smith.

Padron, Bill (t). b. N.O., July 15, 1903; d. N.O., April 9, 1959. Played with the New Orleans Owls and other 1920 bands. Only records are with Owls.

Page, Anthony (vt). b. N.O., before Civil War; d. N.O., *ca.* 1905. Charter member of the Excelsior Brass Band, 1880.

Roy Palmer

Tony Papalia

Russ Papalia

Pajeaud, Willie (c, t). b. N.O., 1895; d. N.O., May 12, 1960. Regularly with the Eureka Brass Band until his death. One of the city's best "readers." Professional since 1915. Worked with Tuxedo Brass Band, 1919; with Maple Leaf Orchestra, John Robichaux, Sam Morgan. In 1929 he was the leader at the Alamo dime-a-dance palace. Worked regularly with his own groups during the Depression. Pupil of Manuel Perez.

Palao, James A. (v, s, ah). b. N.O., ca. 1880; d. ca. 1925. With the Imperial Orchestra in 1906. Active in the district to 1912, especially at 101 Ranch and Villa Cabaret. Left to tour in vaudeville with the Original Creole Orchestra. In 1919 played in Chicago in the Deluxe Cafe. His 1916 business card has the word "jaz" printed on it in several places.

Palisier, John "Pujol" (cl). b. N.O., ca. 1885; d. N.O., ———. In band led by Bill Gallaty, Sr.; cousin of Tony Fougerat. His name is usually misspelled "Pallachais."

Palmer, Roy (tb). b. N.O., 1892; d. Chicago, Ill., 1964. With Richard M. Jones, Sidney Desvigne before moving to Chicago in 1914. With Lawrence Duhé in Original Creole Orchestra in the twenties. Also with Johnny Dodds, King Oliver, Jelly Roll Morton. Strong influence on George Brunies.

Palmisano, Angelo (g). Late version of New Orleans Owls, Halfway House Orchestra.

Papalia, Anthony "Tony" (s, cl, l). b. N.O., 1905; d. N.O., Jan. 25, 1974. Long a well-known society orchestra leader. In early days did lots of theater work and was in Tony Parenti's orchestra.

Papalia, Russ (tb, sb, l). b. N.O., 1903; d. N.O., Oct. 27, 1972. Led society dance orchestra for many

96

Tony Parenti

Slow Drag Pavageau

years. Early career with Tony Parenti, Johnny DeDroit, Irving Fazola, Johnny Bayersdorffer.

Papin, Peter (bjo, vo, l). b. N.O., Sept. 17, 1898. Played in Chris Kelly's band in the 1920s. Popular as a singer and entertainer.

Parenti, Tony (cl). b. N.O., Aug. 6, 1900; d. New York City, April 17, 1972. Child prodigy, he was an established bandsman at twelve. At fourteen he played with ragtime bands and turned down an offer to go north with the Original Dixieland Jazz Band because of his youth. In New Orleans he worked with Papa Laine units and played excursions on the steamer *Majestic* on Lake Pontchartrain. Also was in the Triangle and Alamo theaters, the Pup Cafe and with Johnny DeDroit's band. Became a leader at an early age with both a "symphonic" dance orchestra and a jazz band. In 1925 he formed his Liberty Syncopators, which played at the Liberty Theater and the Lavida Ballroom. This band was recorded on Columbia. In the 1920s Parenti left New Orleans to become a world-renowned jazz star. A major attraction into the 1960s, he played on Broadway, mainly at the Metropole and Jimmy Ryan's. Outstanding recordings of rags on Circle, Riverside, GHB.

Parker, George (p, l). b. N.O., ca. 1905; d. N.O., Sept. 25, 1959. Led small groups during the twenties and thirties, often featuring Creole George Guesnon, Clarence Tisdale, Brother Cornbread Thomas, Coo Coo Talbert.

Parker, Willie (cl, bd). b. N.O., March 4, 1875; d. N.O., Aug. 31, 1965. With James A. Palao, Terminal Brass Band in early 1900s. Became a founding member of Eureka Brass Band, 1920. During the late twenties, he was in the Lyons Brass Band.

Pashley, Frank (bjo). Member of Nat Towles's Creole Harmony Kings in the twenties. Migrated to St. Louis in 1924. Played with Kid Ory and Bunk Johnson in the forties in California.

Paul, Casimir (g). b. N.O. With Harold Dejan, Lester Santiago on the lake cruisers in the early 1930s.

Paul, Emanuel (v, bjo, s). b. N.O., Feb. 2, 1904. First learned music in a church-organized seventeen-piece orchestra. Saxophonist through his professional years since the Depression, although during the twenties he played banjo on dance jobs. Frequently worked on jobs for T-Boy Remy, 1940–1942 and started with the Eureka Brass Band about that time. Joined the Kid Thomas band about 1942. With these two groups for over twenty years.

Paulin, Ernest "Doc" (t). b. N.O., ca. 1902. Nonunion leader of small dance and brass bands for sixty years.

Pavageau, Alcide "Slow Drag" (g, b). b. N.O., March 7, 1888; d. N.O., Jan. 19, 1969. Known to traditional fans as the Grand Marshal of the Second Line. Winner of many dance contests in pre–World War I years. He won his musical reputation as the driving bass man of the Bunk Johnson and George Lewis bands through the forties and fifties. Photogenic and charming, he was the target of tourist and press photographer alike, frequently seen on network TV, albeit anonymously.

Santo Pecora

Sammy Penn

Payen, Joe (ah). b. N.O., *ca.* 1875; d. N.O., 1932. Alto horn in the Excelsior Brass Band, he also managed the organization for some twenty years. When he died, the band collapsed.

Payne, Richard (g). b. N.O., *ca.* 1880. With original Superior Orchestra in 1910.

Peccopia, Pete (c). d. *ca.* 1950. A highly regarded musician of the period 1905–1930. Much used by Papa Laine dance units and in the Reliance Brass Band. In Susquehanna Band, early 1920s.

Peck, Bert (p). b. N.O., July 15, 1906. Prominent in politics. He was a popular dixieland piano man in the 1920s. With Princeton Revellers, Johnny Bayersdorffer, Leon Prima at various times. On SS *President* in 1982.

Pecora, Santo (tb, l). b. N.O., March 21, 1902. The true maestro of the dixieland tailgate style. Played and recorded with the New Orleans Rhythm Kings in 1925. Spent seventeen years barnstorming with both large swing bands (Buddy Rogers, Ben Pollack, Will Osborne) and small dixieland groups (Sharkey, Wingy Manone). Since 1942, he has worked steadily in Louisiana, first in and around Baton Rouge, then in New Orleans at the Famous Door on Bourbon Street.

Pecoraro, Santo (d). b. N.O., Sept. 26, 1906. Nephew of Santo Pecora. Worked frequently with Johnny Wiggs in the days prior to Wiggs's temporary retirement about 1962.

Pellegrini, Pete (c). b. N.O., *ca.* 1885; d. N.O., 1940. With Reliance Brass Band.

Penn, Sammy (d, vo). b. Morgan City, La., Sept. 15, 1902; d. Florida, Sept. 18, 1969. First job in hometown band of Jake Johnson. Came to New Orleans in 1921; with Chris Kelly Brass Band, Kid Rena Brass Band, Eureka Brass Band. He was showy personality and a mainstay of the Kid Thomas band for a quarter century. In the mid-fifties he took a group of his own to Chicago as Penn and His Five Pennies, but was soon back at his post with Thomas. Died on tour with the Preservation Hall Jazz Band.

Penn, William (bjo). b. N.O., ——; d. N.O., *ca.* 1946. Popular solo performer of the 1920s widely known for his specialty act of great virtuosity and repertoire. Cousin of Ernest Roubleau.

Peque, Paul (cl, s). b. N.O., *ca.* 1906. Played with Brownlee band in the 1920s.

Perez, Manuel (c). b. N.O., 1873; d. N.O., 1946. A titan of early jazz. Organized his own Imperial Orchestra in 1900. Joined the Onward Brass Band in 1899 and stayed with it until it broke up thirty years later. Made a brief

Manuel Perez

Joseph Petit

visit to Chicago in 1915 to play at the Arsonia Cafe but returned to New Orleans quickly. Was one of the "big name" leaders of Storyville, mainly at Rice's Cafe. After World War I, he played on the SS *Capitol* and was fairly busy thereafter until the Depression.

Perkins, Dave (tb, d, t, eu). b. N.O., *ca.* 1868; d. N.O., 1926. Active brass band musician from 1895 to about 1912, working with the Reliance Brass Band and the Toca Brass Band. Became one of the great music teachers in New Orleans for both trombone and drums.

Peterson, Harold (d). b. N.O., *ca.* 1900. Pre–World War I dixielander, cousin of Raymond Burke. In Charlie Fishbein Orchestra at Lavida in the 1920s.

Petit, Buddy (c). b. N.O., 1887; d. N.O., July 4, 1931. Actual name Joseph Crawford. Contemporaries acclaim Petit as the equal of Armstrong. In 1916 he was coleader of a band with Jimmy Noone. Preferred to job around on one-night stands, advertising wagons, and dance dates. Roamed the Gulf Coast from Galveston to Mobile; dedicated himself more to high living than to music, financing his peccadilloes with his horn. Played for a while on the riverboats and lake steamers about 1931 and died, according to accounts, from the effects of overeating at a July 4 picnic.

Petit, Joseph (tb, l). b. N.O., *ca.* 1880; d. N.O., 1946. Started playing about 1896. Was in Olympia Orchestra about 1900. Led Security Brass Band, Terminal Brass Band during World War I years. Was in Camelia Orchestra and Brass Band in the early twenties. Usually played in Jefferson City Buzzards' Mardi Gras parades. Stepfather of Buddy Petit.

Peyton, Henry (acc). Leader of the string trio that played for the opening of Tom Anderson's Annex on Basin Street and, reportedly, in 1899 with a group at the Big 25.

Pflueger, Sidney (bjo, g). b. N.O., *ca.* 1905. Played jobs in New Orleans for more than forty years. Was associated in his early days with Burnell Santiago.

One-Eye Babe Philip

Fats Pichon

Philip, Joseph "One-Eye Babe" (sb). b. N.O., 1879; d. N.O., 1960. Active bassist of the early 1920s. Yank Johnson's band, 1920; Foster Lewis' jazz band, 1922; Chris Kelly band, 1923. Jobbed around during the late twenties and the thirties. During the forties and early fifties, he was often seen at Mama Lou's and the Happy Landing. Worked for a time with the Kid Thomas band, with which he recorded for AM in 1951.

Philip, Joseph, Jr., "Gossoon" (bjo). b. N.O., 1912; d. N.O., 1968. Played, 1929–1930, with Buddy Petit. Son of One-Eye Babe Philip.

Phillips, Joe (t). b. N.O., 1893. Worked with King Oliver in 1915.

Phillips, John Henry, Sr. See Fischer, Johnny.

Phillips, Willie (c, d). b. N.O., *ca.* 1885. Played with King Oliver in the Melrose Brass Band, 1907, on drums. Played cornet occasionally during World War I.

Pichon, Walter "Fats" (p). b. N.O., 1905; d. N.O., Feb. 26, 1957. Best known as cocktail piano player during many years at the Absinthe House. In the early 1920s he played band piano for Amos Riley. He led his own band in the mid-twenties, mainly on spot jobs. He played with Sidney Desvigne on the *Island Queen* from 1927 into the 1930s. In 1937 he spent a short time with A. J. Piron. He led a band on the SS *Capitol* in the mid-thirties.

Picou, Alphonse (cl). b. N.O., Oct. 18, 1880; d. N.O., Feb. 4, 1961. Known as the creator of a celebrated chorus in *High Society*. Musical career began in 1892 in a band led by Bouboul Valentin. A year later he organized his own Accordiana Band and, in 1897, the Independence Band. He played for Oscar Duconge in 1899, with Freddie Kep-

Alphonse Picou

Dee Dee and Billie Pierce

pard's Olympia Orchestra in 1906, and with the Excelsior Brass Band. From 1916 to the mid-twenties he played in the Tuxedo Brass Band, with time out to play in the Camelia Orchestra and with John Robichaux. In the late forties he was to be seen at times with the Celestin band, and frequently worked in the Paddock on Bourbon Street. His funeral during Mardi Gras of 1961 was one of the biggest in New Orleans history.

Pierce, Billie (p, vo). b. Marianna, Fla., June 8, 1907; d. N.O., Sept. 29, 1974. Boogie-woogie piano player and blues shouter. Worked with husband Dee Dee Pierce. Sister of Sadie Goodson, who played in Buddy Petit's band.

Pierce, Joseph de la Croix "Dee Dee" (t, vo). b. N.O., Feb. 18, 1904; d. N.O., Oct. 29, 1973. Until he lost his sight, he played with the Tuxedo Brass Band. Afterward, he was with Abby Williams. In the late fifties, he was regularly at Luthjen's. Frequently at Preservation Hall in the sixties. Known for his songs in Creole French.

Pierson, Eddie (tb). b. Algiers, La., 1904; d. N.O., Dec. 17, 1958. Mainly associated with Papa Celestin from 1951 until Celestin's death; he took over leadership of the band's remnants in 1954. Played for Sidney Desvigne on the riverboats in the early thirties, and worked in a group

Eddie Pierson

101

Armand J. Piron

Arthur Pons

that included Louis Barbarin and Emanuel Sayles. With the Sunny South, A. J. Piron, Barbarin, Young Tuxedo orchestras, Great Lakes Naval Station band.

Pinero, Frank (p). b. N.O., *ca.* 1906; d. N.O., 1967. Dixieland piano man who worked with Happy Schilling band in the 1920s. Worked with Leon Prima–Sharkey All-Stars and was on the road in the Louis Prima band.

Pinner, Clay (tu, sb). b. N.O., 1895; d. N.O., June 7, 1969. With New Orleans Owls, Happy Schilling, and the New Orleans police band.

Piron, Armand J. (v, l). b. N.O., 1888; d. N.O., 1943. Crippled by an accident at age seven, Piron was unable to walk for many years. He studied violin and began to play professionally with the Peerless Orchestra about 1912. Played in many dance bands. In 1915, with Clarence Williams, he formed a publishing company where many jazz standards made their debuts. From 1917 until his death, he remained one of the most popular leaders in New Orleans. Well remembered, especially for his years at Tranchina's Restaurant at Spanish Fort. Composer of many outstanding melodies.

Pistorius, Steve (p). b. Port Sulphur, La., Nov. 18, 1954. New Orleans' only specialist in classic piano rags. The "Creole Kid" worked at the Gateway Lounge, 1974–1975 and in other Bourbon Street haunts. In 1976 he did a long turn on the riverboats *Admiral* and *Robert E. Lee* in St. Louis, followed by a couple of years at the Levee in Fort Myers, Fla. Returned to New Orleans a polished musician and into 1981 played at the Gazebo in the French Market and with a unit of the stage production *One Mo' Time*. Recorded a solo album at age nineteen.

Pons, Arthur (g). b. N.O., Dec. 19, 1913; d. N.O., Nov. 29, 1973. Virtuoso soloist who also played with prominent dixielanders in the thirties, forties, and fifties. Was with bands led by Irving Fazola. Also played with Armand Hug, Monk Hazel, Julian Laine.

Poree, Ernest (s). b. N.O., Nov. 9, 1908. Mainly a brass band musician, he played for many years with the George Williams Brass Band. Was in the ERA Orchestra during the mid-thirties.

"Pork Chop." See Smith, Jerome.

Porter, John (bh, ah, sb). b. N.O., *ca.* 1890; d. N.O., Nov. 2, 1958. Well-known brass band musician; started with Holmes Brass Band, Lutcher, La., 1910. Played with Tuxedo Brass Band, Allen Brass Band, Louis Dumaine Brass Band.

Bonnie Pottle

Leon Prima

Pottle, Bonnie (sb). b. N.O., *ca.* 1910; b. N.O., 1940s. Popular dixieland drummer, recorded with a late version of the New Orleans Rhythm Kings (George Brunies, Wingy Manone, Sidney Arodin).

Powell, Shannon (d). b. N.O., April 8, 1962. A child prodigy, strongly influenced by the Barbarin family, he developed exceptional percussion technique by age eleven and was accepted into popular jazz bands before he was in his teens.

Powers, Eddie (s). b. N.O., *ca.* 1900; d. N.O., *ca.* 1955. Participated in first jazz broadcast from New Orleans under Pinky Gerbrecht. Played with Ellis Stratakos' Jung Hotel Roof orchestra.

Predonce, Johnny (b). b. N.O., *ca.* 1895; d. N.O., *ca.* 1939. Led the Silver Leaf Orchestra, 1918, and always had jobs under his own leadership, 1919–1923. In 1923 he worked for a while with Chris Kelly and then retired from music to pursue an active and profitable career as a bartender at the Big 25 Club on Franklin Street.

Prescott, Dewey (p). b. N.O., ——. Spent most of his musical life in California.

Preston, Walter (bjo). b. N.O., *ca.* 1880. Part of Kid Punch Miller's original band in 1915.

Prestopnik, Irving. See Fazola, Irving "Faz."

Prevost, James (sb). b. Houma, La., Feb. 7, 1919. One of the city's most skilled bass players, he became active in jazz after experience in large swing bands. Played at the Paddock on Bourbon Street in 1961 with Octave Crosby's band, and into 1982 was a regular at Preservation Hall.

Price, Fonce (v). Pre–World War I dixielander.

Prima, Leon (t). b. N.O., July 28, 1907. Led his own bands for many years and was coleader, with Sharkey, of a swing band in the 1930s. During the forties, fifties, and sixties, he was a successful nightclub operator and led combos in his own spots. Brother of Louis Prima.

Prima, Louis (t, vo). b. N.O., Dec. 7, 1911; d. N.O., Aug. 24, 1978. In 1923 led his own "kid's band" which featured ten-year-old Irving Fazola. Went to work in the Saenger Theater pit band in 1928; became popular in the mid-thirties as leader of large swing band. Made several films. Produced several outstanding discs on Brunswick and Vocalion with a small combo. Composer of "Sing, Sing, Sing."

Provenzano, Johnny (p, v, g, vo). b. N.O., *ca.* 1878; d. N.O., Dec. 26, 1972. One of the earliest dixieland piano players. Heard in the 1900s with Johnny Lala, Tony

Alton Purnell

Snoozer Quinn

Giardina, and the Brunies clan. Played solo piano in cabarets of the "tango belt" (a group of cafes surrounding the Storyville district), 1905–1925.

Purnell, Alton (p). b. N.O., *ca.* 1911. Best known for his recordings with Bunk Johnson in 1945 and for his years in the George Lewis band during the late forties and early fifties. He settled in California.

Purnell, Theodore "Ted" (s, cl). b. N.O., *ca.* 1903; d. N.O., Nov. 25, 1974. With David Jones at Lavida Ballroom, 1925. On the historic Jones-Collins Astoria Hot Eight session in 1929. In 1932 he was working riverboats with Sidney Desvigne. Sometimes seen in street parades; played at the Paddock occasionally into the 1950s.

Quinn, Edwin McIntosh "Snoozer" (g, v, vo). b. McComb, Miss., Oct. 18, 1906; d. N.O., 1952. As a very young child, he played professionally in a local trio at Bogalusa, La. In his teens, worked with Paul English Traveling Shows, then joined Claude Blanchard's orchestra and the Jack Wilrich band before working with Johnny Wiggs in Peck Kelly's Jazz Band, Houston, Texas, 1924.

Jobbed around New Orleans for a few years. Went on tour with Paul Whiteman, 1928. Cut four sides with Bix Beiderbecke and Frank Trumbauer on Columbia, which were lost. Recorded in 1931 with hillbilly singer Jimmie Davis, later governor of Louisiana. He made four sides issued by Johnny Wiggs in the early fifties. In his later professional years, he played guitar and violin and sang scat vocals with Earl Crumb's band at Beverly Gardens. Considered by some prominent New Orleans jazzmen to have been the greatest guitarist of all time.

Ragas, Henry W. (p). b. N.O., 1897; d. New York City, Feb. 18, 1919. Original pianist of the Original Dixieland Jazz Band. Jobbed around New Orleans from 1910, playing solo in the "tango belt." From about 1913, he was associated with Johnny Stein's band. Left town with Stein and the Original Dixieland Jazz Band men to start his months of glory. Made the first Original Dixieland Jazz Band discs. Succumbed in flu epidemic as band was preparing to go to Europe.

Henry Ragas

Eblen Rau

Ragas, Herman (sb). b. N.O., ———. Early dixielander who played in Papa Laine dance bands. Brother of Original Dixieland Jazz Band's Henry Ragas.

Ramos, Florenzo (s). b. Mexico, D.F., ca. 1865; d. N.O., July 7, 1931. Came to U.S. with Mexican band for Sugar and Cotton Exposition, 1885, and remained. One of the founders of the musicians union. Introduced the saxophone to New Orleans. Played with everyone, from the band at the French Opera House to Stalebread Lacoume.

Ramos, "Sou Sou" (g). Played with Stalebread Lacoume's Razzy Dazzy Spasm Band, 1904–1908.

Rando, Doc (cl). b. N.O., 1910. Played with the Bob Crosby orchestra.

Rankins, Sam (g). b. N.O., ———; d. N.O., Feb. 17, 1971. Member of the Noon Johnson bazooka trio in the 1950s.

Raphael, Bernard (tb). b. N.O., ca. 1883; d. N.O., ———. A member of the Melrose Brass Band in 1907. Worked in the district until about 1913. Also in the Excelsior Brass Band in 1913.

Raphael, Peter (d). b. N.O., 1905; d. N.O., May 5, 1963. Rhythm man of the Eureka Brass Band.

Rapp, Butler "Guyé" (tb, g, bjo). b. N.O., ca. 1898; d. N.O., 1931. Played trombone with Onward Brass Band in the early 1920s; banjo with Sam Morgan until 1925. Worked in the late twenties with Chris Kelly, the Magnolia Orchestra, and Eddie Jackson.

Rau, J. Eblen (v). b. N.O., Sept. 3, 1898. Entire musical career linked with the Invincibles String Band, which became the New Orleans Owls. Gave up music as a profession as soon as the group took "professionalism" seriously.

Ray, Phil (sb). b. N.O., ca. 1888. Pre–World War I dixielander.

Raymond, Henry (s, cl). b. N.O., ca. 1895; d. July 24, 1949. With Johnny DeDroit, Ellis Stratakos.

Reason, Lionel (p). b. N.O., ca. 1909. Played very little in New Orleans, though he worked all over the U.S. with New Orleans bands, including Ory on the West Coast and King Oliver in the Midwest. In 1932 was on tour in large band led by Polo Barnes.

Lionel Reason

Kid Rena

Reed, Howard (t). b. N.O., March 27, 1906. Started in 1922 with the Extra Half Jazz Band. Through the twenties and thirties, he played in Dixola novelty band and was with Irving Fazola in the forties. Led his own band for short time in the early fifties before retiring from music.

Reiner, Jules (p). b. N.O., ——. An early dixieland pianist associated with Papa Laine dance groups before World War I.

Reininger, Johnny (s, cl). b. N.O., Aug. 19, 1908. Popular dance-band leader, he was one of the Dawn Busters on New Orleans radio station WWL for many years. During the early thirties, he played with Ellis Stratakos at the Jung roof, and frequently with Leon Prima. Had house band at L'Enfant's during the early fifties.

Remy, Dominique "T-Boy" (t). b. N.O., ca. 1886. Played many dance jobs during the forties and became leader of the Eureka Brass Band about 1946. Migrated to Los Angeles in the early fifties.

Rena, Henry "Kid" (t). b. N.O., Aug. 30, 1898; d. N.O., April 25, 1949. With Louis Armstrong at the Waif's Home, Rena was taught by Armstrong's teacher, Peter Davis; later studied with Manuel Perez. Rival to

Buddy Petit and Chris Kelly, he worked for a while for Kid Ory. Then put together his own Dixie Jazz Band, which worked steadily in New Orleans during the 1920s and made successful trips to Chicago on several occasions. Later, he played in the Tuxedo Brass Band and during the Depression led his own brass band. He had a group, including Alphonse Picou and Alec Bigard, that played at the Brown Derby, a dime-a-dance palace. He made only one disc session, 1940, on the Delta label, but contemporaries agree he did not sound his best. Forced to quit music because of ill health, he died two years later.

Rena, Joseph (d). b. N.O., March 11, 1897; d. N.O., Dec. 26, 1973. Jobbed with his brother, Kid Rena, in his teens. Was in Wesley Don's Liberty Bell Orchestra in 1920 and was with his brother's Dixie Jazz Band in 1923 and 1924. Made Delta session with his brother in 1940 and stayed with him until about 1945, when he retired from music to become an Evangelical Baptist preacher.

Richardson, Eddie (t). b. N.O., April 18, 1903. Paraded with Kid Rena's brass band. Played in Mandeville with Earl Foster, 1929–1930, and was in the WPA and ERA music programs in the mid-Depression years. Recorded with Eureka Brass Band for Pax. Played in Gibson Brass Band.

Jeff Riddick

Bebé Ridgley

Amos Riley

Riddick, Jeff (p). b. Oakland, Miss., June 3, 1907. Long-time mainstay of Sharkey's best band. Led small groups of his own on dance jobs and performed at the Famous Door through the early fifties in a memorable trio that included Ray Burke, Sherwood Mangiapane. Infrequently recorded. Brother of Johnny Riddick.

Riddick, Johnny (p). b. Oakland, Miss., Nov. 12, 1901; d. 1971. Member of the two great recording bands of the mid-twenties centered in Mobile—the Arcadian Serenaders and the Crescent City Jazzers. Brother of Jeff Riddick.

Riddick, Richard "Dick" (har). b. Oakland, Miss., Feb. 1, 1904; d. Los Angeles, Calif., 1975. Worked steadily with Borrah Minevitch Harmonica Rascals, won a "World Harmonica Championship" in Berlin (1905).

Ridgley, William "Bebé" (tb). b. N.O., Jan. 15, 1882; d. N.O., May 28, 1961. Founder of the Tuxedo Brass Band and the original Tuxedo Orchestra, in which he worked for many years, sometimes with, sometimes separate from, Papa Celestin. Started with the Silver Leaf Orchestra about 1907. Remained musically active until 1936, when he retired because of ill health. Made his last public appearance at the age of seventy-nine as a mourner at the funeral of Alphonse Picou.

Zue Robertson

Sleepy Robertson

Riley, Amos (t). b. N.O., *ca.* 1879; d. N.O., 1925. Organizer and leader of the long-popular Tulane Orchestra, one of the best known pre–World War I dance bands.

Riley, Theodore (t). b. N.O., May 10, 1924. With George Williams Brass Band in the 1950s. In 1965 he took over leadership of the band following William's death. Son of Amos Riley. Active in the 1980s.

Robertson, C. Alvin "Zue" (tb). b. N.O., March 7, 1891; d. Watts, Calif., 1943. Pupil of his cousin, Baptiste Delisle. During his few Crescent City years, he worked in Storyville with King Oliver, John Robichaux, A. J. Piron, Richard M. Jones, Clarence Williams. Frequently at Pete Lala's in the district. Drafted in 1918, discharged the following year. Worked in carnivals and circuses.

Robertson, Henry "Sleepy" (d). b. N.O., *ca.* 1890; d. N.O., 1962. Longtime parade bass drummer last seen in the 1960s with the Young Excelsior Brass Band.

Robichaux, Joe (p). b. N.O., March 8, 1900; d. N.O., Jan. 17, 1965. Much influenced by Steve Lewis, Burnell Santiago. Before World War I, he sometimes played solo for private parties. Joined Tig Chambers in Chicago in 1917; soon returned to New Orleans. Joined the Black Eagles on the "country circuit," 1922–1923. Recorded in 1929 with Jones-Collins Astoria Hot Eight. Short stint with Willie O'Connell at the Music Box, then organized his own band for the Entertainers Club. Made session for

Joe Robichaux   *Photo by Grauman Marks*

Vocalion. Invaded big band market in the thirties, increasing to fifteen pieces. During the forties and fifties, he was at Davilla's behind Lizzie Miles. Ultimately replaced Alton Purnell in George Lewis band.

Jim Robinson

Emmett Rogers

Robichaux, John (v, sb, d, acc, l). b. Thibodaux, La., Jan. 16, 1866; d. N.O., 1939. Began career as bass drummer for the Excelsior Brass Band in 1891. From 1893 to 1939 he was the most continuously active dance band leader in New Orleans. Led band at Lyric Theater, 1918–1927. La Louisiane restaurant.

Robichaux, John (d). b. N.O., May 16, 1915. Nephew of famed band leader of same name. Played with Kid Shots Madison in 1944. During the fifties, he was at times with Kid Thomas. In the eighties with *One Mo' Time* orchestra and the New Orleans Ragtime Orchestra.

Robinson, Ed "Rabbit" (d). b. LaPlace, La., *ca.* 1882. Drummer in Kid Ory's first band.

Robinson, Frank (tu, sou). b. N.O., ——. Bass man during the 1920s for the Excelsior Brass Band.

Robinson, Isaiah "Big Ike" (tb). b. Thibodaux, La., March 16, 1892; d. N.O., 1962. Played guitar in local Thibodaux band, 1911. With Kid Milton band, 1920, and in the Camelia Brass Band and Orchestra. Studied with Dave Perkins on trombone and joined Chris Kelly in 1924, remaining until the latter's death in 1929. Worked for a while in dance halls and with Kid Rena's brass band. Retired about 1938.

Robinson, Nathan "Jim" (tb). b. Deer Range, La., Dec. 25, 1892; d. N.O., May 4, 1976. Studied guitar as a kid, but took up trombone while in the army. On his return to New Orleans in 1919, he was good enough to join the Sam Morgan band in which he was a fixture for a

dozen years. Studied with Sunny Henry and worked with Lee Collins in the Golden Leaf Band. Stayed active through the Depression mainly with Kid Howard and was a regular in the George Lewis band. Recorded with Sam Morgan in the twenties; was in on the Kid Rena Delta session in 1940; is also on most of Bunk Johnson's records.

Robinson, Oscar (bjo, sb). b. N.O., *ca.* 1888. With Silver Leaf Orchestra, 1909.

Robinson, Sam (s). b. N.O., 1891. Alto sax man of the 1920s. Worked with Young Morgan Band and with Kid Howard. Brother of Jim Robinson.

Roddy, Ruben (as). b. Joplin, Mo., May 5, 1906; d. N.O., 1960. Joined Eureka Brass Band in 1946 after career with Count Basie, Bennie Moten, and Walter Page. Played in the fifties in dance bands led by Kid Thomas.

Rogers, Emmett (d). b. N.O., *ca.* 1898; d. N.O., *ca.* 1947. Legal name, John McCloskey. One of the big names among dixieland drummers. Worked steadily at Halfway House in Abbie Brunies' band, and was usually considered the Brunieses' drummer. Played at the Doghouse with Harry Shields about 1940. Nephew of Buck Rogers.

Ernest Rogers

Leon Roppolo

Rogers, Ernest (d). b. N.O., April 19, 1891; d. N.O., Aug. 26, 1956. Began his career with Edward Clem, 1910. In 1913 was in the Crescent Orchestra. Joined the Silver Leaf Orchestra and stayed until World War I. Was with the Lyons Brass Band from its inception, and played through the thirties and forties in other brass bands, including the Young Tuxedo. Worked at Luthjen's in the forties. Made records with Bunk Johnson, Big Eye Louis Nelson, 1949.

Rogers, Everett "Buck" (p, d). b. N.O., Apr. 18, 1891; d. N.O., Aug. 28, 1952. Worked with Abbie Brunies, Johnny Wiggs. First drummer with Dukes of Dixieland. Uncle of Emmett Rogers.

Roppolo, Leon (cl, s, g). b. Lutheran, La., March 16, 1902; d. N.O., Oct. 5, 1943. His family name is often incorrectly spelled Rappolo. Roppolo is among the jazz immortals though his career spanned less than a decade. At age fourteen he left New Orleans with the Bee Palmer vaudeville troupe. Back home, he joined the Brunies brothers' band. Played with Halfway House Orchestra. Won fame with the New Orleans Rhythm Kings in Chicago during the early twenties. Shares composer credit for "Tin Roof Blues," "Farewell Blues." Spent eighteen years in a sanitarium before succumbing to various ills.

Rose, Freddie (p). b. N.O., ca. 1892. A dixieland pianist associated with Merritt Brunies, Emile Christian, with whom he worked in the New Orleans Jazz Band before World War I.

John Royen

Ross, Sam (c, l). b. Algiers, La., ca. 1878; d. Algiers, La., 1921. An early bandleader, the first to employ Jimmie Noone. His group was active for eleven years, playing only dances.

Rotis, Joe (tb). b. N.O., Oct. 30, 1917; d. Apr. 24, 1965. Came to national attention during the 1950s with the Basin Street Six. Also worked extensively with Sharkey, Phil Zito.

William Russell

Jim Ruth

Roubleau, Ernest (bjo). b. N.O., *ca.* 1897; d. June 7, 1973. Cousin of celebrated William Penn. Worked with many jazz revival groups.

Rouchon, Tete (sb, tu). b. Algiers, La., *ca.* 1860; d. N.O., *ca.* 1932. Member of the Pickwick Band about 1882 and the Algiers Brass Band. Played with Henry Allen, Sr., before 1910; in 1916 worked with Elton Theodore. His final professional jobs were with Chris Kelly in the late 1920s.

Rouse, Morris (p, vo). b. N.O., ——. Member of Louis Dumaine's Jazzola Eight recording band.

Rousseau, August (tb). b. N.O., *ca.* 1894; d. N.O., *ca.* 1956. Member of the original Tuxedo Orchestra before World War I. Sometimes played alto horn in the Tuxedo Brass Band.

Rouzon, Oscar (s). b. N.O., Jan. 10, 1912. With Young Tuxedo Brass Band and many dance bands from the 1920s to the 1980s. Frequently with Papa Celestin in the forties and fifties. In many groups led by Danny Barker.

Rowling, Red (cl). b. N.O., *ca.* 1894. Pre–World War I Dixielander. Played frequently in bands with the Brunies family. In Chicago in 1916 wit Morgan's Euphonic Band.

Royen, John (p). b. Washington, D.C., March 29, 1955. Student of Don Ewell. In the 1980s, employed at the Gazebo in the French Market, playing outdoors. Regular piano with the Louisiana Repertory Jazz Ensemble.

Russ, Henry (d, t, sb). b. N.O., Aug. 7, 1903. During the late 1920s, a bandleader at the dime-a-dance halls or worked with Peter Lacaze's NOLA Band. During the Depression, he switched to trumpet and worked with WPA and ERA groups. During World War II was in the Algiers Naval Station Brass Band.

Russell, Bud (sb). b. N.O., ——. Played with Golden Leaf Band in 1920 and led his own band in later twenties.

Russell, Luis (p, l). b. Careening Cay, Panama, Aug. 5, 1902; d. New York, N.Y., *ca.* 1962. Played at Tom Anderson's in 1920 with Albert Nicholas, Paul Barbarin. To Chicago in 1925 with Doc Cooke, King Oliver. Led his own band until 1948, touring the country and recording. It was Russell's band that Louis Armstrong fronted from 1935 to 1943.

Russell, William (v). b. Canton, Mo., Aug. 26, 1905. Distinguished jazz archivist, writer, composer, and classically trained musician. Regular member of the New Orleans Ragtime Orchestra.

Ruth, Jim (g, bjo, mdl). b. N.O., *ca.* 1880; d. N.O., 1957. Pioneer rhythm man, half brother of the Shields family. Played with the earliest dixieland groups, including Ernest Giardina's band, Papa Laine, the Barrocco brothers, King Watzke.

St. Cyr, Johnny (bjo, g). b. N.O., April 17, 1889; d. Los Angeles, Calif., June 17, 1966. Led his own band, the Young Men of New Orleans, on the miniature river steamer *Mark Twain* at Disneyland. A jazz star of the first magnitude. He worked in 1917 with Piron. On the SS *Capitol* under Fate Marable. In the mid-twenties, he made the fabulous Armstrong Hot Five and Hot Seven discs. Worked with King Oliver, Jelly Roll Morton, and all the top names of his era.

Johnny St. Cyr

Burnell Santiago

Santiago, Burnell (p). b. N.O., Sept., 1915; d. Jan. 6, 1944. Billed himself as the King of Boogie Woogie in the 1930s, but was a skilled musician, held by many contemporaries to be the finest of his era. Worked mainly as soloist or in a trio with Ollie Papa, string bass, and Sidney Pflueger, guitar. Brother of Lester, nephew of Willie Santiago.

Santiago, Lester "Blackie" (p). b. N.O., Aug. 14, 1909; d. N.O., Jan. 18, 1965. Began his career in the late 1920s with Arnold Depass. Mainly associated with Paul Barbarin; led groups and recorded extensively. Sometimes did vocals in Creole patois. Nephew of Willie, brother of Burnell.

Santiago, Willie (bjo, g). b. N.O., ca. 1887; d. N.O., 1945. One of the great rhythm men of New Orleans, he was with the top Storyville bands and, 1919–1920, with the Maple Leaf Orchestra. Uncle of Lester and Burnell Santiago. Played with Louis Armstrong at Anderson's in 1920, later with Arnold Metoyer, Paul Barbarin. Worked at the Bungalow, 1925–1931. Is on the Kid Rena Delta recordings.

Blackie Santiago

Emanuel Sayles   *Courtesy Preservation Hall*

Tony Sbarbaro

Sayles, Emanuel (bjo, g). b. Donaldsonville, La., Jan. 31, 1905. Studied violin, viola with Dave Perkins. Son of banjoist George Sayles. Joined a band in Pensacola, Fla., 1923; returned to a stint with Bebé Ridgley's Tuxedo Orchestra at the Pelican Hall, 1925. Worked the riverboats with Fate Marable, and on the SS *J. S.* under A. J. Piron. Member of famed Jones-Collins Astoria Hot Eight disc session. Played with Sidney Desvigne at the Pythian roof garden. From 1939 to 1949, led his own group, mainly in Chicago. Worked with George Lewis band, 1959. Recorded extensively on Altantic, Riverside, and other labels. In 1966 at Jazz Ltd. in Chicago. A regular at Preservation Hall in the seventies and eighties. His TV biodocumentary, *This Cat Can Play Anything*, appeared on PBS in 1980.

Sayles, George (g, bjo). b. N.O., *ca.* 1880. Played with Silver Leaf Orchestra before the Spanish-American War. After the war, continued with same group until 1918, when it disbanded. Retired from music soon after. Father of Emanuel.

Sbarbaro, Tony (d, kazoo). b. N.O., June 27, 1897; d. New York, N.Y., Oct. 29, 1969. Known also as **Tony Spargo**. Youngest member of Original Dixieland Jazz Band; considered by many to be the greatest dixieland drummer. Replaced Johnny Stein in Original Dixieland Jazz Band at Chicago in June, 1916. Had already worked in New Orleans with the Brunies brothers at the Tango Palace and was a member of Ernest Giardina's ragtime band. Played kazoo mounted in a large horn. In later years was seen frequently at Nick's and on jobs with the Phil Napoleon band.

Scaglione, Nunzio (cl). b. N.O., *ca.* 1890; d. N.O., May 12, 1935. Early dixielander, veteran of Papa Laine groups. Recorded on famous Bayersdorffer sides for Okeh.

Schellang, August "Augie" (d). b. N.O., March 1, 1905; d. N.O., Oct. 16, 1958. Played with most of the top dixieland and dance bands during the twenties and thirties, including Ellis Stratakos, the Prima-Sharkey orchestra, the New Orleans Rhythm Masters, Wingy Manone. Nephew of Tony Parenti.

Schilling, George, Sr., "Happy" (tb, g, l). b. N.O., April 26, 1886; d. N.O., Feb. 28, 1964. Important early dixieland influence. Led his own brass band and dance orchestra. He and another noted leader, Johnny Fischer, used to play in each other's bands. Also led the band at Heineman's ball park for New Orleans Pelicans' games.

Schilling, George, Jr. (s, cl). b. N.O., ——. d. N.O., Feb. 28, 1978. Son of Happy Schilling. Played with his dad's orchestra and brass band. Also was with Slim Lamar's Argentine Dons.

Tony Schiro

Jake Sciambra

Bud Scott

Schiro, Luke (cl). b. N.O., *ca.* 1903. Seldom-heard New Orleans clarinetist. Rarely worked professionally, but was seen frequently during the fifties at the New Orleans Jazz Club. Taught Irving Fazola.

Schiro, Tony (g, bjo). b. N.O., April 18, 1899; d. N.O., 1981. Veteran dixielander who studied with John Marrero, Johnny St. Cyr. Played in Triangle Band, 1917–1925. Later with Sharkey.

Schreiner, Tony (d). b. N.O., *ca.* 1912. Played with the best of his era, notably Tom Brown, the Triangle Band. Worked during the 1960s uptown at Munster's under the leadership of Tony Fougerat. Also in Lyons Brass Band.

Sciambra, Jacob "Jake" (p, cl). b. N.O., Sept. 23, 1910. Well-known attorney, active with Johnny Wiggs during the late fifties. Continued with informal group into the eighties.

Scioneaux, Louis (tb). b. N.O., *ca.* 1931. Became popular as trombonist with George Girard's New Orleans Five during the 1950s. For many years he was with Sam Butera's Witnesses, a rock-and-roll act occasionally fronted by Louis Prima.

Arthur Seelig, Sr.

Scott, Alex (sb). b. N.O., *ca.* 1895; d. N.O., *ca.* 1943. Active bassist who began about 1915 with the Tulane Orchestra but was mostly active during the 1920s with George Lewis, Earl Humphrey, Lee Collins.

Scott, Arthur "Bud" (g, bjo, vo). b. N.O., Jan. 11, 1890; d. Los Angeles, Calif., July 2, 1949. Between 1905 and 1912, he played mainly in the district with Freddie Keppard, Kid Ory. Also worked with Buddy Bolden's and John Robichaux's orchestras. Recorded with King Oliver. From 1927, he worked in Chicago with Erskine Tate, Oliver, Jimmie Noone. Moved to California at the beginning of the Depression and worked frequently with Mutt Carey and Kid Ory. Was with Ory when he died in 1949.

Seelig, Arthur, Sr. (sb). b. N.O., Apr. 8, 1908. Dixieland and dance musician, active especially during the 1930s. At Famous Door with Santo Pecora in 1966.

Seelig, Arthur, Jr. (p). b. N.O., Apr. 9, 1929. Younger dixieland musician, played with Dukes of Dixieland, George Girard.

Shannon, Harry (t). b. N.O., *ca.* 1885. Dixieland trumpet player of the early 1900s. Played in Fischer's Brass Band about 1905.

Shannon, Tony (tu, sou). b. N.O., ———. Original tuba player in Fischer's Brass Band.

Sharkey Bonano

Sharkey (t). b. N.O., April 9, 1904; d. N.O., March 27, 1972. Real name Joseph Bonano. Dixieland band leader from 1922. On tour with Jean Goldkette, 1927. Trademarks: brown derby, high-pitched vocals, and impromptu "cootchie" dances. He employed top New Orleans dixieland stars and toured with them in Europe, Asia, South America. Once, for a short time, he replaced Bix Beiderbecke in the Wolverines orchestra. He also replaced Nick La Rocca in the Original Dixieland Jazz Band.

Sherman, Herman E. (as, ts). b. N.O., 1923. Played in George Williams brass band in the fifties, Eureka in the sixties. Became leader of the Young Tuxedo Brass Band, 1972. Continued into the eighties.

Shields, Bernard Saxon "Bernie" (g, md, bjo, z, org). b. N.O., May 6, 1893; d. N.O., Feb. 20, 1978. Began playing with Six and 7/8 String Band about 1910. Had long vaudeville career. Not related to other Shieldses listed.

115

Herman Sherman

Harry Shields

Eddie Shields

Shields, Eddie (p). b. N.O., 1896; d. N.O., 1938. Brother of Larry and Harry. Played with members of Original Dixieland Jazz Band before they went north.

Shields, Harry (cl, bs). b. N.O., June 30, 1899; d. N.O., Jan. 18, 1971. One of the great New Orleans clarinets. Played baritone sax in the Norman Brownlee band after World War I; clarinet with Johnny Wiggs, Sharkey, Tom Brown. Brother of Larry, Eddie Shields. Much recorded.

Shields, Larry (cl). b. N.O., Sept. 13, 1893; d. Hollywood, Calif., Nov. 21, 1953. Celebrated clarinetist of the Original Dixieland Jazz Band. Star of the very first jazz record date. Also played with Tom Brown's Five Rubes in vaudeville. Shares composer credit for "Tiger Rag," "Original Dixieland One-Step," "Clarinet Marmalade," "Lazy Daddy," and others.

Shields, Pat (g). b. N.O., ca. 1891. A member of King Watzke's dixieland band, 1904–1908. Played with his many brothers.

Shields Family. A large uptown family of musicians and music teachers of which only the most prominent jazzmen are listed here. Among the brothers was half brother Jimmy Ruth.

Larry Shields

Omer Simeon

Simeon, Omer (cl). b. N.O., July 21, 1902; d. New York, N.Y., Sept. 17, 1959. Pupil of Lorenzo Tio, Jr. Probably never worked in New Orleans. In Chicago in the twenties with Charlie Elgar, King Oliver, Erskine Tate. Played and recorded with Jelly Roll Morton. Played in the pit at the Regal Theater in 1931. Six years with Earl Hines until 1937; also, until 1940 with Walter Fuller, Horace Henderson, Coleman Hawkins. With the Jimmy Lunceford orchestra, 1942–1950. With Wilbur DeParis at Jimmy Ryan's in New York, 1951–1958. He recorded many times; cut his last record—for Audiophile—three weeks before his death.

Simpson, Duke (d). b. Algiers, La., ——. d. ——. Snare drummer with the Pacific Brass Band before World War I.

Simpson, Ron (g, bjo). b. London, Eng., Jan. 17, 1935. Society Jazz Band.

Sims, George (bh). b. Algiers, La., *ca.* 1872. Manager and baritone horn, Pacific Brass Band from about 1900 to about 1910.

Singleton, Arthur "Zutty" (d). Bunkie, La., May 14, 1898; d. New York, N.Y., July 14, 1975. Tuxedo Brass Band, 1916; Maple Leaf Band, 1916; John Robichaux orchestra, 1917. With Big Eye Louis Nelson, Steve Lewis trio before 1920. On riverboats with Charlie Creath, Fate Marable, early twenties. In Chicago with Doc Cooke, Carroll Dickerson, Louis Armstrong, Jimmie Noone, Dave Peyton. Remained in the forefront of jazz drummers through the thirties, forties, and fifties.

Small, Freddie "Blind Freddie" (cl, har). b. N.O., *ca.* 1898. Worked bars with trio or duet for many years. In the 1920s worked with Wesley Don's Liberty Bell Orchestra. Continued into the 1970s with gospel singing.

Smilin' Joe. See Joseph, Pleasant.

Smith, Jerome "Pork Chop" (d). b. Dec. 26, 1895. Played in the 1920s with Sam Morgan, Kid Rena. Moved to Chicago about 1928. Played with Lee Collins, Eurreal Montgomery, Natty Dominique.

Smith, John (p, bjo). b. N.O., Oct. 21, 1910. Played with Wooden Joe Nicholas' Camelia Orchestra in the late 1920s. Nephew of trumpeter Sugar Johnny Smith. Played at Preservation, Dixieland halls in 1965.

Smith, John "Sugar Johnny" (c). b. N.O., *ca.* 1880; d. Chicago, Ill., 1918. Worked in group with Lorenzo Staulz in the district in 1902. Later led a small band at Groshell's Dance Hall and worked in Richard M. Jones's Four Hot Hounds, at Abadie's, 1913–1914. Went to Chicago in 1917; played briefly in vaudeville act with Lawrence Duhé's band, then worked for Duhé at the Deluxe Cafe. Succumbed to pneumonia in 1918.

Monk Smith

Edmond Souchon

Smith, Lester "Monk" (g, cl, s, l). b. N.O., May 23, 1898; d. Bay St. Louis, Miss., Sept. 5, 1952. Member of Invincibles String Band, 1912–1920. A founder and onetime leader of the New Orleans Owls.

Snaer, Albert (t). b. N.O., 1902; d. Los Angeles, Calif., 1962. One of the best technicians on brass New Orleans ever produced. Played in Excelsior Brass Band and, between 1926 and 1928, led the Moonlight Serenaders. His later career was spent touring with big swing bands— Andy Kirk, Horace Henderson, Edgar Hayes. In the 1950s he was doing studio work in Los Angeles.

Son, Babe (bjo). b. N.O., *ca.* 1897. Played banjo with Kid Rena, 1918–1919, for dances and advertising wagons. In the mid-twenties he was active with Chris Kelly's band. During the Depression he worked taxi-dance halls with Willie Pajeaud.

Songier, Leo (bjo). b. Covington, La., *ca.* 1900. With Foster Lewis Jazz Band in the 1920s.

Souchon, Edmond "Doc" (bjo, g, vo). b. N.O., Oct. 25, 1897; d. N.O., Aug. 24, 1968. Obstetrician, as well as skilled musician. In his teens he helped organize the Six and 7/8 String Band. One of the most recorded jazz musicians, he appeared on discs with many of the great New Orleans jazzmen. He contributed to the musi-

cal development of some outstanding banjo and guitar players. As founder of the *Second Line* and the New Orleans Jazz Museum, he brought many great jazzmen to deserved prominence. For others, too poor to afford the services of a doctor, he provided free medical care.

Spargo, Tony (d). See Sbarbaro, Tony.

Spears, A. B. (s). b. N.O., ———; d. N.O., Aug. 24, 1965. Sax player for and manager of the Gibson Brass Band.

Spitlera, Joseph P., Jr. "Pee Wee" (cl). b. N.O., Dec. 21, 1937. An animated youngster frequently seen in the "kid bands" of the 1950s, especially under the leadership of George Girard, Murphy Campo. Now regular clarinetist with Al Hirt.

Stafford, Greg (t, vo). b. N.O., 1958. Armstrong-oriented musician developed by Danny Barker in the Fairview Baptist band. Played in Hurricanes Brass Band as a youngster and went on to fill in on adult jobs.

Starr, Frederick (cl, s). b. Cincinnati, Ohio, March 24, 1940. Former vice-president in charge of academic affairs at Tulane University. Author of *Red and Hot: Jazz in the USSR* and *A Jazz Atlas of New Orleans*. Coleader of the Federal Jazz Commission band in Washington, D.C. Played with the Queen City Jazz Band in Cincinnati and the Tin Rainbow Jazz Band of New Haven, Conn. Founder and leader of the Louisiana Repertory Jazz Ensemble.

Staulz, Lorenzo (g, bjo). b. N.O., *ca.* 1880; d. N.O., *ca.* 1928. Highly regarded but erratic. Played irregularly in the Bolden band in early 1900s. With Buddy Petit in the

Coo Coo Talbert

Eagle Band, 1916. Worked in the district first with Freddie Keppard, then with Kid Ory at Lala's until 1918. Finished his active career about 1925 with Bob Lyons's Dixie Jazz Band.

Stein, Johnny (d). b. N.O., June 15, 1891; d. N.O., Sept. 30, 1962. Legal name John Philip Hountha. Organizer and first leader of the Original Dixieland Jazz Band but lost the leadership before band scored its big success because of personality conflicts. Organized the original New Orleans Jazz Band for Jimmy Durante. Played in New York and Chicago for most of his career.

Stephens, Joe (d). b. N.O., ——; d. N.O., 1974. Son of the great drummer Ragbaby Stephens. Joe was active during the 1930s, especially in a band led by Henry Belas and featuring Raymond Burke.

Stephens, Mike "Ragbaby" (d). b. N.O., ca. 1885; d. Richmond, Ind., ca. 1927. Sometimes called the "father of dixieland drums," he was a fixture in Papa Laine units and in the Reliance Brass Band.

Stevens, Arthur (tb). b. N.O., ——. Manager and trombone for the Bulls Club Brass Band in the early 1920s.

Stevenson, Burke (sb, tu, t). b. Plaquemine, La., Aug. 14, 1899. Pupil of Professor Jim Humphrey. Played trumpet with Eclipse Brass Band, Deer Range Brass Band. Came to New Orleans in 1917; played mostly for dances, frequently with Little Dad Vincent, Walter Decou. Was in Kid Rena's brass band. Played trumpet in ERA Orchestra in the mid-thirties. Worked in Kid Thomas band for many years.

Stewart, Alonzo (d). b. N.O., April 13, 1919. Plays regularly in Preservation Hall in the bands of Kid Thomas and Harold Dejan. With Thomas on tour of Poland and Soviet Union.

Stewart, George (cl). With Camelia Orchestra in the 1920s. Earlier in Excelsior Brass Band.

Stratakos, Ellis (tb). b. N.O., Dec. 1, 1904; d. Gulfport, Miss., Jan. 25, 1961. Early dixieland contemporary of the DeDroit brothers, Tony Parenti, Johnny Wiggs. Fronted dance band at the Jung Hotel Roof for many years. Popular along Mississippi Gulf Coast. Recorded on Vocalion.

Summers, Eddie (tb). b. N.O., Sept. 15, 1903; d. N.O., Oct. 27, 1977. Began in neighborhood bands. Joined Augustin-Snaer Moonlight Serenaders in the late 1920s, then worked with the same group under the leadership of A. J. Piron. Was with Eureka and Young Tuxedo brass bands.

Surgi, Stanley (d). b. N.O., Sept. 18, 1907. Active in the thirties, forties, and fifties. Longtime standby at the New Orleans Jazz Club. In early years was frequently with Tony Fougerat's band.

Suter, Marion (p). b. N.O., ca. 1903; d. N.O., August 3, 1974. Played for four decades in most of the dixieland bands from the twenties to the sixties.

Talbert, Elmer "Coo Coo" (t). b. N.O., Aug. 8, 1900; d. N.O., Dec. 13, 1950. Did not begin career until 1929 with Arnold Depass dance orchestra. Trained by Kid Rena; sometimes worked in Rena's brass band. Worked with the George Lewis band. In 1935 he was with Polo Barnes. Worked his last jobs in 1950 with the Albert Jiles group.

Taranto, Joe (g). Dixielander of the 1900s.

Tervalon, Clement (sb, tb). b. N.O., Nov. 13, 1915. Most frequently seen in the forties and fifties at the Paddock under Octave Crosby's leadership or with the Young Tuxedo Brass Band. Led a band on Bourbon Street in the sixties.

Blanche Thomas

Bob Thomas

Theodore, Elton (bjo, s). b. Algiers, La., *ca.* 1897; d. N.O., Sept. 11, 1972. Popular bandleader of the 1920s, "across the river," with whom Kid Thomas played.

Thomas, Blanche (vo). b. N.O., *ca.* 1918; d. N.O., April 20, 1977. One of New Orleans' rare singers of authentic blues. During the sixties and seventies, she was the only one of her genre working in jazz circles in the city. She began singing on Bourbon Street in 1944 and was featured in the sixties at Dixieland Hall and in the seventies at Heritage Hall. Exceptional ability to work with her accompanists. Appeared in State of Louisiana film *Jazz Age to Space Age* and recorded on the Louisiana Department of Commerce and Industry record series, "All That Jazz."

Thomas, Bob (tb). b. N.O., *ca.* 1898; d. N.O., Feb. 26, 1960. Worked in the early 1920s with Evan Thomas' (no relation) Black Eagles band, touring Louisiana and East Texas. Long a popular jazzman, he was seen most often, in his later years, with Paul Barbarin, with whom he recorded and went on frequent tours.

Thomas, Charles. See "Ollie Papa."

Thomas, Evan (t). b. Crowley, La., *ca.* 1890; d. Rayne, La., Nov. 21, 1931. Reportedly equal to Armstrong. Thomas never played New Orleans, preferring to lead his Black Eagles band, manned with New Orleans jazz stars, through the hinterlands. Stabbed to death on a bandstand.

Thomas, George W. (p, l). b. Texas, *ca.* 1885; d. Chicago, Ill., 1938. Bandleader of the World War I period who composed the "New Orleans Hop Scop Blues."

Played at Fewclothes Cabaret in the district. Had music publishing firm on Franklin Street.

Thomas, Joe "Brother Cornbread" (cl). b. N.O., Dec. 3, 1902; d. N.O., 1981. Cornbread worked in the Joe Harris Dixieland Band in the mid-twenties and spent a lot of time on tour in the late twenties and thirties. In 1951 he joined the Papa Celestin band and continued with the group after Papa's death, first under the leadership of Eddie Pierson, then Albert French.

Thomas, Kid (t). b. Reserve, La., Feb. 3, 1896. Legal name Thomas Valentine. Played in the Hall family band at home until about 1923, when he joined the Elton Theodore band in Algiers, La. He has led his own band actively since 1926.

Thomas, Son (bjo). b. N.O., *ca.* 1903; d. N.O., *ca.* 1933. Played with the Young Eagles Band, 1918–1919, and through the mid-twenties with Kid Rena's dixie jazz band.

Thomas, Worthia "Showboy" (tb). b. Napoleonville, La., Feb. 26, 1907. Called Showboy because he's always been ready to leave town with any circus or tent show that comes along. Usually seen, when in New Orleans,

120

Kid Thomas

Wilbert Tillman

with the George Williams Brass Band. Sometimes works dance jobs.

Tillman, Cornelius (d). b. N.O., *ca.* 1887. One of Buddy Bolden's favorite rhythm men.

Tillman, Wilbert (s, t, tu, sb). b. N.O., March 31, 1898; d. Feb. 11, 1967. With Eureka Brass Band; Young Tuxedo Brass Band. During Depression years, he was in ERA music program, and in the forties, he led a band jointly with Kid Avery.

Tio, Lorenzo, Sr. (cl). b. Mexico, D.F., *ca.* 1865; d. Jackson, Miss., *ca.* 1920. Played in Excelsior Brass Band in the 1880s. Organized a dance band with Anthony Doublet that was active until about 1892. Active as a teacher until the early 1900s. Brother of Luis, father of Lorenzo, Jr.

Tio, Lorenzo, Jr. (cl). b. N.O., 1884; d. New York, N.Y., Dec. 1, 1933. Most famed as teacher of Jimmie Noone, Albert Nicholas, Barney Bigard, Omer Simeon, Emile Barnes, Albert Burbank, Louis Cottrell, Jr., Johnny Dodds, Wade Whaley. Worked in 1910 with the Onward Brass Band and in 1913 with Papa Celestin's Original Tuxedo Orchestra. First performed as a concert musician under

his father and Theogene V. Baquet. Went to Chicago with Manuel Perez, 1915–1916. Back to Celestin, 1917–1918. In 1918 he began a long stand with the A. J. Piron Orchestra, with which he made his only recordings. Son of Lorenzo, Sr., and nephew of Luis Tio.

Tio, Luis "Papa" (cl). b. Mexico, D.F., *ca.* 1863; d. N.O., 1927. With Excelsior Brass Band in the 1880s. Mainly a concert musician, he turned to jazz after 1910, working in the district with Manuel Manetta, Peter Bocage, Henry Peyton. He also played in dance bands with John Robichaux, A. J. Piron.

Tisdale, Clarence (g, bjo). b. N.O., *ca.* 1900. Usually associated with Kid Rena, especially in the 1930s. Sometimes played with trios for dancing.

Toca, Lawrence (t). b. N.O., *ca.* 1900; d. N.O., July 2, 1972. Worked with Bill Hamilton's Oriental Orchestra during the 1920s. During the Depression, he was with many small groups, notably Kid Milton and Polo Barnes in Little Woods. At Harmony Inn through the mid-forties; later at Happy Landing with Albert Jiles, Emma Barrett. Played for a short time with George Lewis. Recorded with Dee Dee Pierce in 1951. Retired about 1955.

Lawrence Toca

Todd, Camilla (p). b. N.O., *ca.* 1888; d. N.O., 1969. Prominent piano teacher. Played mainly with concert groups, but was a member of the Maple Leaf Orchestra, 1919–1920. Played in NOLA Band.

Toms, Ricky (tb). Dixielander of pre–World War I era. Played with Nick La Rocca, Yellow Nunez, and Papa Laine groups.

Torregano, Joseph (cl). b. N.O., Feb. 28, 1952. Played with Doc Paulin band 1971–1972; Fairview Baptist Brass Band, 1971–1972. Played with Gibson, Young Tuxedo, Onward and Olympia Brass Bands. Was associate curator of the New Orleans Jazz Museum in the seventies. Taught music at University of New Orleans.

Tortorich, Tony (d). b. N.O., *ca.* 1900. With Dixola Jazz Band in the 1920s.

Touro, Pinchback (bh, g, v). b. St. James Parish, La., *ca.* 1870; d. early 1940s. Always a bandleader, Touro invariably called his many outfits by the name of the Lincoln Band. Was most active during the Depression, when he headed the WPA Brass Band.

Towles, Nat (sb). b. *ca.* 1900. During the early 1920s was leader of the Creole Harmony Kings.

Joseph Torregano

Toyama, Yoshio (t). b. Tokyo, Japan, March 5, 1944. No oriental has ever had as much impact on the musicians of the city. Arrived with his wife, **Keiko**, an expert banjoist, in the 1960s and thrilled locals with his Bunk Johnson–style horn. Returned to Japan in 1968 to organize an authentic New Orleans jazz band. Toured the U.S. and Europe with Barry Martyn's "Legends of Jazz" and spent a long time on the road with Alton Purnell and Louis Nelson. Returned to Japan because of immigration restrictions.

Yoshio Toyama

Ninesse Trepagnier

Eddie Tschantz

Trepagnier, Ernest "Ninesse" (d). b. N.O., ca. 1885; d. N.O., April 11, 1968. Started with Olympia Orchestra in 1909. Worked before 1920 with Robichaux, Celestin, and the Gaspards. In 1916 joined the Tuxedo Brass Band and stayed with it until 1928, winning his reputation as the greatest bass drummer of them all. During the Depression, he was in the ERA Orchestra and the WPA Brass Band.

Treveque, Jack (bjo). b. N.O., ca. 1899. During the 1920s worked with Alfred Laine's orchestra.

Tschantz, Eddie (d). b. N.O., Jan. 7, 1911. Popular dixieland drummer. Nephew of Tom Brown. Frequently led small combinations for dancing.

Tujague, Joe (sb, gu, g). b. N.O., ca. 1891. Pre–World War I dixielander.

Tujague, John (sb). b. N.O., ca. 1893. Pre–World War I dixielander.

Turner, Benny (p). b. N.O., ca. 1908; d. N.O., Oct. 8, 1973. Worked during the thirties with Kid Rena. During the forties, he was frequently at Luthjen's; worked many dance jobs with small groups in the forties and fifties. Seen in the sixties at Preservation Hall.

Turnis, Arthur (bd). b. N.O., ——. Lyons Brass Band in the late 1920s.

Vache, Alphonse (tu). Played in Melrose Brass Band with King Oliver in 1907.

Valentin, Bouboul (vt). b. N.O., ca. 1870; d. N.O., ca. 1925. Led Accordiana Band in 1894. In 1897 played in Alphonse Picou's Independence Band. Sometimes worked with Henry Peyton. Sat in frequently with the bands on Iberville Street in the district.

Lawrence Veca

Cajun Verret

Valentin, Punkie (c). b. N.O., *ca.* 1866; d. Calif., *ca.* 1951. A dentist, Bouboul's elder brother was only a part-time musician, but a virtuoso. Frequently marched with the Excelsior, Onward, and Melrose brass bands. Moved to California in the forties.

Valentine, Thomas. See Thomas, Kid.

Veca, Lawrence (c). b. N.O., 1889; d. N.O., 1911. Considered by many contemporary musicians the greatest of the dixieland cornetists. Veca was leader of Papa Laine's No. 1 ragtime band and a star of the Reliance Brass Band. Played all instruments. Name usually misspelled Vega.

Verret, Irving "Cajun" (tb). b. Alexandria, La., *ca.* 1906. Verret has been an outstanding big band musician and studio star for many years. Played with Sidney Arodin. He is of particular interest because of his discs with Wingy Manone.

Verrett, Harrison (bjo, g). b. N.O., Feb. 27, 1907; d. Oct. 18, 1965. Pupil of Dave Perkins. Made his debut in 1924 with Johnny Brown's band. During the late twenties, he worked taxi-dance places in New Orleans and Mississippi; in the thirties, he continued with his own group at the Fern Cafe. Worked with Papa Celestin, 1945–1951; made a successful tour with Fats Domino. Best known in last years as part of Noon Johnson bazooka trio.

Vidacovich, Irvine "Pinky" (cl). b. N.O., 1905; d. N.O., July 5, 1966. Known to a generation of Or-

leanians as the voice of Cajun Pete in a popular radio commercial. Was with the New Orleans Owls and, earlier, the Princeton Revellers. Was a member of WWL staff band, the Dawn Busters, and recorded for Southland.

Vigne, John (d). b. N.O., *ca.* 1865. Dance band drummer in turn-of-century days. Played with Olympia Orchestra in 1901; with Peerless Orchestra under Bab Frank, 1903–1908; and also under A. J. Piron until about 1912. Also worked with the Golden Rule Orchestra and about 1906 with the Imperial Orchestra.

Vigne, John "Ratty" (d). b. N.O., *ca.* 1885. Played with Jack Carey, about 1912, and on jobs in the district with Clarence Williams in 1913. He was also at Fewclothes Cabaret with Freddie Keppard in the same year, and played with King Oliver at Pete Lala's cafe in 1915.

Vigne, Sidney (cl). b. N.O., *ca.* 1903; d. N.O., Dec. 24, 1925. A promising young clarinetist who played with the Golden Leaf Band, Bob Lyons' Dixie Jazz Band, the Maple Leaf Orchestra in the early twenties. Killed by a truck on Christmas Eve, 1925.

Pinky Vidacovich

Vincent, Clarence "Little Dad" (bjo). b. Baton Rouge, La., 1899; d. N.O., 1960. Lilliputian Little Dad was barely four feet tall. He was well known for work with Buddy Petit and Chris Kelly before he was twenty. Played at the West End in Amos White's New Orleans Creole Jazz Band, 1923–1924. In the twenties, he joined Herb Morand to work in Yucatan, Mexico. During the Depression, he worked at times with Louis Dumaine and with Octave Crosby.

Vinson, Eddie (tb). b. N.O., ca. 1885. In 1910 Vinson was a member of the Olympia Orchestra and the Excelsior Brass Band. He left New Orleans with the Original Creole Orchestra, led by Bill Johnson, for a vaudeville tour. He remained in the North thereafter.

Waelde, Bill (sb). b. N.O., 1892; d. N.O., 1959. Dixielander who frequently worked with Abbie Brunies. Also with Albert Artigues' French Market Gang. Brother of Henry Waelde.

Waelde, Henry (g). b. N.O., Aug. 10, 1892; d. N.O., June 14, 1975. Onetime leader of the Melon Pickers. Worked with Alfred Laine and Leon Prima.

Walters, Albert (t). b. N.O., July 19, 1905; d. N.O., Oct. 20, 1980. Began his musical career about 1929. In 1931 organized, with Albert Jiles, the Crescent City Serenaders, which was active through the early Depression years. Afterwards, he played with most of the best bands in town and was frequently in parades, especially with the George Williams Brass Band.

Ward, Benny (p). A Storyville "professor."

Albert Warner

Warner, Albert (tb). b. N.O., Dec. 31, 1890; d. N.O., Sept. 10, 1966. Known almost exclusively as a brass band musician. Was with Kid Rena's brass band, the Young Tuxedo Brass Band, and since 1932, the Eureka Brass Band. In the early forties, he recorded with Bunk Johnson. In earlier days, he played in dance bands, notably with Big Eye Louis Nelson.

Warner, Willie (cl). b. N.O., ca. 1865; d. N.O., ca. 1908. Member of the original Buddy Bolden band. Also played with Charlie Galloway and with the Pelican Brass Band.

Warnick, Louis (s, cl). b. N.O., ca. 1890. Warnick played jobs in brass bands in his teens. In 1918 he joined A. J. Piron for a ten-year stand at Spanish Fort; he recorded with the orchestra, 1923–1925. In 1928 he played with the Creole Serenaders, one of the city's most successful bands; he broadcast regularly over station WWL.

Washington, Edward "Son White" (d). b. Natchez, Miss., Oct. 12, 1902; d. N.O., 1964. Known mainly as a brass band drummer, especially with the George Williams Brass Band. He was also a dance drummer who studied with Dave Perkins in 1920 and went to work for the Foster Lewis band. In later years he was associated with Joe Avery and with Wilbert Tillman.

Louis Warnick

Joe Watkins

Eddie Watson

Washington, Fred (p). b. N.O., 1888. A Storyville "professor." Moved to California in 1919. Played, irregularly, for many years. Recorded on first Kid Ory session.

Washington, George (tb). b. N.O., *ca.* 1900; d. N.O., *ca.* 1942. First job in Kid Lindsey's band, alongside Louis Armstrong, 1916. Later identified with Buddy Petit in early 1920 period.

Watkins, Joe (d, vo). b. N.O., Oct. 24, 1900; d. N.O., Sept., 1969. Real name Mitchell Watson. Internationally known drummer in the George Lewis band during its peak years. In 1964 he toured Japan with the band and was a frequent performer at Preservation Hall. Nephew of Johnny St. Cyr. Stopped playing in 1966 because of failing health.

Watson, Eddie (g). b. Pass Christian, Miss., July 13, 1904. One of Edmond Souchon's early teachers. Began with his three brothers in a spasm band that later merged with the John Handy band.

Watson, Joseph (cl). b. N.O., *ca.* 1895; d. N.O., *ca.* 1925. A member of Sam Morgan's first band in 1916.

Watson, Mitchell. See Watkins, Joe.

Watzke, Alex "King" (v, l). b. N.O., *ca.* 1880; d. N.O., 1918. Led popular band before 1908. Another claimant to composer credit for "Tiger Rag," which he actually played in 1904, calling it "No. 2." Died in flu epidemic.

Whaley, Wade (cl). d. N.O., 1895. At the Bungalow before 1916. Another protégé of the Tios. Before he left New Orleans in 1919, he had worked in the bands of A. J. Piron, John Robichaux, Manuel Perez, Manuel Manetta, Jack Carey. In California he worked with Jelly Roll Morton and Kid Ory; led his own band in California from the mid-twenties until the Depression. Recorded with Bunk Johnson in 1944.

White, Amos (c). b. Kingstree, S.C., Nov. 6, 1889; d. Calif., 1980. Came to New Orleans in 1919 after army

Wade Whaley

Johnny Wiggs

discharge. Played first at the Cadillac Bar with Harrison Verrett, then joined Celestin's Tuxedo Brass Band. Worked on boats with Fate Marable and on Marable's Okeh disc, 1924. In 1924 he organized his New Orleans Creole Jazz Band, which played for dancing opposite Tranchina's. As late as 1960 White played a concert in California, where he settled.

White, Benjamin "Benjy" (cl, s, v). b. N.O., Aug. 30, 1901. Played with Invincibles String Band before taking up clarinet and saxophone. Was an original member of the New Orleans Owls. Never played with anyone else; when group disbanded, he quit music.

White, Michael (cl). b. N.O., Nov. 29, 1954. Later generation of the famous jazz family that included Papa John and Kaiser Joseph. He has an ability to improvise harmonies on the clarinet that is rare in the late twentieth century. Talent became obvious with the Young Tuxedo Brass Band. Sometimes with Louisiana Repertory Jazz Ensemble. Played in Doc Paulin's Brass Band (1975–1979);

Danny Barker's Fairview Baptist Church Brass Band (1976–1979). Also with Imperial, Tuxedo, Royal, and Magnolia Brass Bands. Sometimes in *One Mo' Time* theater band.

Wicker, Chester (p). b. N.O., 1904; d. N.O., Dec. 21, 1970. With Tony Fougerat, Tony Almerico, Irving Fazola, Digger Laine from about 1919.

Wiggs, Johnny (c, l). b. N.O., July 25, 1899; d. N.O., Oct. 9, 1977. Legal name John Wigginton Hyman, he also performed under the name **Johnny Hyman**. Worked in the early 1920s with Happy Schilling's band, Tony Parenti, Norman Brownlee. Recorded for Victor in 1927 with his own Bayou Stompers band. In the early thirties with Ellis Stratakos. The revival of jazz from 1946 on is due largely to his efforts. He founded the New Orleans Jazz Club and brought many a great jazzman out of involuntary retire-

Abby Williams

Alfred Williams

ment. As a teacher he turned out distinguished pupils— including George Girard, Pete Fountain, Jack Delaney, Sam Butera, and many others—for a new jazz generation. He operated his own music school and directed music education in the New Orleans public school system. Widely recorded in the 1950s when his power and creativity were at their peak, he retired in 1960, remaining the ideal of purists around the world. In 1965 he began making appearances at Preservation Hall.

Williams, Abby (d). b. N.O., Sept. 22, 1906; d. N.O., June 29, 1977. Led the Square Deal Social Club Brass Band in the late twenties, Abby Williams Happy Pals brass band in the forties and fifties.

Williams, Alfred (d). b. N.O., Sept. 1, 1900; d. N.O., April 30, 1963. First job playing snare drum in the Tuxedo Brass Band in 1920. In the early twenties, he worked in the Sam Morgan band. From 1925 to 1927, he was with Manuel Perez; joined A. J. Piron on the SS *Capitol* in 1929. Left New Orleans in 1936; returned in 1951, playing small dance jobs and marching with the Eureka Brass Band. Was frequently at Preservation Hall before his death.

Williams, "Black Benny" (d). b. N.O., *ca.* 1890; d. N.O., 1924. Though better known as an underworld

character, Williams was quite a drummer. Played bass drum for the Onward Brass Band before World War I. Sometimes marched with the Tuxedo Brass Band or sat in with Louis Armstrong on a job. Stabbed to death by a woman.

Williams, Byers "Buzzy" (p). b. Birmingham, Ala., 1892; d. Mobile, Ala., Oct. 20, 1980. Early dixielander popular in dance bands. Played with Stalebread Lacoume in Charlie Fishbein's Orchestra at the La Vida ballroom and worked with Sharkey, Johnny Wiggs, Emmett Hardy in later years. Played in the Absinthe House as a soloist in the twenties.

Williams, Claiborne (c, l). Leader of early concert orchestra and brass band, mainly in Baton Rouge area in early 1900s.

Williams, Clarence (p, vo, l). b. Plaquemine, La., Nov. 8, 1893; d. New York, N.Y., Nov. 6, 1965. Began playing in Storyville brothels about 1914 and occasionally had a job with A. J. Piron. Went to Texas with Sidney Bechet via boxcar, but the trip proved unproductive. Went into music publishing business with Piron in 1915. Migrated to Chicago about 1917 and became an important factor in the publishing and recording business. Through

Freddie Williams

Spencer Williams

the twenties and thirties produced great records on Okeh and Columbia, including the famous Blue Five discs that brought Louis Armstrong and Sidney Bechet together on wax. For more than twenty years, he operated a hobby shop in Harlem.

Williams, Dave (p). b. N.O., La., Aug. 26, 1920; d. N.O., March 12, 1982. Occasional performer at Preservation, Dixieland halls during the 1960s.

Williams, Freddie (d). b. N.O., ca. 1887; d. N.O., April 30, 1963. Early dixielander; an official in the New Orleans police department. Played with Emile Christian, George and Merritt Brunies in pre–World War I era.

Williams, George (bd). b. N.O., Oct. 25, 1910; d. N.O., Aug. 27, 1965. Leader of the George Williams Brass Band, active in New Orleans for the past twenty years. Worked at the Paddock with Bill Matthews in the 1950s.

Williams, George (c). Before World War I played in Excelsior Brass Band.

Williams, George (g). Worked in the district about 1910–1913, mainly with the Primrose Orchestra.

Williams, Nolan "Shine" (d). b. N.O., ca. 1902; d. N.O., ca. 1942. First major job with the Sam Morgan band, 1926–1927; recorded with the band in spring, 1927. Went on to work in Clarence Desdunes Joyland Revelers, mainly traveling through Louisiana and nearby states.

Williams, Norwood "Giggy" (g). b. N.O., ca. 1880. Member of Bill Johnson's Original Creole Orchestra that left New Orleans for history-making Pantages vaudeville tour.

Williams, Spencer (p). b. N.O., Oct. 14, 1880; d. New York, N.Y., July, 1965. Reared by the notorious madam, Lulu White, he worked as a "professor" for a while in his early years. Is best known as a composer. Wrote "Basin Street Blues," "Mahogany Hall Stomp," "Tishomingo Blues," and "Shim-Me-Sha-Wabble."

Willigan, Bill (d). b. N.O., ———. Early drummer in Buddy Bolden's band.

Willigan, Jim (d). b. N.O., ca. 1902; d. N.O., ca. 1930. One of the best of the New Orleans drummers. First noted in 1923 with Nat Towles's Creole Harmony Kings and then with Papa Celestin's Original Tuxedo Orchestra. Selected by Louis Dumaine for the celebrated Jazzola Eight session of 1927. Joined Lee Collins just before the Depression.

Willis, Joshua F. "Jack" (t, mel, ah). b. Galena, Ill., April 15, 1920. Active member of marching bands in recent years—Young Tuxedo Brass Band, George Williams

Clive Wilson

Brass Band. Played with George Lewis and at Preservation and Dixieland halls.

Wilson, Alfred (p). One of the best musicians among the Storyville bordello "professors."

Wilson, Clive (t, l). b. London, Eng., Aug. 19, 1942. Arrived in New Orleans in 1965 and surprised the music people with his developed and authentic lead horn. He studied with Johnny Wiggs and had no trouble finding jobs, especially with the Albert French Tuxedo Orchestra. In the 1970s he organized an excellent and stable band, the New Camelia Jazz Band, much in demand.

Wilson, Johnny (bh). Charter member of the Eureka Brass Band. Brother of Willie Wilson.

Wilson, Udell (p). Though not a Louisianian, Wilson was active in the district as a band piano man before World War I working at Fewclothes Cabaret, with Big Eye Louis Nelson, and at 101 Ranch. Worked with Maple Leaf Orchestra, 1919, and with Manuel Perez, 1922. Replaced Luis Russell at Anderson's in 1924.

Wilson, Willie (t). b. N.O., ca. 1890. Founder of the Eureka Brass Band. Worked in the ERA program during the Depression.

Winkler, Martin "Bull" (d). b. N.O., ca. 1890; d. N.O., ca. 1955. Dixieland drummer with the Papa Laine, Bill Gallaty, Frank Christian bands.

Winstein, Dave (s). b. N.O., Dec. 18, 1909. Active in the late twenties and early thirties. Worked with the Sharkey–Leon Prima All-Stars and with Louis Prima. Later, as president of Local 174 of the Musicians Mutual Protective Union, he made his local a model for those in

Willie Wilson

other cities. Became president of Local 174 of the American Federation of Musicians.

Wolfe, Joe (p). b. N.O., 1892; d. Dec. 13, 1961. Most noteworthy connections were Johnny Bayersdorffer in the twenties, Ellis Stratakos in the thirties.

Woods, Alvin (d). b. N.O., Feb. 1, 1909; d. May 14, 1975. With Kid Sheik Colar, Narvin Kimball. Played with Joe Robichaux orchestra in the late thirties. Also with Kaiser Joseph.

Wynn, Albert (tb). b. N.O., July 29, 1907; d. Chicago, Ill., 1975. Never played in New Orleans, but his career was closely associated with the jazz of his native city. Although he lived in Chicago, he played for over forty years with the most celebrated Crescent City jazzmen.

Yancy, Melvin (b). b. N.O., June 9, 1922. Established veteran of over forty years in jazz bands. In the Society Jazz Band with Andrew Hall in 1982.

Young, Austin "Boots" (tb, tu, sb). b. N.O., ca. 1885; d. N.O., ca. 1954. With his brother Sport on sax and Willie Pajeaud on trumpet, he formed the nucleus of a

Boots Young

Chester Zardis *Photo by Mary Tunis*

group that worked dance halls from the late twenties through the Depression years. He recorded in 1942 with Bunk Johnson for "Jazzman" in 1945 and 1949.

Young, Sport (s). Brother of Boots Young. Worked with his brother and Willie Pajeaud in taxi-dance halls for fifteen years.

Ysaguirre, Robert (tu, sb). b. N.O., *ca.* 1895. Longtime bassist with A. J. Piron Orchestra.

Zanco, Manuel "Moose" (c). b. N.O., Feb. 12, 1929. Regular with the Last Straws.

Zardis, Chester (sb). b. New Iberia, La., May 27, 1900. Outstanding bassist with Buddy Petit in Mandeville in 1920. Saw duty with Chris Kelly, Kid Rena, Kid Howard. Was with Sidney Desvigne, 1930–1931, then had his own band from 1935 to 1938. He recorded with the George Lewis band in 1943. Regular performer at Preservation Hall.

Zeno, Henry (d). b. N.O., *ca.* 1880; d. N.O., *ca.* 1918. Early drummer with the Buddy Bolden band, 1900. Worked frequently with Edward Clem, Manuel Manetta in the years around 1906–1907; joined Duson's Eagle Band in 1908. Played in the Olympia Orchestra with A. J. Piron, 1913–1914, and was at Pete Lala's with King Oliver in 1916. Just before his death he was working with the Original Tuxedo Orchestra.

Zimmerman, Gus (c). b. N.O., *ca.* 1887. Member of Reliance Brass Band. With Barocco brothers in 1919.

Zimmerman, Roy (p). b. N.O., Oct. 23, 1913; d. Gulfport, Miss., July 7, 1969. Best known as pianist with Basin Street Six during the 1950s. Often seen with Sharkey. Was with Pete Fountain and his Three Coins.

Roy Zimmerman

Zimmerman, Tom (p). b. N.O., *ca.* 1886; d. Dec. 4, 1923. Considered by many the greatest ragtime piano player of the "tango belt." Apprenticeship as movie house musician. He was a popular soloist in cabarets for most of his active days. In the 1920s he played with Tony Parenti and with the Johnny DeDroit orchestra.

Zito, Phil (d). b. N.O., Aug. 8, 1914. Active bandleader of the late forties and early fifties. Recorded with his own band called the International Dixieland Express.

A JAZZ BAND BALL

Here is a cavalcade of New Orleans bands that made jazz history. They came in all sizes and varieties, with as many approaches to the music as there were leaders. All of those listed and pictured are not purely jazz bands. Some are, of course, but others, not similarly oriented, nevertheless *sometimes* played the real jazz. Band personnels, as given, are partial and collective. It must be understood that there were frequent changes and also circumstances in which a musician worked regularly with more than one group.

A word of explanation is necessary about our use of terms to describe these musical groups.

First, when we use the term *jazz band*, we mean a group of musicians playing in 2/4 or 4/4 time, improvising collectively on a theme. Usually these bands emphasized counterpoint rather than conventional harmony.

By a *dixieland band*, we mean a group of from five to eight musicians, consisting of a front line of cornet or trumpet, clarinet and trombone, plus a rhythm section. The group will have memorized certain parts of each tune in its fixed repertoire. (This is what is called a head arrangement.) The band will do some collective improvisation but usually is more occupied with "hot" solos. Sometimes there is a saxophone in a dixieland band.

When we say *dance orchestra* in the New Orleans jazz sense, what we mean is any group of musicians capable of reading written scores and employed to play for dancing. However, such orchestras could also play a number of tunes *without* music, in the dixieland tradition.

A *novelty orchestra* is one that depends largely on showmanship, odd or homemade instruments, slapsticks, and other items of "skiffle" origin. Frequently, however, such groups produce excellent jazz.

String bands, of course, are just what the name specifies. *Brass bands* are a big enough classification to be covered elsewhere in this volume as a separate group.

Co-op bands like the Bob Crosby Orchestra and the Casa Loma Orchestra were organized and incorporated by groups of musicians who hired a leader to "front" the band. The leader was not necessarily a member of the corporation. This was a phenomenon in the North during the swing era.

The names of bands were not protected by copyright; therefore, two different organizations sometimes had the same name. For example, Charlie Deichmann's Moonlight Serenaders was an all-white orchestra. Another band called the Moonlight Serenaders had several black members. The latter group had no official leader but appeared under the leadership of the musician who secured the job for a particular date.

Our first knowledge of an organized jazz band using conventional instruments dates back to 1889 when a group headed by guitarist Charlie Galloway played for dances and social activities. However, the authors disclaim here and now any implication that this was, in truth, the first jazz band. In fact, we are convinced that the development of jazz was so gradual as to make specious any such claim as related to an individual or group. The Papa Laine Reliance Band organized in 1892 was the first group we know of to play the style now known as "authentic jazz."

Accordiana Band (1894), dance orchestra. Nucleus: Henry Peyton, acc, l; Alphonse Picou, cl; Punkie Valentin, c; Bouboul Valentin, vt.

Albert, Tom (1910), jazz band. Tom Albert, t, v, l; Eddie

Atkins, tb; Albert Gabriel, cl; Manuel Manetta, p, v; Skeeter Jackson, g; Lutzie Rubean, b; Son Hamilton, d.

Alcorn, Alvin, Trio. A long-standing fixture on weekday afternoons in the Marriott Hotel lobby and for Sunday brunch at Commander's Palace, this superior trio consists of leader Alcorn, t; Clarence Ford, cl; and Irving Charles, g. This is probably uptown New Orleans most beloved group.

American Stars (1908–1917), jazz band. Willie Hightower, c, l; Roy Palmer, tb; Wade Whaley, cl; Robert Smith, g; Udell Wilson, p; Baby Dodds, d. Sometimes a violin was added.

Andrus, Dutch, dance orchestra. Dutch Andrus played trumpet with varied personnel. Frequently employed on the steamer *President*.

Arcadian Serenaders (mid-1920s), dixieland band. Mainly composed of Orleanians, the group was active on the Gulf Coast, especially Mobile, Ala. Wingy Manone or Stirling Bose, t; Avery Loposer, tb; Cliff Holman, cl, s; Johnny Riddick, p; Slim Leftwich or Bob Marvin, bjo; Felix Guarino, d.

Banjo Bums (1950s), string band. John Chaffe, Malcolm Genet, bjo; Edmond Souchon, g; Sherwood Mangiapane, sb.

Banner Band (1920s), jazz band. Traveling band in Louisiana country towns, composed of varied personnel, usually including Gus Fortinet, v, l; Bunk Johnson, t; Lawrence Duhé, cl; Kid Avery, tb; Pop Hamilton, bh; Chester Zardis, b.

Barbarin, Paul, jazz band. Partial collective personnel: John Brunious, Ernie Cagnolatti, Albert Walters, t; Bob Thomas, Frog Joseph, Clement Tervalon, tb; Willie James Humphrey, Louis Cottrell, Jr., cl; Lester Santiago, Joe Robichaux, p; Danny Barker, bjo; Paul Barbarin, d, l.

Basin Street Six (1950s), dixieland-comedy band. Co-op group comprising George Girard, t, vo; Joe Rotis, tb; Pete Fountain, cl; Roy Zimmerman, p; Bunny Franks, b; Charlie Duke, d.

Bayersdorffer, Johnny (1920s–1930s), dixieland band. Partial collective personnel: Johnny Bayersdorffer, t, l; Tom Brown, Charlie Hartmann, tb; Nunzio Scaglione, Lester Bouchon, Harry Shields, Elery Maser, Bill Creger,

cl, s; Johnny Miller, Joe Wolfe, p; Nappy Lamare, Freddie Loyacano, Steve Loyacano, bjo, g; Chink Martin, b; Leo Adde, Ray Bauduc, d.

Bienville Roof Orchestra (1928), dixieland band. Sharkey, t; Sidney Arodin, cl; Hal Jordy, s; Freddie Neumann, p; Joe Capraro, g; Luther Lamar, b; Monk Hazel, d, mel, c, l.

Black and Tan Orchestra (1920s), jazz band. Buddy Petit, t, l; George Washington, tb; Edmond Hall (later, Pill Coycault), cl; Sadie Goodson, p; Buddy Manaday, bjo; Chester Zardis, sb; Eddie "Face-O" Woods (later, Chinee Foster), d.

Black Devils (1920s), jazz band. Played in and around Plaquemine, La. Leader, Dennis Williams, father of pianist Clarence Williams, played string bass.

Black Diamond Orchestra (1930s), dance orchestra. Albert Walters, t; Frank Crump, s; Eddie Summers, tb; Boy Bigeou, bjo; George Henderson, d, l.

Black Eagles (1921–1933), jazz band. Partial collective personnel: Evan Thomas, t, l; Bunk Johnson, c; Bob Thomas, Kid Avery, Harrison Brazlee, tb; Lawrence Duhé, George Lewis, Sam Dutrey, Jr., cl; Robert Goby, s; Abraham Martin, bjo; Walter Thomas, Chinee Foster, d.

Bolden, Buddy (1893–1907), ragtime band. Played for dances, parades, parties, with flexible personnel according to the nature of the job. Among the bandsmen were Buddy Bolden, t, l; Bunk Johnson, t; Willie Cornish, Frank Duson, Vic Gaspard, tb; Frank Lewis, Willie Warner, Big Eye Louis Nelson, Sam Dutrey, Sr., cl; Manuel Manetta, Alcide Frank, James A. Palao, v; Bab Frank, pc; Charlie Galloway, Brock Mumford, Lorenzo Staulz, g; Jimmy Johnson, Bob Lyons, Albert Glenny, Bebé Mitchell, sb, tu; Bill Willigan, Henry Zeno, John MacMurray, Cornelius Tillman, d.

Brownlee, Norman (1920s), dixieland, novelty band. Partial collective personnel: Emmett Hardy, Johnny Wiggs, Sharkey, c, t; Tom Brown, tb; George Barth, c, t, tb; Harry Shields, Lester Bouchon, cl, s; Billy Braun, mel, s; Norman Brownlee, p, s, l; Behrman French, Bill Eastwood, Freddie Loyacano, bjo; Alonzo Crombie, tb, d; Frank Christian, tu; Paul Peque, s.

Brown's, Tom, Band from Dixieland (1915). As it left for Chicago in 1915, the band included Ray Lopez, t;

Happy Schilling's Orchestra (1915)
Kneeling are Fred Dantagnan (left) and Don Sanderson. Others, left to right, are Johnny Frisco, Happy Schilling, Bob Aquilera, Johnny Lala, Henry Knecht, Jack Pipitone, John Goety, Lefty Eiermann.

Stalebread Lacoume's Band (1906)
Stalebread (extreme right, with guitar) brought his band to the lake at old West End to play for this family picnic. Of the other musicians, only Sou Sou Ramos, the mandolin player, is identified. Members of this gang were usually tagged with such bizarre nicknames as Warm Gravy, Chinee, Family Haircut, and Cajun.

The Original Tuxedo Orchestra (1924)
Seated, left to right, are Polo Barnes, Joe Strohter (whose local fame was based more on his playing of the slide whistle than on his drums), Bebé Ridgley, Papa Celestin, John Marrero. Standing, left to right, are Henry Pajeaud, Simon Marrero, Manuel Manetta, and Kid Shots Madison.

The Louisiana Shakers (mid-1920s)
Seated, left to right, are Roy Evans, Lionel Ferbos, Kid Keifer, Edmund Bottley, unknown. Standing are George Clark, Sidney Pflueger, Captain John Handy, Benny Clark, Henry Kimball.

Tom Brown, tb, l; Gussie Mueller, cl; Deacon Loyacano, sb, p; Billy Lambert, d. Larry Shields replaced Mueller on clarinet in late 1915.

Brunies New Orleans Jazz Band (ca. 1918). See Original New Orleans Jazz Band.

Camelia Dance Orchestra (1917–mid-1920s). Same as Camelia Brass Band, but Ike Robinson switches to guitar and Joe Parone, string bass, replaces Buddy Luck. Billy and Lawrence Marrero, string bass and banjo, respectively, sometimes played in the band. Other personnel included Albert Warner, tb; Johnny Predonce, b; George Henderson, d; Elmer Talbert, Sr., t; George Stewart, cl; Clarence Tisdale, g, bjo.

Celestin, Papa. See Original Tuxedo Orchestra.

Christian Ragtime Band (ca. 1910–1918). Partial collective personnel: Harry Nunez, v; Ernest Giardina, v, vo; Frank Christian, t, tu, l; Emile Christian, c; Charlie Christian, tb; Bill Gallaty, vt; Yellow Nunez, Achille Baquet, Tony Giardina, Leon Goureaux, cl; Manuel Gomez, g; Willie Guitar, sb; Kid Totts Blaise, Bull Winkler, d.

Columbus Band (1898), jazz band. Tig Chambers, t, l; Willie Eli Humphrey, cl; Willie Cornish, tb; Bob Lyons, sb; Bill Willigan, d.

Crawford-Ferguson Night Owls. One of the very best of the mid-century authentic jazz bands. The Night Owls played regularly for many years on the steamer *President*. Organized by Paul Crawford and Leonard Ferguson, the group produced a couple of the best LPs of the jazz revival. With certain changes the group has survived, working irregularly as the schedules of the musicians permit. Among the collective personnel are Jack Bachman, t; Paul Crawford, tb; Hank Kmen, Raymond Burke, cl; Bill Humphries, Edmond Souchon, Les Muscutt, bjo, g; Sherwood Mangiapane, sb; Leonard Ferguson, s.

Creole Harmony Kings (1922–1927), jazz band. Herb Morand, t; Bill Matthews, tb; Kid Moliere, cl; Wallingford Hughes, s; Frank Pashley, bjo; Nat Towles, sb, l; Louis Mahier (later, Jim Willigan), d.

Creole Serenaders (from 1928), dance orchestra. Peter Bocage, t, v, l; Henry Bocage, t; Lorenzo Tio, Jr., cl; Louis Warnick, s; Steve Lewis, Dwight Newman, p; John Marrero, Charlie Bocage, bjo; Paul Barbarin, Cié Frazier, Henry Martin. Since 1928 all Bocage-led groups have been called Creole Serenaders.

Crescent City Jazzers (mid-1920s). This name was used only for recording purposes. Same personnel as Arcadian Serenaders plus Eddie Powers, s, and minus Wingy Manone, t.

Crescent City Serenaders (1931–1934), dance orchestra. A group built around a four-man nucleus that changed personnel according to the size of the job. The basic four: Albert Walters, t; Frank Crump, s; Boy Bigeou, bjo; Albert Jiles, d.

Crescent Orchestra (1913–1920), jazz band. Partial collective personnel: Mutt Carey, Punch Miller, t; Jack Carey, tb, l; Wade Whaley, Willie Eli Humphrey, Georgia Boy Boyd, cl; Charlie Moore, Tom Benton, g; Wiley King, Pops Foster, sb, tu; Li'l Mack Lacey, Tubby Hall, Baby Dodds, Ernest Rogers, Ram Hall, d.

Crosby, Octave (1940s to 1963), jazz band. Crosby was house bandleader at the Paddock on Bourbon Street for many years. In his band have been: Alvin Alcorn, Papa Celestin, Lee Collins, Thomas Jefferson, t; Bill Matthews, Frog Joseph, Bob Thomas, Clement Tervalon, tb; Alphonse Picou, Albert Burbank, Willie James Humphrey, Ted Purnell, cl; Ricard Alexis, Narvin Kimball, Richard McClean, bjo; Happy Goldston, Alfred Williams, George Williams, d.

DeDroit, Johnny (1917–late 1950s), dance orchestra. Johnny DeDroit, t, l; Russ Papalia, Ellis Stratakos, tb; Tony Parenti, Henry Raymond, cl, s; Rudolph Levy, as; Frank Cuny, Tom Zimmerman, Frank Froeba, p; George Potter, bjo; Paul DeDroit, d.

Dejan's Moonlight Serenaders (1920s and 1930s), dance orchestra. Early version of rock-and-roll band. Leo Dejan, t, l; Harold Dejan, Henry Casenave, s; Sidney Cates, bjo; Arnaul Thomas, d.

Desdunes, Clarence, Joyland Revelers (1927–1931), dance orchestra. Usual personnel: Clarence Desdunes, v, l; Alvin Alcorn, George McCullum, Jr., George Montgomery, t; Ray Johnson, Ray Brown, tb; Oliver Alcorn, cl, ss; Lucien Johnson, Harold Dejan, s; Harry Fairconnetue, bjo; Henry Kimball, sb; Ransom Knowling, tu; Little Brother Montgomery, p.

Desvigne, Sidney (1925–1931), dance orchestra. Worked on the Streckfus line steamers. Among the personnel from New Orleans were Sidney Desvigne, t, l; Red Allen, Gene Ware, t; Bill Matthews, Louis Nelson, tb; Tats Alexander, Ted Purnell, Henry Julian, Eddie Cherie, s;

The Eagle Band (Feb. 28, 1916)
Left to right are Big Eye Louis Nelson, Chinee Foster, Frank Duson, Buddy Petit, Lorenzo Staulz, Dandy Lewis.

Sam Dutrey, Sr., s, cl; Walter Pichon, William Houston, p; Pops Foster, Sylvester Handy, Al Morgan, Ransom Knowling, sb, tu; Emanuel Sayles, Rene Hall, H. E. Minor, Johnny St. Cyr, g, bjo; Louis Barbarin, d.

Dixie Jazz Band (1918–1925), jazz band. Ricard Alexis, c; Sidney Vigne (later Big Eye Louis Nelson), cl; Ernest Kelly or Paul Ben, tb; Lorenzo Staulz, bjo; Little Dad Vincent, g; Little Joe Lindsey, d; Bob Lyons, b, l.

Dixieland Roamers (1920s). In 1923 this group made the first live jazz broadcast from New Orleans, from the Joe Uhalt station atop the Southern Electric Company building next to the DeSoto Hotel. Pinky Gerbrecht, t, l; Ellis Stratakos, tb; Eddie Powers, s; Frank Mutz, p; Ray Bauduc, d; Ed McCarthy, vo.

Dixie Rhythm Band (1930–1936), dance orchestra. Small group that played on lake steamers; it was led by saxman, Harold Dejan and included Casimir Paul, bjo; Lester Santiago, p.

Dixola Jazz Band (mid-1920s–early 1930s), dance orchestra. Howard Reed, t; Chick Johnson, Elwood Taylor, s; Count Cómes, p; Tony Tortorich, d; Leo Donegan, d; Harold Wirth, bjo; Axson Riley, tu.

Dukes of Dixieland (1950 to present), dixieland-novelty. One of the nation's big-name bands, built around the Assunto family. Papa Jac played bjo, tb; son Frank, the leader, played trumpet; and Freddie played trombone. Among the New Orleans musicians who worked in the band are Harry Shields, Tony Parenti, Raymond Burke, Pete Fountain, cl; Stanley Mendelson, Arthur Seelig, Jr., p; Willie Perkins, Buck Rogers, Roger Johnston, d; Tony Balderas, g; Henry Barthels, Martin Abraham, Jr., sb.

Dumaine, Louis, Jazzola Eight (1927–1929), jazz band. Collective personnel: Louis Dumaine, t, l; Earl Humphrey, Yank Johnson, tb; Kaiser Joseph, cl; Clarence Gabriel, g; Leonard Mitchell, bjo; Morris Rouse, p; Joe Howard, sb, tu; Willie Ledet, Jim Willigan, d; Louis James, b.

Revised Original Dixieland Jazz Band (1956)
Making an appearance with Garry Moore on the *I've Got a Secret* TV program are, left to right, J. Russel Robinson, Tony Parenti, Phil Napoleon, Daddy Edwards, Tony Sbarbaro.

Superior Orchestra (1910)
Seated, left to right, are Walter Brundy, Peter Bocage, Richard Payne. Standing, Buddy Johnson, Bunk Johnson, Big Eye Louis Nelson, Billy Marrero.

Louis Armstrong's Hot Five (1926)
Left to right are Johnny St. Cyr, Kid
Ory, Louis Armstrong, Johnny Dodds,
Lil Hardin Armstrong.

The Henry Belas Orchestra (1930s)
Left to right are Henry Belas, Al Moore, Joe Stephens, Raymond Burke, Pee Wee ———. Singer unknown.

140

Papa Celestin's Band (1950s)
Left to right are Happy Goldston, Papa Celestin, Octave Crosby, Alphonse Picou, Roger Wolfe (disc jockey, emcee), Ricard Alexis, Bill Matthews.

The Crawford-Ferguson Night Owls (1963)
Left to right, seated, are Edmond Souchon (not a regular member), Bill Humphries, Leonard Ferguson. Standing, Paul Crawford, Jack Bachman, Hank Kmen, Sherwood Mangiapane.

Sharkey and His Kings of Dixieland (1949)
Left to right are Santo Pecora, Monk Hazel, Chink Martin, Sharkey, Jeff Riddick, Lester Bouchon.

The Johnny Wiggs Orchestra (1950)
Left to right, Edmond Souchon, Ray Bauduc, Johnny Wiggs, Stanley Mendelson, Harry Shields, Tom Brown, Sherwood Mangiapane.

The Dixola Novelty Orchestra (1924)
In the Tip-Top Room at the Grunewald Hotel are, left to right, Howard Reed, Leo Donegan, Axson Riley, Count Cómes, Harold Wirth, Chick Johnson, Elwood Taylor.

Dumaine-Houston Jazz Band (1930s), dance orchestra. Louis Dumaine, t, and Fats Houston, d, led the band jointly. They booked jobs and hired musicians to fill them. Willie Joseph, cl, was a steady employee.

Eagle Band (1900–1917), jazz band. Partial collective personnel: Bunk Johnson, Tig Chambers, Joe Johnson, King Oliver, Frank Keelin, Edward Clem, Buddy Petit, t; Frank Duson, tb, l; Willie Parker, Frank Lewis, Sidney Bechet, Johnny Dodds, Big Eye Louis Nelson, cl; Dandy Lewis, Bill Johnson, Pops Foster, Bob Lyons, sb, tu; Lorenzo Staulz, Brock Mumford, g; Henry Zeno, Chinee Foster, Baby Dodds, d.

Emergency Relief Administration Orchestra (mid-30s). Some ninety musicians on a federal Depression relief project were led first by Pinchback Touro, later by Louis Dumaine. As many as possible of the musicians are identified on the photograph in this volume.

Five Southern Jazzers (about 1919–1924). This band, which played in Chicago, was composed of Frank Christian, t, l; Frank L'Hotag, tb; Johnny Fischer, cl; Ernie Erdman, p; Anton Lada, d. L'Hotag and Erdman are midwesterners.

Fougerat, Tony (early 1920s to 1966), dixieland band. This bandleader supplied music to Orleanians for over forty years. Some of those who worked in his bands are Nappy Lamare, g; Charlie Christian, tb; Willie Guitar, sb; Lester Bouchon, Harry Shields, cl.

Four Hot Hounds (1909–1911), jazz band. A Storyville group usually at Abadie's. Sugar Johnny Smith, c; Wooden Joe Nicholas, cl; Richard M. Jones, p, l; Ernest Rogers, d. Sometimes King Oliver replaced Smith.

French Market Jazz Band. Street band playing for tips in French Quarter in ancient tradition. Wes Mix, Frank Minyard, t; Scott Hill, tb, l; Otis Bazoon, cl; David Lastie, s; Les Muscutt, bjo, g; Pete Vriondes, tu; Walter Lastie, d.

Friars' Society Orchestra. See New Orleans Rhythm Kings.

Gehl, Buddy, and His Eight Winds. A college-boy band of the 1920s, composed mainly of Tulane students, that played many dance and theater dates over a five-year span. Most of its members have become New Orleans business or professional men. Its steadiest members were Herman Kohlmeyer, Dick Mackie, t; Gerald "Skinny" Andrus, Dede Newman, cl, s; Louis Kohlmeyer, tu; Preacher Wadsworth, p; Rene Gelpi, bjo; Buddy Gehl, d, l.

Golden Leaf Band (1920–1921), jazz band. Lee Collins, t; Jim Robinson, tb; Sidney Vigne, cl; Sidney Brown, v; Bud Russell, sb; Arthur Ogle, d, g; Jesse Jackson, bjo, l. Sometimes Punch Miller, t, and Happy Goldston, d, substituted.

Golden Rule Orchestra (1905), dance orchestra. Alcide Frank, v, l; Adolphe Alexander, Sr., t; Big Eye Louis Nelson, cl; James Brown, sb; Joe Brooks, g; John Vigne, d. A revival of the band in 1920 included Dennis Harris and

The Irving Fazola Orchestra
At Tony's Cafe on Canal Boulevard are, left to right, Joe Rotis, Howard Reed, Irving Fazola, Charlie Duke, Ogden Lafaye.

Louis Cottrell, Jr., cl, s; Lawrence Marrero, bjo; Cié Frazier, d.

Halfway House Orchestra (1923–1928), dance orchestra. Partial collective personnel: Abbie Brunies, c, l; Leon Roppolo, Charles Cordilla, Sidney Arodin, cl, s; Joe Loyacano, as; Merritt Brunies, vt; Bill Eastwood, Angelo Palmisano, bjo; Mickey Marcour, Red Long, p; Deacon Loyacano, Chink Martin, Bud Loyacano, sb; Monk Hazel, d, mel, c; Leo Adde, Emmett Rogers, d.

Hamilton, Pop, Band (1930s). This band, which lasted almost a year before being killed off by the Depression, included Lumas Hamilton, l, t; Andrew Johnson, d; Al Smith, ts; Pop Hamilton, tu; Pinky Alberts, t; Patty Whisker, p; and others.

Hightower, Willie. See American Stars.

Hill City Band (1906), dance orchestra. Andrew Kimball, c; John Hime, Hamp Benson, tb; Charles McCurdy, cl; Charles Pierson (sometimes Coochie Martin), g; Cato, d.

Hollywood Orchestra (1929–1931), dance orchestra. A large dance band headed by Mike Delay, c, featuring Louis Nelson, tb, and Andrew Morgan, cl, s.

Hyman, Johnny, Bayou Stompers (1927), dixieland recording band. Johnny Wiggs, c, l; Charlie Hartmann, tb; Elery Maser, cl; Alvin Gautreaux, har; Horace Diaz, p; Nappy Lamare, g; Monk Hazel, d.

Imperial Orchestra (1901–1908), dance orchestra. Partial collective personnel: Manuel Perez, c, l; George Filhe, Buddy Johnson, tb; George Baquet, Big Eye Louis Nelson, cl; James A. Palao, v; Adolphe Alexander, Sr., bh; Rene Baptiste, g; Jimmy Brown, sb; John Vigne, John Mac-Murray, d.

Invincibles String Band (1912–1921). This group evolved into the New Orleans Owls. Collective personnel: Johnny Wiggs, Eblen Rau, Frank Ferrer, Benjy White, Ed Pinac, Donald Coleman, v; Bill Kleppinger, mdl; Fred Overing, bjo, mdl; Ernest Guidry, 6-string bjo; Rene Gelpi, 5-string bjo; Charles Hardy, tar, u; Monk Smith, g, u; Rollo Tichenor, Lorimer Neff, g; Red Mackie, sb, g, bjo; Mose Ferrer, p; Earl Crumb, d.

Jazzola Eight. See Dumaine, Louis, Jazzola Eight.

Jazzola Six (1919–1921), dixieland band. Johnny Bayersdorffer, c, l; Paul Cinquemano, tb; Johnny Beninate, cl; Billy Braun, p; Roscoe Legnon, sb; Buster Klein, d.

Dejan's Original Moonlight Serenaders (early 1930s)
Left to right are Arnaul Thomas, Leo Dejan, Harold Dejan, Henry Casenave, Sidney Cates.

Jones-Collins Astoria Hot Eight (1927). Organized for a single recording session. Lee Collins, t, coleader; Sidney Arodin, cl; Ted Purnell, as; David Jones, ts, co-leader; Joe Robichaux, p; Emanuel Sayles, bjo; Al Morgan, b; Albert Martin, d.

Laine, Alfred, Orchestra (late 1920s–early 1930s), dixieland band. Alfred Laine, t, c, l; Sanford Mello, tb; Red Lagman, cl, s; Bud Loyacano, sb, tu; Jack Treveque, bjo; Charlie Kuhl, p; Jimmy Cozzens, d. Sometimes Harry Shields or Raymond Burke, cl, joined the band.

Last Straws (1950s–1960s). Moose Zanco, c; Nick Gagliardi, tb; Bris Jones, cl; Bill Lee, ss; Bob Casey or Frank de la Houssaye, p; Al Lobre or John Chaffe, bjo; Bob Ice, sb, tu, l; Bob McIntyre or J. J. Joyce, d.

Lewis, Foster, Jazz Band (early 1920s). Dude Foster, t; Zeb Lenares, cl; Tink Baptiste, p; Leo Songier, bjo; One-Eye Babe Philip, sb; Foster Lewis, d, l.

Lewis, George, Ragtime Jazz Band (from early 1940s). Partial collective personnel: Percy Humphrey, Thomas Jefferson, Coo Coo Talbert, Kid Howard, Punch Miller, t; Jim Robinson, Albert Warner, Louis Nelson, tb;

George Lewis, cl, l; Alton Purnell, Joe Robichaux, Charlie Hamilton, p; Lawrence Marrero, Emanuel Sayles, Creole George Guesnon, g, bjo; Slow Drag Pavageau, Papa John Joseph, sb; Joe Watkins, Baby Dodds, Edgar Mosley, d.

Liberty Bell Orchestra (1919–1920), jazz band. Wesley Don, t, l; Jack Blount, v, mgr; Freddie Miller, tb; Bill Dimes, cl, mgr; Little Dad Vincent, bjo; Eddie Gilmore, sb; Joe Rena, d. Sometimes Jim Robinson, tb; Blind Freddie Small, cl, har.

Lincoln Band (1930s), large concert or dance orchestra. This title was always used for bands led by Pinchback Touro, v. Willie Pajeaud, t, and Sunny Henry, tb, were mainstays. Sometimes Lawrence Duhé played clarinet.

Lindsey's, Kid, Jazz Band (1917–1918). Louis Armstrong, t; Maurice French, tb; Louis Prevost, cl; Son Carr, b; Little Joe Lindsey, d, l; various guitarists, banjoists.

Louisiana Five (early 1919), dixieland band. This band, organized just to make records, never played in New Orleans. Its two Orleanians were Yellow Nunez, cl, and Anton Lada, d, l.

145

The Jazzola Six (1918)
Left to right are Roscoe Legnon, Billy Braun, Johnny Beninate, Johnny Bayersdorffer, Paul Cinquemano, Buster Klein.

Pop Hamilton's Orchestra (1930)
Patty Whisker sits at the piano. Others, left to right, are leader Lumas Hamilton, Andrew Johnson, Dave ——, Al Smith, Pop Hamilton, Pinky Alberts, —— Johnson (emcee), —— Kelley.

Jelly Roll Morton's Red Hot Peppers (1920s)
Jelly Roll, seated, lectures band members, left to right, Omer Simeon, André Hillaire, John Lindsay, Johnny St. Cyr, Kid Ory, George Mitchell. All but Mitchell are native Orleanians.

Louisiana Repertory Jazz Ensemble. Formed in 1980, originally as a project of the Tulane University Jazz Archive, this organization dedicated itself to recreating the sounds of the classic New Orleans jazz band of the twentieth century, with emphasis on the music of Jelly Roll Morton, King Oliver, Armand J. Piron, and Sam Morgan, using as its repertoire arrangements from the archive's extensive collection. The band's home base has been the Maple Leaf Bar on Oak Street in Carrollton, where it has played on Wednesday nights since its debut. Collective personnel has included Norbert Susemihl, Wes Mix, Leroy Jones, t; Tom Ebbert, Freddie Lonzo, tb; Fred Starr, Michael White, reeds; John Royen, Steve Pistorius, Morten Gunnar Larsen, p; John Chaffe, bjo, g, mdl; Curt Jerde, sb, tu; Sherwood Mangiapane, sb; J. J. Joyce, d.

Louisiana Shakers (early 1930s), rock-and-roll band. A forerunner of today's mechanized, commercial groups, organized by sax player John Handy and including his bassist brother Sylvester.

Magnolia Orchestra (1909–1914), dance orchestra. Partial collective personnel: Emile Bigard, v, l; King Oliver, c; Willie Pajeaud, c, t; Big Boy Goudie, Dave Depass, Lorenzo Tio, Sr., George Baquet, cl; Zue Robertson, Honore Dutrey, Yank Johnson, tb; Louis Keppard, Johnny St. Cyr, g, bjo; Pops Foster, Thomas Copland, sb; Arnold Depass, Happy Goldston, d.

Magnolia Sweets (1910), jazz band. Tig Chambers, c, l; Ernest Kelly (sometimes Yank Johnson) tb; Zeb Lenares, cl; various rhythm sections.

Maple Leaf Orchestra (1918–late 1920s), dance orchestra. Collective personnel: Emile Bigard, v; Hippolyte Charles, Willie Pajeaud, Sidney Desvigne, t; Vic Gaspard, tb; Lorenzo Tio, Jr., Albert Nicholas, Sidney Vigne, Sam Dutrey, Sr., cl; Willie Bontemps, Willie Santiago, bjo; Camilla Todd, Steve Lewis, Udell Wilson, p; Oak Gaspard, sb, l; Louis Cottrell, Sr., Alec Bigard, Dave Ogden, d.

Marable, Fate (1910–1925), dance orchestra. Marable ran the Streckfus steamship lines band, sometimes called **Marable's Ten Bold Harmony Kings,** The **SS** *Capitol* **Harmony Syncopators, Marable's Cotton Pickers, Marable's** *Capitol* **Revue Orchestra.** Among the New Orleans musicians who played in the Marable orchestras were Louis Armstrong, Red Allen, Peter Bocage, Manuel Perez, Joe Howard, Amos White, Albert Duconge, Sidney Desvigne, t; Honore Dutrey, Bebé Ridgley, Bill Matthews, tb; Willie James Humphrey, Johnny Dodds, Sam Dutrey, Sr., cl; David Jones, s, mel; Willie Foster, g; Johnny St. Cyr, bjo; Pops Foster, Albert Morgan, Henry Kimball, Wellman Braud, sb, tu; Baby Dodds, Walter Brundy, Zutty Singleton, d.

Melody Masters. Band that played for dancing on the steamer *Greater New Orleans.* Leon Prima, Sharkey, t;

The Peerless Orchestra (about 1911)
Posing in City Park, New Orleans, are: front row, left to right, John Vigne, Charles McCurdy, Armand J. Piron, Coochie Martin; back row, Vic Gaspard, Andrew Kimball, Oak Gaspard.

Digger Laine, tb; Charlie Cordilla, cl, s; Nino Picone, Joe Loyacano, s; Freddie Neumann, p; Freddie Loyacano, bjo; Chink Martin, sb, tu; Leo Adde, d.

Melon Pickers (late 1920s–early 1930s), dance orchestra. Bill Naquin, t; Raymond Burke, cl; Julius Chevez, p; Henry Welde, g, l; John Bell, sb; Al Doria, d.

Miller, Johnny, Frolickers (1927–1928). Sharkey, t; Sidney Arodin, cl; Hal Jordy, s; Johnny Miller, p, l; Steve Brue, bjo; Martin Abraham, Sr., b; Leo Adde, d.

Miller, Punch, Jazz Band (1920), jazz band. Punch Miller, c, l; Eddie Morris, tb; Georgia Boy Boyd, cl; Walter Preston, bjo; Joe Gable, sb; Arnold Depass, d.

Moonlight Serenaders (1926–1935), dance orchestra. Originally led by George Augustin, sb, bjo, later by Armand J. Piron, v. Among its regulars: Albert Snaer, t; Eddie Summers, tb; Alfred Williams, d.

Morgan, Sam (1920s), dance orchestra. Collective personnel: Sam Morgan, t, l; Isaiah Morgan, t; Jim Robinson, Yank Johnson, tb; Joseph Watson, cl; Andrew Morgan, cl, ts; Earl Fouché, cl, as; Tink Baptiste, Walter Decou, p; Sidney Brown, Tom Copland, sb; Johnny Dave, Guyé

Rapp, Creole George Guesnon, g, bjo; Shine Williams, Alfred Williams, Rudolph Bodoyer, Roy Evans, d.

Morgan's Euphonic Syncopators (1917). All but the pianist in this Chicago band are Orleanians: Fred Neuroth, c; Emile Christian, tb; Red Rowling, cl; Ernie Erdman, p; Billy Lambert, d.

National Orchestra (1914–1932). Collective Personnel: Martin Manuel Gabriel, Sr., Freddie Keppard, c; Zue Robertson, Adolphe White, Vic Gaspard, August Lanoix, Earl Humphrey, tb; Wade Whaley, Martin Gabriel, Jr., Dude Gabriel, cl; Manny Gabriel, Jr., cl, d; Paul Beaulieu, Alberta Gabriel, Clarence Gabriel, p; Johnny St. Cyr, g; Clarence Gabriel, Jr., bjo; Tom Copland, August Lanoix, Jim Glenne, Oak Gaspard, Thomas Mitchell, Percy Gabriel, b; Joe Welch, d.

Naylor's Seven Aces (1920s), recording group. Oliver Naylor, v, p, l; Pinky Gerbrecht, c; Charles Hartmann, tb; Jerry Richel, s; Jules Bauduc, bjo; Ray Bauduc or Louis Darrough, d. Sometimes Newton Richardson played tenor sax.

New Camellia Jazz Band. Organized in 1978 by English trumpeter, Clive Wilson, this band is really a lineal

The Sam Morgan Jazz Band (1920s)
Seated, left to right, are Shine Williams, Isaiah Morgan, Sam Morgan, Earl Fouché, Andrew Morgan, and Johnny Dave. Jim Robinson and Sidney Brown stand at rear.

descendant of the Original Tuxedo Orchestra, which survived under the successive leaderships of Papa Celestin, Eddie Pierson, and Albert French. It plays frequently at the Duke's Place on the roof of the Monteleone Hotel. Personnel has included leader Wilson, Frog Joseph, tb; Brother Cornbread Thomas, Tony Mitchell, cl; Jeannette Kimball (of the Original Tuxedo Orchestra), p; Les Muscutt, g, bjo; Chester Zardis, Frank Fields, sb; Louis Barbarin, d.

New Leviathan Oriental Fox-Trot Orchestra. A large orchestra playing tunes of the period 1890–1920, including classic rags and Jelly Roll Morton numbers. Plays numerous sellout concerts in New Orleans area. Talented comic vocalist, George Schmidt.

New Orleans Creole Jazz Band (1925), dance orchestra. Played for dancing at Spanish Fort. Amos White, t, l; Willie Willigan, c; Sunny Henry, tb; Barney Bigard, cl; Willa Bart, Red Dugie, p; Bob Ysaguirre, sb.

New Orleans Harmony Kings (1920s), dixieland band. Sharkey, t; Sidney Arodin, cl; Freddie Neumann, p; Joe Capraro, bjo; Chink Martin, tu; Augie Schellang, d.

New Orleans Jazz Band (1918–1922), dixieland band. Co-op band composed of Frank Christian, c; Frank L'Hotag, tb; Achille Baquet, cl; Jimmy Durante, p; Johnny Stein, d. Durante (the comedian) and L'Hotag are not from New Orleans.

New Orleans Joymakers. Sensationally successful on European tours. Percy Humphrey, t; Louis Nelson, tb; Orange Kellin, cl; Lars Edegran, p; Father Al Lewis, g, bjo; Chester Zardis, b; Louis Barbarin, d.

New Orleans Owls (1922–1929), dance orchestra. Collective personnel: Dick Mackie, Red Bolman, Johnny Wiggs, Bill Padron, c; Frank Netto, tb; Jimmy Rush, Pinky Vidacovich, Eddie Miller, cl, s; Johnny Carughi, Eblen Rau, Benjy White, v; Siegfried Christensen, Mose Ferrer, Ar-

The Jimmy Palao Band (about 1900)
Band members seated behind the two unidentified children are, left to right, Edward "Chico" Claiborne, Louis Rodriguez, Joe Smith, and Rene Baptiste. Standing are Willie Parker, James A. Palao, and Toby Nuenutt.

The Original Tuxedo Orchestra (about 1928)
Left to right are Bill Matthews, Guy Kelly, leader Papa Celestin, Jeannette Salvant (Kimball), Narvin Kimball, Joe Lawrence, Chinee Foster, Joe Rouzon, Simon Marrero, Clarence Hall.

Sidney Desvigne's SS *Capitol* Orchestra (about 1931)
Left to right are Louis Nelson, Eugene Porter, Gene Ware, Emanuel Sayles, Adolphe Duconge, leader Desvigne, Marcellus Wilson, Ransom Knowling, Tats Alexander, Ted Purnell, Walt Cosby.

mand Hug, p; Dan Leblanc, Red Mackie, tu, sb; Rene Gelpi, Monk Smith, Nappy Lamare, Angelo Palmisano, bjo, g; John Laporte, d; Earl Crumb, d, l.

New Orleans Ragtime Orchestra (organized 1967). Plays classic rags, cakewalks, other material of the era 1890–1915. Performs over United States and Europe. Bill Russell, v; Lionel Ferbos, t; Paul Crawford, tb; Orange Kellin, cl; Lars Edegran, p, l; Walter Payton, Jr., b; John Robichaux, d, vo.

New Orleans Rhythm Kings (early 1920s), dance orchestra. Also known as **Friar's Society Orchestra**. Partial collective personnel: Paul Mares, c, l; Wingy Manone, t; George Brunies, Santo Pecora, tb; Leon Roppolo, Charles Cordilla, cl, s; Red Long, p; Steve Brown, Deacon Loyacano, Bonnie Pottle, Chink Martin, sb, tu; Leo Adde, Monk Hazel, d.

Nola Band (1920s), dance orchestra. Peter Lacaze, t, l; Ricard Alexis, t; Henry Russ, t, c; Mercedes Fields, p; Charles McCurdy or Alphonse Picou would frequently play clarinet. The other musicians were pickup, depending on the occasion.

Noone-Petit Orchestra (1916), jazz band. Buddy Petit, c, coleader; Honore Dutrey, tb; Jimmie Noone, cl, coleader, were the front-line men. Rhythm sections added as convenient.

Olivier, Adam, Orchestra (1892–1910), dance orchestra. Many small dance groups played under this name, led by cornetist-violinist Olivier. Most of the musicians were not jazzmen, but both Bunk Johnson (c) and Tony Jackson (p) made their debuts in this band.

Olympia Orchestra (1900–1914), dance orchestra. Partial collective personnel: Freddie Keppard, c, l; King Oliver, c; Joseph Petit, Zue Robertson, Eddie Atkins, Eddie Vinson, tb; Big Eye Louis Nelson, Alphonse Picou, Lorenzo Tio, Jr., Sidney Bechet, Charles McCurdy, cl; Armand J. Piron, v, l (1912); Louis Keppard, Willie Santiago, Bud Scott, g, bjo; Steve Lewis, Clarence Williams, p; John Lindsay, Billy Marrero, sb; John Vigne, Louis Cottrell, Sr., Ninesse Trepagnier, Henry Zeno, d.

Olympia Orchestra (2) (1927–1932), jazz band. Basic personnel: Coo Coo Talbert or Dee Dee Pierce, t; George Lewis, cl; Lester Santiago, p; Arnold Depass, d.

151

Prima-Sharkey Orchestra (1930)
At the Little Club are, front row, left to right, Charlie Hartmann, Sharkey, Leon Prima, Irving Fazola, Dave Winstein, Nino Picone. Standing at back are Augie Schellang, Louis Masinter, Freddie Loyacano, Frank Pinero.

Don Albert's Orchestra (about 1933)
Left to right are Ferdinand Dejan, Arthur Derbigny, Albert Martin, Jimmy Johnson, Hiram Harding, Don Albert, Herb Hall, Louis Cottrell, Jr., Frank Jacky, Albert Freeman, Sidney Hansell.

152

The Woodland Band (1905)
Kid Ory's first band poses at LaPlace, La. Left to right are Rabbit Robinson, Kid Ory, Chif Matthews, Raymond Brown, Stonewall Matthews, Foster Lewis.

Oriental Orchestra (1928–1938), jazz band. Lawrence Toca, t; Eddie Summers, tb; Melvin Frank, cl; Bill Hamilton, g, l; Albert Jiles, d.

Original Creole Orchestra (*ca.* 1913–1917), vaudeville band. Collective personnel: Freddie Keppard, c; James A. Palao, v; Eddie Vinson, George Filhe, tb; George Baquet, Jimmie Noone, Big Eye Louis Nelson, cl; Bill Johnson, sb, l; Giggy Williams, g; Dink Johnson, d.

Original Dixieland Jazz Band (1915–early 1920s). Collective personnel: Nick La Rocca, Sharkey, c, t; Daddy Edwards, Emile Christian, tb; Yellow Nunez, Larry Shields, cl; Henry Ragas, p; Johnny Stein, d, l; Tony Sbarbaro, d. This band made the first jazz records.

Original New Orleans Jazz Band (*ca.* 1916). Merritt Brunies, c, l; Emile Christian, tb; Johnny Fischer, cl; Freddie Rose, p; Freddie Williams, d.

Original Tuxedo Orchestra (from 1913). Partial collective personnel: Papa Celestin, t, vo, l; Guy Kelly, Kid Shots Madison, t; Ricard Alexis, t, sb; Bill Matthews, Eddie Pierson, tb; Clarence Hall, Cecil Thornton, Brother Cornbread Thomas, Tats Alexander, Alphonse Picou, cl, s; Mercedes Fields, Emma Barrett, Jeannette Kimball, Lester Santiago, Joe Robichaux, p; Sidney Brown, sb; Albert French, Narvin Kimball, bjo; Louis Barbarin, Happy Goldston, d; Joe Strohter, d, slidewhistle. See also Ridgley's Original Tuxedo Jazz Band.

Peerless Orchestra (1905–1913), dance orchestra. Collective personnel: Andrew Kimball, Nenny Coycault, c; Vic Gaspard, George Filhe, Hamp Benson, tb; Charles McCurdy, cl; Armand J. Piron, v, l (1910); Peter Bocage, v; Bab Frank, pc; Coochie Martin, g; Oak Gaspard, Bill Johnson, sb; Walter Brundy, John Vigne, Bebé Matthews, d.

Piron, A. J., Orchestra (1918–1928), dance orchestra. Partial collective personnel: Peter Bocage, Willie Edwards, c, t; John Lindsay, tb, sb, tu; Lorenzo Tio, Jr., Louis Warnick, cl, s; Charles Bocage, John Marrero, Johnny St. Cyr, bjo, g; Steve Lewis, Arthur Campbell, p; Bob Ysaguirre, Henry Bocage, sb, tu; Louis Cottrell, Sr., Paul Barbarin, Cié Frazier, Bill Matthews, d; A. J. Piron, v, l.

Primrose Orchestra (1912), dance orchestra. A small band that worked in Storyville cabarets. Herb Lindsay, v, l; Joe Johnson, c; Hamp Benson, tb; George Williams, g, bjo; Cato, d.

Razzy Dazzy Spasm Band (1890s). A skiffle band made up of teenage boys under the leadership of Stalebread Lacoume.

Reliance Band (*ca.* 1892–1913), dixieland band, dance orchestra. Papa Laine operated as many as six units of this organization simultaneously. Front lines were drawn from members of the Reliance Brass Band. Others added for dance units included Henry Ragas, Norman Brownlee, Johnny Provenzano, Jules Reiner, Tom Zimmerman, p;

Frank Christian's New Orleans Jazz Band (1921 or 1922)
The band was appearing in Chicago. Left to right are Anton Lada, Frank L'Hotag, Frank Christian, Johnny Fischer, Ernie Erdman.

Alfred Laine's Orchestra (1920s)
Left to right, seated, are Jimmy Cozzens, Red Lagman, Alfred Laine, Charlie Kuhl. Standing are Samford Mello, Bud Loyacano, Jack Treveque.

Johnny Bayersdorffer's Orchestra (about 1922)
At Tokyo Gardens, Old Spanish Fort, are, left to right, Chink Martin, Tom Brown, Johnny Bayersdorffer, Leo Adde, Johnny Miller, Steve Loyacano, Nunzio Scaglione.

Dominick Barocco, Joe Guiffre, Stalebread Lacoume, Jim Ruth, g, bjo; Joe Barocco, Steve Brown, Jules Cassard, John Guiffre, Willie Guitar, Deacon Loyacano, Bud Loyacano, sb, tu; Herman Ragas, sb; Dave Perkins, Tim Harris, Buster Klein, Anton Lada, Buddy Rogers, Emmett Rogers, Tony Sbarbaro, Johnny Stein, Diddie Stephens, Ragbaby Stephens, d.

Ridgley's Original Tuxedo Jazz Band (1925), dance orchestra. A group that split from the Celestin-led Tuxedo Orchestra. Partial collective personnel: Kid Shots Madison, Ricard Alexis, t; Bebé Ridgley, tb, l; Kaiser Joseph, cl, s; Emma Barrett, p; Willie Bontemps, bjo; Simon Marrero, sb, tu; Bill Willigan, Bebé Matthews, d.

Robichaux, John (1895–1927), dance orchestra. Partial collective personnel: John Robichaux, v, l; Wendell MacNeil, v; Arnold Metoyer, James MacNeil, James Williams, Andrew Kimball, Charlie Love, George McCullum, Sr., c, t; Baptiste DeLisle, Harrison Barnes, Vic Gaspard, Honore Dutrey, John Lindsay, tb; Charles McCurdy, Alphonse Picou, Lorenzo Tio, Jr., Sam Dutrey, Sr., Wade Whaley, George Baquet, cl; Henry Kimball, Oak Gaspard, Paul Dominguez, Sr., George Augustin, Albert Glenny, sb; Bud Scott, Coochie Martin, g; Lawrence Marrero, bjo; Albert Carroll, Paul Beaulieu, p; Dee Dee Chandler, Happy Bolton, Cié Frazier, Alec Bigard, Louis Cottrell, Sr., Walter Brundy, Zutty Singleton, d.

Ross, Sam, Orchestra (1910–1921). This band from "over the river" was distinguished mainly by the presence of Jimmy Noone who started his career playing in it at Cut Off, Louisiana, his hometown. Personnel at its peak period consisted of Sam Ross, c, l; Milton Martin, tb; Jimmie Noone, cl; Jackson Butler, b; Skeeter Jackson, g; Sonny Hampton, d.

Schilling, Happy (1910–1926), dance orchestra. Partial collective personnel: Johnny Wiggs, Richie Brunies, Johnny Lala, Henry Knecht, Arnold Metoyer, c, t; Monk Hazel, c, mel, d; Bob Aquilera, tb; Happy Schilling, tb, l; Achille Baquet, George Schilling, Jr., Johnny Fischer, Elery Maser, cl, s; Clay Pinner, tu; Frank Pinero, p; Freddie Loyacano, g, bjo; Johnny Frisco, d.

Security Orchestra (1900s), dance orchestra. A small, short-lived group, organized, led, and managed by trombonist Joseph Petit.

Silver Leaf Orchestra (1897–1917), dance orchestra. Hippolyte Charles, c; Adam Lambert, vt; Sam Dutrey, Sr., cl; Albert Baptiste, v, l; Oscar Robinson, bjo, g; Johnny Predonce, sb, l; Ernest Rogers, d. Others who sometimes played instead of the regulars: Honore Dutrey, tb; Phil Nickerson, bjo; George Sayles, g; Paul Barbarin, d. Johnny Predonce took over the leadership of this band in 1918.

New Orleans Owls (early 1920s)
Left to right are Monk Smith, leader Earl Crumb, Benjy White, Mose Ferrer, Rene Gelpi, Eblen Rau, Dick Mackie.

Original New Orleans Jazz Band (1916–1917)
Band Members appearing in Chicago are, left to right, Johnny Fischer, Freddie Rose, Merritt Brunies, Emile Christian, Freddie Williams.

New Orleans Owls (1928)
Left to right, standing, are John Laporte, Eddie Miller, Frank Netto, Armand Hug, Bill Padron. Angelo Palmisano is seated at front.

Happy Schilling's Orchestra (about 1924)
Happy Schilling sits holding the euphonium. Others, left to right, are Elery Maser, Monk Hazel, Johnny Wiggs, Clay Pinner, Freddie Loyacano, George Schilling, Jr., Frank Pinero.

Norman Brownlee Orchestra (about 1921)
Bill Eastwood, seated, is surrounded by, left to right, Alonzo Crombie, Emmett Hardy, Billy Braun, Norman Brownlee, and George Barth.

Tony Parenti's Symphonic Dance Orchestra (1922–1923)
Appearing at the Cave in the Grunewald Hotel are, left to right, Johnny Bayersdorffer, George Traiy, Charlie Hartmann, Wilbur Dinkel, Tony Parenti, Sam LaNasa, Bill Miller, Joe Hartman.

The Melon Pickers (1930s)
Left to right are leader Henry Waelde, John Bell, Raymond Burke, Al Doria, Bill Naquin, Julius Chevez.

Six and 7/8 String Band (from 1911). Original group: Bob Reynolds, g; Harry Reynolds, mdl; Hilton "Midget" Harrison, Roland Rexach, v; Charles Hardy, u, tar; Bill Gibbens, g, mdl; Bernie Shields, bjo, mdl, steel g, z; Shields O'Reardon, mdl; Edmond Souchon, 12-string g. Partial collective personnel: Earl Crumb, bjo, d; Albert Moustier, u; Wilfred Sancho, mdl, v, u; Howard McCaleb, g, vo; Alton Nall, g, u; Bill Kleppinger, mdl; Red Mackie, sb; Percy McCay, Thompson McCay, g, sb; Marie Souchon, p, vo; Ed Pinac, v; Ruth Hardy, p, vo.

Society Jazz Band. An international band with Tony Fougerat (t), Ernest Poree (s), and Melvin Yancy (b) of New Orleans; Ron Simpson (g, bjo) and Andrew Hall (d) of England; and Frank Naundorf (tb) of Germany. This band has been playing regularly since 1974 at the Maple Leaf Club in the Carrollton section of New Orleans.

Stratakos, Ellis, Orchestra (late 1920s–early 1930s), dance orchestra. Partial collective personnel: Johnny Wiggs, Louis Prima, Howard Reed, c, t; Ellis Stratakos, tb, v, l; Irving Fazola, Dave Winstein, Johnny Reininger, Joe Loyacano, Eddie Powers, cl, s; Joe Wolfe, Freddie Neumann, p; Frank Federico, Al Hessemer, Freddie Loyacano, g, bjo; Freddie Chretien, v; Louis Masinter, Don Peterson, tu, sb; Augie Schellang, Von Gammon, d.

Superior Orchestra (ca. 1908–1913), dance orchestra. Collective personnel: Bunk Johnson, Nenny Coycault, c; Buddy Johnson, tb; Big Eye Louis Nelson, George Baquet, cl; Adolphe Alexander, Sr., bh; Peter Bocage, v, l; Richard Payne, g; Billy Marrero, sb, mgr; Walter Brundy, d.

Susquehanna Band (1923–1925). Worked on the lake steamer *Susquehanna.* Its basic members were: Pete Peccopia, t; Benny Deichman, tb; Johnny Palisier, cl; Bill Farrell, p; Dominick Barocco, g, bjo, mdl, l; Joe Barocco, sb, tu; Ferdie Knecht, d.

Theodore, Elton, Orchestra (early 1920s), jazz band. Among the members of this Algiers, La., based band were Kid Thomas, t; Loochie Jackson, tb; Steve Angrum, cl; Elton Theodore, bjo, l; Tete Rouchon, sb, tu; Tommy Henderson, d.

Tio-Doublet Orchestra (1888–1890), dance orchestra. Charles Doublet, c; Anthony Doublet, v; Anthony Page, tb; Lorenzo Tio, Sr., Luis Tio, cl; Dee Dee Chandler, d.

Tio-Doublet String Band (1889), dance quartet. A. L. Tio, Anthony Doublet, v; Professor William J. Nickerson, viola; Paul Dominguez, Sr., sb.

The Elton Theodore Orchestra (1921)
Seated, left to right, are Tommy Henderson, Steve Angrum, Kid Thomas. Standing, Loochie Jackson, Elton Theodore, Tete Rouchon. The band was from Algiers, La.

Red Bolman Orchestra (1931)
On the bandstand at the Little Club are, left to right, Digger Laine, Luther Lamar, Steve Brue, Red Bolman, Monk Hazel, Gene Meyer, Joe Wolfe, Nino Picone, Sal Scorsone.

The Princeton Revellers (about 1922)
Seated, left to right, are Vic Leglise, Steve Brue, Bert Peck. Standing are Bill Padron, Paul Pique, Pinky Vidacovich.

Triangle Band (1917–1925). Dominated the jazz activities in the Irish Channel during its period. Basic personnel: Tony Magiotta, c; Charles Christian, tb; Sal Magiotta, cl, s; Tony Schiro, g, bjo; Bud Loyacano, sb, tu; Louis Stephens, d.

Tulane Orchestra (1906–1919), jazz band. Loosely organized group that played irregularly, led by Amos Riley, t. Usually included Alcide Landry, t; Kid Avery, tb; Sam Dutrey, Sr., cl; Alex Scott, sb; Big Cato, bjo; Cato, d.

Tuxedo Orchestra (from 1910), dance orchestra. Partial collective personnel: Papa Celestin, t, l; Ricard Alexis, Kid Shots Madison, Guy Kelly, Kildee Holloway, Joe Howard, t; August Rousseau, Yank Johnson, Bebé Ridgley (l), George Filhe, Bill Matthews, Eddie Pierson, tb; Polo Barnes, Sidney Carriere, Clarence Hall, Cecil Thornton, Joe Rouzon, Tats Alexander, Willard Thoumy, Brother Cornbread Thomas, cl, s; Jeannette Kimball, Emma Barrett, Mercedes Fields, Lester Santiago, p; John Marrero, Willie Bontemps, Johnny St. Cyr, Albert French, g, bjo; Simon Marrero, Narvin Kimball, Jim Little, sb, tu; Henry Zeno, Chinee Foster, Happy Goldston, Louis Barbarin, d.

Watzke, King (1903–1908), dixieland band. Played lots of original material by the leader. None of the tunes had names—just numbers. Basic personnel: King Watzke, v; Jimmy Kendall, t; Freddie Burns, cl; Buzz Harvey or Emile Bigard, sb; Jimmy Ruth or Pat Shields, g. Sometimes Larry Shields played with this band.

Wiggs, Johnny, and His New Orleans Music (from about 1949). Wiggs's early bands are listed under either Johnny Hyman or the Bayou Stompers. Partial collective personnel: Johnny Wiggs, c, l; Tom Brown, Digger Laine, Santo Pecora, Charlie Miller, Emile Christian, Paul Crawford, tb; Raymond Burke, Harry Shields, Boojie Centobie, Lester Bouchon, Irving Fazola, cl; Armand Hug, Stanley Mendelson, Julius Chevez, Jeff Riddick, Jake Sciambra, p; Edmond Souchon, g, bjo; Chink Martin, Deacon Loyacano, Sherwood Mangiapane, sb, tu; Ray Bauduc, Von Gammon, Buck Rogers, Freddie King, Eddie Tschantz, Santo Pecoraro, d.

Young Eagles Band (1918), jazz band. Lee Collins, t; Earl Humphrey, tb; John Casimir, cl; Son Thomas, bjo; Pops Foster, sb, tu; Joe Casimir, d.

The New Orleans Harmony Kings (1920s)
Left to right are Freddie Neumann, Chink Martin, Sharkey, Augie Schellang, Sidney Arodin, Joe Capraro.

Ellis Stratakos Orchestra (1929)
Left to right are Louis Masinter, Johnny Reininger, Irving Fazola, Augie Schellang, Ellis Stratakos, Frank Federico, Freddie Neumann, Louis Prima, Dave Winstein.

Young Morgan Band (1921–1925), dance orchestra. Isaiah Morgan, t, l; Jim Robinson, tb; Andrew Morgan, cl; Earl Fouché, Sam Robinson, s; Johnny Dave, bjo; Sidney Brown, sb, tu; Rudolph Bodoyer, d.

Young Olympians (1917–1918), jazz band. Band led by Buddy Petit, c.

Young Superior Band (early 1920s), jazz band. Arthur Derbigny, t; Leonard Bechet, tb, l; Andrew Morgan, cl; Whitey Arcenaux, bjo; Tommy Hudson, sb, tu; Arthur Joseph, d.

Young Tuxedo Orchestra (1920), dance orchestra. Bush Hall, t; Paul Ben, Bob Thomas, tb; Louis Cottrell, Jr., Polo Barnes, Henry Julian, cl, s; Dwight Newman, p; Lawrence Marrero, bjo, l; Eddie Marrero, sb; Cié Frazier, Milford Dolliole, d.

The Original Dixieland Jazz Band (1916)
Left to right are Tony Sbarbaro, Daddy Edwards, Nick La Rocca, Yellow Nunez, Henry Ragas.

The Halfway House Orchestra (1923)
Left to right are Charlie Cordilla, Mickey Marcour, Leon Roppolo, Abbie Brunies, Bill Eastwood, Joe Loyacano, Leo Adde.

Buddy Bolden's Band (about 1902)
Standing, left to right, are Willie Warner, Willie Cornish, Buddy Bolden, Jimmy Johnson. Seated are Frank Lewis, Brock Mumford. This photograph looks as if it had been reversed because the photographer posed the bass and guitar players as though they were playing lefthanded.
Courtesy Bella Cornish

The New Orleans Rhythm Kings (about 1922)
Orleanians in this group are George Brunies, trombone; leader Paul Mares, trumpet; Leon Roppolo, saxophone (seated next to Mares); Steve Brown, sousaphone, string bass. Others are Ben Pollack, drums; Mel Stitzel, piano; Volly De Faut, saxophone; Lew Black, banjo.

The Olympia Orchestra (1915)
Shown are Joe, Ricard, and Peter Alexis.
Courtesy Danny Barker

Johnny Stein's Original Dixieland Jazz Band (1916)
The band was appearing in Chicago. Left to right are Yellow Nunez, Daddy Edwards, Henry Ragas, Nick La Rocca, leader Johnny Stein.
Courtesy Mrs. John P. Hountha

The Original Creole Orchestra (about 1914)
Front row, left to right, are Dink Johnson, leader James A. Palao, Giggy Williams. Rear, Eddie Vinson, Freddie Keppard, George Baquet, Bill Johnson.

Frank and McCurdy's Peerless Orchestra (1906)
Left to right are John Vigne, George Filhe, Charles McCurdy, Andrew Kimball, Bab Frank, Coochie Martin.

Stalebread's Razzy Dazzy Spasm Band (1899)
Second from left is Stalebread Lacoume.

Courtesy Anna Lacoume

The Imperial Orchestra (about 1905)
Left to right are John MacMurray, George Filhe, James A. Palao, Big Eye Louis Nelson, Rene Baptiste, Manuel Perez, Jimmy Brown.

The Original Dixieland Jazz Band in England (1919)
Left to right are Tony Sbarbaro, Emile Christian, Nick La Rocca, Larry Shields, and English pianist Billy Jones.

Nat Towles's Creole Har-mony Kings (1926)
Left to right are Bill Matthews, Herb Morand, Louis Mahier, Wallingford Hughes, Frank Pashley, Nat Towles.

Buddy Petit's Jazz Band (1920)   *Courtesy George Hoefer*
In Mandeville, La., left to right, are Leon René, Eddie "Face-O" Woods, George Washington, Buddy Petit, Buddy Manaday, Edmond Hall, Chester Zardis.

Johnny Bayersdorffer's Orchestra (1924)
At the Tokyo Gardens, left to right, are Charlie Hartmann, Ray Bauduc, Johnny Bayersdorffer, Joe Wolfe, Nappy Lamare, Lester Bouchon, Bill Creger.

Johnny Dodds's New Orleans Jazz Band (1930)   *Courtesy Duncan Schiedt*
In Chicago are, left to right, Baby Dodds, Natty Dominique, Johnny Dodds, Rudolph Reynaud, Lonnie Johnson, Lil Hardin Armstrong.

King Oliver's Creole Jazz Band (early 1920s)
Kneeling in front playing the slide trumpet is Louis Armstrong. The others, left to right, are Honore Dutrey, Baby Dodds, King Oliver, Lil Hardin Armstrong, Bill Johnson, Johnny Dodds.

Four New Orleans Jazz Babies (about 1920)
At the Halfway House are, left to right, Buck Rogers, Abbie Brunies, Mickey Marcour, Stalebread Lacoume.

Courtesy Anna Lacoume

The Crescent City Jazzers (about 1926)
Left to right are Felix Guarino, Stirling Bose, Johnny Riddick, Avery Loposer, Slim Leftwich, Cliff Holman.

The Invincibles (about 1916)
In front, left to right, are Fred Overing, Bill Kleppinger, Monk Smith, Ernest Guidry. In the rear are Lorimer Neff, Frank Ferrer, Rollo Tichenor.

Ridgley's Original Tuxedo Jazz Band (about 1925)
Standing is Jesse Thomas. The others, left to right, are Bill Matthews, Bebé Ridgley, Kid Shots Madison, Kaiser Joseph, Emma Barrett, Arthur Derbigny, unknown saxophonist, Robert Hall, Willie Bontemps.

Armand J. Piron's Society Orchestra (about 1923)
Left to right are Bob Ysaguirre, Lorenzo Tio, Jr., Charlie Bocage, Louis Cottrell, Sr., Piron, Peter Bocage, Steve Lewis, John Lindsay, Louis Warnick.

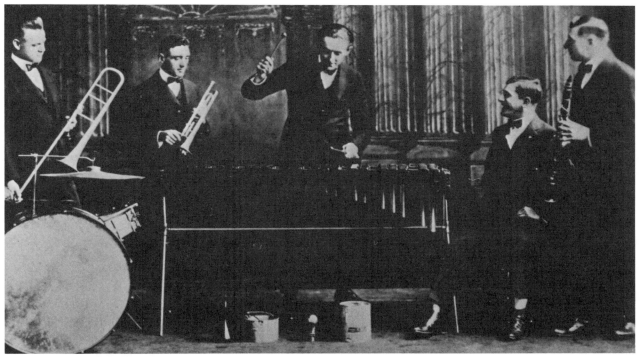

Five Southern Jazzers (1921 or 1922)
Left to right are Frank L'Hotag, Frank Christian, Anton Lada, Ernie Erdman, Johnny Fischer.

Johnny DeDroit Orchestra (about 1921)
Johnny DeDroit is seated at the piano. Looking on are, left to right, Paul DeDroit, Henry Raymond, Frank Froeba, Ellis Stratakos, George Potter.

Dejan's Black Diamond Orchestra (1928)
Seated, left to right, are leader Leo Dejan, Alvin McNeal, Eddie Johnson, Herb Leary, Reese Cobette, Harold Dejan. Standing are emcee Sherman Cook, Eddie Pierson, Sidney Montegue, Rube McClennon, August Lanoix.

The Creole Serenaders (1930)   *Courtesy Danny Barker*
Left to right are leader Peter Bocage, Henry Bocage, Louis Warnick, Dwight Newman, Henry Martin, Charlie Bocage.

Bunk Johnson's Band (1944)
Left to right are Jim Robinson, Bunk Johnson, Baby Dodds, Lawrence Marrero, George Lewis, Slow Drag Pavageau.

Manuel Perez Jazz Band (1923)
At the Pythian Roof are, left to right, Alfred Williams, Earl Humphrey, Tats Alexander, Maurice Durand, Osceola Blanchard (kneeling), Manuel Perez, Caffrey Darensburg, Eddie Cherie, Jimmy Johnson.

The Dominos (about 1929)
Nappy Lamare's brother Jimmy is seated at the piano for this picture, though he wasn't a musician. The others, left to right, are Tony Burrella, Charles Christian, Tony Fougerat, Willie Guitar, Lester Bouchon, Nappy Lamare.

176

Johnny DeDroit's Jazz Band (1920)
The band was appearing at Kolb's Restaurant. Left to right are Tony Parenti, Johnny DeDroit, Paul DeDroit, Mel Berry, Tom Zimmerman.

Preservation Hall All-Star Jazz Band (1963)
Posing just before a four-month tour of Japan are, left to right, Papa John Joseph, Louis Nelson, Joe Watkins, Kid Thomas (didn't make the trip), Kid Punch Miller, Joe Robichaux, George Lewis.

Clarence Desdunes Joyland Revelers (about 1929)
Lined up next to the band's bus are, left to right, Harry Fairconnetue, Harold Dejan, George McCullum, Jr., Shine Williams, Ray Brown.

Courtesy Duncan Schiedt

Jimmie Noone's Orchestra (1930s)
Plenty of New Orleanians could be found in Chicago during the Depression. Here with Noone (clarinet) are Baby Dodds, John Lindsay, Lee Collins, who is almost hidden behind Preston Jackson, John Henley. The guitarist is unidentified.

178

The Six and 7/8 String Band (1964)
Left to right are Charles Hardy, Edmond Souchon, Bill Kleppinger, Red Mackie, Bernie Shields. They began playing together in 1912 or 1913.

The Last Straws (1963)
Left to right are Bob Casey, Bill Lee, J. J. Joyce, Bris Jones, Al Lobre, Moose Zanco, Bob Ice, and Nick Gagliardi.

The Susquehanna Band (1924)
Left to right are Benny Deichman, Dominick Barocco, Pete Peccopia, Johnny Palisier, Junius Boudreaux, Louis Uhle, Joe Barocco. Deichman and Dominick Barocco are holding each other's instruments. The photo was taken on an excursion up the river to the Godchaux Plantation.

The John Robichaux Orchestra (1896)
Seated, left to right, are Dee Dee Chandler, Charles McCurdy, Robichaux, Wendell MacNeil. Standing, Baptiste DeLisle, James Wilson, James MacNeil, Oak Gaspard.

Christian Ragtime Band (1915)
On Quarella's Pier at Milneburg are, left to right, Willie Guitar, Manuel Gomez, Harry Nunez, Yellow Nunez, Frank Christian, Charlie Christian, Kid Totts Blaise.

Photo by Johnny Donnels

The French Market Jazz Band
Band members are Otis Bazoon, clarinet; Frank Minyard, trumpet; Art Langston, tuba; leader Scott Hill, trombone; Walter Lastie, drums; Les Muscutt, banjo; David Lastie, saxophone.

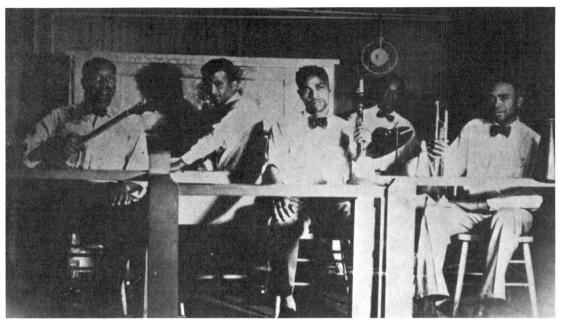

George Parker's Orchestra (about 1925)
Left to right are Clarence Tisdale, Parker, Brother Cornbread Thomas, Sidney Jackpierre, Coo Coo Talbert.

The New Orleans Joymakers (1972)
The band was in London on tour. In front are Louis Nelson (left) and Father Al Lewis. Rear, Percy Humphrey, Orange Kellin, Chester Zardis, Louis Barbarin, Lars Edegran.

The New Leviathan Oriental Fox-Trot Orchestra
Center, with baton, is Dick Mackie, later director of the Baton Rouge Symphony. Bruce Pollack, eighth from right, was leader during most of the seventies. Sixth from right, vocalist George Schmidt, is well-known as a painter.

The Arcadian Serenaders (1920s)
These Orleanians played at the Arcadian Ballroom in St. Louis and recorded on Okeh. Seated, left to right, are Wingy Manone, Felix Guarino, Cliff Holman. Standing are Johnny Riddick (left) and Slim Leftwich.

Naylor's Seven Aces (1924)
In the back row are, left to right, Bill Creger, Charles Hartmann, Jules Bauduc, Oliver Naylor. In front are Louis Darrough, Newton Richardson, Pinky Gerbrecht.

The Young Tuxedo Orchestra (about 1925)
Left to right are Cié Frazier, Paul Ben, Bush Hall, Dwight Newman, Lawrence Marrero, Simon Marrero (standing), Louis Cottrell, Jr., Pop Hamilton.

Murphy Campo and the Jazz Saints
Left to right are Johnny Sansone, Lucien Jourdan, Campo, Oscar Davis, Joseph Morton.

Photo by Bill Russell

The Emile Barnes Band (1951)
Left to right are Harrison Brazlee, Cié Frazier, Lawrence Toca, Billie Pierce, Dee Dee Pierce, Barnes, Albert Glenny.

A Preservation Hall Band

Alfred Williams, drums; Homer Eugene, trombone; August Lanoix, string bass; Peter Bocage, trumpet; Joe Robichaux, piano; Louis Cottrell, Jr., clarinet.

Courtesy the New Orleans Jazz Museum

An Evening at Preservation Hall

Bill Matthews, trombone; Chester Jones, drums; Jerry Greene, string bass; Ernie Cagnolatti, trumpet; John Casimir, clarinet.

Courtesy the New Orleans Jazz Museum

The New Orleans Ragtime Orchestra (1970)
Left to right are Lionel Ferbos, Bill Russell, Cié Frazier, Paul Crawford, Orange Kellin, James Prevost, Lars Edegran.

Photo by Dan Leyrer, courtesy Arhoolie Records

All-Stars at Preservation Hall
Cié Frazier, drums; Slow Drag Pavageau, string bass; Jim Robinson, trombone; Kid Thomas, trumpet; Billie Pierce, piano; Dee Dee Pierce, trumpet; George Lewis, clarinet; Narvin Kimball, banjo.

Courtesy Preservation Hall

The A. J. Piron Orchestra (about 1925)
The orchestra was appearing at Old Spanish Fort. Front row, left to right, are Peter Bocage, Steve Lewis, Louis Cottrell, Sr., Piron. Back row, John Marrero, Louis Warnick, Lorenzo Tio, Jr., and John Lindsay.

The Camelia Dance Orchestra (about 1918)
Standing are Albert Warner (left) and Johnny Predonce. Seated, left to right, are George Henderson, Elmer Talbert, Sr., George Stewart, Clarence Tisdale.

Dominick Barocco's Band (1958)
Left to right are Barocco, unknown, Tom Mujera, Sal Gutierrez, Tony Fougerat, Raymond Burke, Paul Crawford, Sal Magiotta.

Emergency Relief Administration Band (1935)

The photo was taken in Jackson Square. Front row, left to right: first five unknown, Wilfred Ledet, Happy Goldston, Cié Frazier, Louis Dumaine, Dave Ogden, Abby Williams, Judge Riley, Raymond ———, ——— Ridgley, Alphonse Johnson. Second row: Paul Moliere, Jimmy Clayton, unknown, Richard McLean, Raymond Glapion, Son Thomas, Lionel Tapo, Ninesse Trepagnier, Peter Raphael, Emile Knox, Sam Morgan, unknown, Douglas Hood, Eddie Morgan, Leo Songier, Ernest Penn, Alcide Landry, Kid Shots Madison. Third row: unknown, unknown, Bob Antler, Kid Harrison, Gilbert Young, unknown (almost hidden), unknown, Ricard Alexis, Charlie Peterson, unknown, Burke Stevenson, next three unknown, Henry Russ, unknown, Sonny Williams, Wilbert Tillman, George McCullum, Jr., unknown, William Brown, unknown. Fourth row: Albert Ganier, unknown, Frank Duson, Oscar Henry, Sunny Henry, Joe Harris, Isaiah Robinson, Israel Gorman, Melvin Frank, next four unknown, Albert Jones, ——— Green, unknown, Arthur ———, Joe Morris. Fifth row: Pinchback Touro, unknown, Tom Steptoe, unknown, John Anchor, unknown, ——— Taylor, Eddie Morris, unknown, unknown, Andrew Morgan, Manuel Paul, unknown, Alan "Hunter" Gordet, unknown, unknown, Eddie Edward, Harold Davis, unknown, unknown, Ernest Poree, Frank Crump, Tats Alexander.

The Original Dukes of Dixieland
Pictured are Freddie, Jac, and Frank Assunto.

Andrew Hall's Society Jazz Band
Actor Robert Morley looks on during filming for a British Airways commercial. Left to right are Teddy Johnson, Ernest Poree, leader Andrew Hall, Chris Burke, standing in front of Keith Smith, Greg Stafford. Hall, Burke, and Smith are Britishers who settled in New Orleans.

THE BRASS BANDS

There's nothing original about the idea of brass bands in western culture. Every small town has had its firemen, police force, high school, or civic group organize a dozen or so uniformed men with instruments. They usually performed outdoors to help celebrate occasions for which their appearance seemed appropriate. Universally they have specialized in military airs and have been most in evidence on patriotic holidays.

While New Orleans also found use for such groups as early as the 1850s, the city's exotic cultural pattern developed broader uses for them and involved them more closely in daily life. Only in New Orleans does the brass band figure regularly in funeral plans. Only here do the bands turn out in force mainly on Mother's Day rather than the Fourth of July. Almost every fraternal lodge makes regular provision for the music of the brass band.

Not only is the brass band used unconventionally in the Crescent City, but its music owes little debt to John Philip Sousa and Arthur Pryor. Peace-loving Orleanians prefer popular tunes, jazz standards, and blues, along with an occasional solemn dirge or hymn when these are warranted by the circumstances. Our music-loving public relates to its brass bands with affection unparalleled in American culture. It has been known to make folk heroes of its favorites. The likes of Buddy Bolden, Manuel Perez, and Lawrence Veca were the Mickey Mantles, Willie Mayses, and Babe Ruths of their era. In other climes the brass band on parade has stationary spectators who stand on sidewalks and watch the band go by. But in New Orleans, the "Second Line"—a mass audience of extroverted enthusiasts—follows along with the musicians, dancing in figures little removed from the calindas and bamboulas of the century past. From the ranks of the Second Line have been recruited the great names of New Orleans jazz. Little Louis Armstrong proudly carried the horns of Bunk Johnson and King Oliver in the street. George Lewis took his turn tagging along, as did Pete Fountain and the rest.

The brass bands represent the happiest, most beloved phase of the music of New Orleans.

Allen, Henry, Brass Band (1907–1940s). Henry Allen, Sr., t, l; Peter Bocage, Joe Howard, Papa Celestin, Louis Dumaine, t; Jack Carey, Buddy Johnson, Yank Johnson, Harrison Barnes, tb; Lawrence Duhé, cl; Wallace Collins, bh; James A. Palao, ah; Bebé Matthews, Ramos Matthews, sn; Clay Jiles, Red Allen, bd.

Bulls Club Brass Band (late teens–early 1920s). Manuel Calier, t, l; Arthur Stevens, tb. King Oliver and George McCullum, Sr., sometimes played with this group.

Camelia Brass Band (1917–1923). Wooden Joe Nicholas, t, l; Buddy Petit, t; Big Ike Robinson, Joseph Petit, Eddie Morris, tb; Alphonse Picou, Israel Gorman, Johnny Brown, cl; Buddy Luck, sou; Arthur Ogle, sn; Booker T. Glass, bd.

Columbia Brass Band (1897–1900). Partial personnel: Punkie Valentin, c; Alcibiades Jeanjacques, t; Bouboul Valentin, tb; Edward Boisseau, bh; Alphonse Picou, cl; Isidore Barbarin, ah; Dee Dee Chandler, bd.

The Tonic Triad Band (1928)

Front row, left to right: unknown, Albert Francis, Albert Francis, Jr., Albert Jones, James Smith, Ace Williams. Middle row: Isidore Barbarin, unknown, unknown, Albert Warner, Red Clark, Ronald Lopice, Chicken Henry, John Ever, unknown, J. T. Dalmas. Of those in the back row, the first three are not musicians. Remaining, left to right, are Gertrude Daily, Ophelia Grigsby, James Harris, Pop Hamilton, Melvin Frank, Geneva Moret, Bea Acheson, Lumas Hamilton, Willie Pajeaud, Alcide Landry, and the director, Professor Henry Pritchard.

Crescent City Brass Band (1880s). This band, organized by Professor Jim Humphrey, was perhaps the first to feature syncopated band arrangements.

Deer Range Band. Jim Humphrey organized this band in a small town near Magnolia plantation in the nineteenth century. It made frequent appearances in New Orleans and introduced the superior trumpet playing of Chris Kelly and his brother Ben.

Diamond Stone Brass Band (1897). An uptown band that used mostly nonjazzmen but included Edward Clem, c, and Frank Jackson, bd.

Eclipse Brass Band (1900–1917). "Official" band of the Magnolia Plantation, directed by Professor Jim Humphrey. It included Chris Kelly, t; Sunny Henry, Harrison Barnes, tb.

Eureka Brass Band (1920–present). Partial collective personnel: Fats Houston (grand marshal); Willie Wilson, t, organizer and first l; Tom Albert, Alcide Landry, Kid Shots Madison, Percy Humphrey, T-Boy Remy, Willie Pajeaud, Eddie Richardson, Kid Sheik Colar, t; Adolphe Alexander, Sr. (founding member), c; Willie Cornish, Jim Robinson, Earl Humphrey, Albert Warner, Eddie Summers, Louis Nelson, Sunny Henry, Chicken Henry, Kid Avery, tb; George Lewis, Willie Parker (founding mem-

ber), Albert Burbank, Willie James Humphrey, cl; Alphonse Johnson, ah; Johnny Wilson, bh; Red Clark (mgr.), Wilbert Tillman, sou, tu; Alfred Williams, Cié Frazier, Happy Goldston, Son Fewclothes Lewis, d; Tats Alexander, Emanuel Paul, Ruben Roddy, s. T-Boy Remy and Percy Humphrey, in order, succeeded Wilson as leader.

Excelsior Brass Band (1880–1928). Partial collective personnel: Theogene V. Baquet, c, first l; George Moret, Edward Clem, Frank Jackson, Fice Quire, James MacNeil, James Williams, George Hooker, Arnold Metoyer, Nelson Jean, Paul Thomas, Adolphe Alexander, Sr., Peter Bocage, Hippolyte Charles, Sidney Desvigne, George McCullum, Jr., t; Aaron Clark, Anthony Page, Harrison Barnes, Baptiste Delisle, Honore Dutrey, Bernard Raphael, Buddy Johnson, Eddie Vinson, Sunny Henry, tb; George Baquet, Alphonse Picou, Lorenzo Tio, Sr., Lorenzo Tio, Jr., Luis Tio, Charles McCurdy, Sam Dutrey, Sr., Willie James Humphrey, cl; Hackett Brothers, Joe Payen (last leader), ah; Edward Boisseau, Vic Gaspard, George Hooker, bh; Isidore Barbarin, Ralph Montegue, ah; Frank Jackson, Frank Robinson, tu; John Robichaux, Clay Jiles, Louis Cottrell, Sr., Dee Dee Chandler, d.

Fairview Baptist Church Brass Band. Organized in the 1960s by Danny Barker to encourage children in the tradition of New Orleans music, it became a well-trained unit, familiar in New Orleans parades, and sent many musicians on to jazz careers.

The Reliance Brass Band (1906)
Seated are Manuel Belasco (left) and Joe Alexander. Standing, left to right, are Dave Perkins, Vincent Barocco, Sidney Moore, Peter Pellegrini, Freddy Neuroth, and leader Papa Laine.

Fischer's Brass Band (1910). Partial collective personnel: George Barth, Harry Shannon, Richie Brunies, Manuel Mello, t, c; Leonce Mello, Cack Riley, Happy Schilling, Henny Brunies, Merritt Brunies, tb; Johnny Fischer, cl, l; Tony Shannon, bh; Freddie Williams, Charles Hazel, d.

Gibson Brass Band (mid-1950s–1965). Eddie Richardson, Johnny Wimberley, Leon Bajeon, t; Carroll Blunt, Fred Thompson, Eddie Morris, tb; George Sterling, David Bailey, d; Louis Keppard, tu; A. B. Spears, Robert Davis, s.

Holmes Band of Lutcher (1910). Professor Anthony Holmes, c, l; Joe Porter, c; Henry Sawyer, tb; Dennis Harris, cl; Papa John Joseph, s; John Porter, bh; Floyd Jackson, tu; David Jones, sn, mel, s; Nub Jacobs, bd. This band from Lutcher, La., played many carnivals and tent shows, besides parades in New Orleans.

Hurricanes Brass Band. Organized in the 1970s as an outgrowth of Danny Barker's Fairview Baptist Church Band, the band was made up of teenagers, many of whom later became professional jazzmen. Leroy Jones, Greg Stafford, t, and Lucien Barbarin, tb, began here. Jules L. Cahn, faithful photographic chronicler of countless parades and other jazz events, sponsored the Hurricanes and produced their first LP.

Lincoln Band (1890s). An offshoot of the Excelsior Brass Band with fewer personnel, assembled by Professor Jim Humphrey.

Lyons Brass Band (1928). Pop Hamilton, t, l; Alcide Landry, Manuel Trapp, t; Maurice French, Tom Steptoe, tb; Willie Parker, cl; Lumas Hamilton, fh; "Sheik-O," bh; Ernest Rogers, sn; Arthur Turnis, bd.

Masonic Brass Band (1930s). A Masonic organization kept a stock of band caps and hired men who were available for parade jobs. Some of the regulars were Red Clark, tb; Ophelia Grigsby, s; A. B. Spears, bd.

Melrose Brass Band (1900–1910). Regular members: King Oliver, c; Bernard Raphael, Honore Dutrey, tb; Paul Beaulieu, cl; Alphonse Vache, tu; Willie Phillips, sd. Sometimes Adam Olivier, Bunk Johnson, c; Sam Dutrey, Sr., cl.

Onward Brass Band (1889–1930). Partial collective personnel: Manuel Perez, c; Andrew Kimball, Peter Bocage, Oscar Duconge, James MacNeil, Bellevue Lenair, Sylvester Coustaut, King Oliver, Maurice Durand, c, t; Buddy Johnson, Vic Gaspard, George Filhe, Baptiste Delisle, Steve Johnson, Earl Humphrey, Guyé Rapp, tb; Lorenzo Tio, Jr., Luis Tio, George Baquet, cl; Joseph Bruno, Isidore Barbarin, Adolphe Alexander, Sr., Bartholomew Bruno, ah; Eddie Atkins, Aaron Clark, bh;

The Works Progress Administration Band (1936)

Courtesy New Orleans Jazz Society, London

This government program provided steady employment for a host of jazz greats during the Depression. At the left stands the leader, Pinchback Touro. Seated in the front row, left to right: Willie Humphrey, Albert Mitchell, Israel Gorman, Richard McNeal, Sidney Cates, Leon Saulny, Leo Songier, George McCullum, Jr., Manuel Coustaut. Second row: Son Johnson (holding sax), Howard Davis, John Casimir, Emanuel Paul, Andrew Morgan, Eddie Johnson(s), Tats Alexander, Raymond Glapion. Third row: Edward Johnson(t), Henry Hardin, Manny Gabriel, Sam Lee, Sunny Henry, Chicken Henry, Harrison Barnes. Standing in the back row: Albert Glenny, Sidney Montegue, Cié Frazier, Ninesse Trepagnier, Joe Howard, William Brown, Alcide Landry, Kid Shots Madison, Gilbert Young, Ricard Alexis, Henry Russ, Albert Ganier, Louis Dumaine.

Eddie Jackson, Frank Jackson, Albert Tucker, tu; Bebé Matthews, Dee Dee Chandler, sn; Black Benny Williams, Henry Martin, Dandy Lewis, Mike Gillin, Clay Jiles, Happy Goldston, bd.

Pacific Brass Band (1900–1912). Basic personnel of this Algiers, La., band included George Hooker, Manuel Manetta, c; Buddy Johnson, Frank Duson, tb; Dude Gabriel, cl; George Sims, George Hooker, bh; Duke Simpson, sn; George Davis, bd.

Pelican Brass Band (organized 1889). Professor J. Dretsch, leader. Jim Humphrey worked in this band and eventually became its leader.

Pickwick Brass Band (1898–1901). Norman "Deuce" Manetta, c, was leader of this band from LaPlace, La. Other members: Jules Manetta, c; Edward Love, tb; Levi Bailey, f; Dennis Williams, Tete Rouchon, tu. Others not known.

Reliance Brass Band (ca. 1892–1913). Owned, managed, and booked by Papa Laine. Partial collective personnel: Manuel Mello, Freddie Neuroth, Joe Lala, Johnny Lala, Richie Brunies, Gus Zimmerman, Merritt Brunies, Abbie Brunies, Nick La Rocca, Pete Pellegrini, Frank Christian, Lawrence Veca, George Barth, Harry Shannon, Pete

Dientrans, Ray Lopez, Johnny DeDroit, c; Leonce Mello, Dave Perkins, Daddy Edwards, George Brunies, Emile Christian, Marcus Kahn, Bill Gallaty, Sr., Ricky Toms, Jules Cassard, Henny Brunies, Tom Brown, Happy Schilling, tb; Yellow Nunez, Achille Baquet, Martin Kirsch, Sidney Moore, Clem Camp, Johnny Fischer, Larry Shields, Tony Giardina, Gussie Mueller, John Palisier, Red Rowling, Leon Roppolo (elder), cl; Pantsy Laine, Vincent Barocco, Merritt Brunies, ah; Manuel Belasco, bh; Joe Alexander, Chink Martin, tu; Papa Laine, Tim Harris, Ragbaby Stephens, Johnny Stein, Tony Sbarbaro, Billy Lambert, Diddie Stephens, Emmett Rogers, d.

St. Joseph Brass Band (1888–1895). Though based in Donaldsonville, La., this band frequently played for carnival and parades in New Orleans. Partial collective personnel: Claiborne Williams, c, l; William Dailey, Sullivan Sproul, Edward Duffy, Israel Palmer, Lawrence Hall, c; George Williams, Ernest Hime, Harrison Homer, tb; Marble Gibson, Ben Bauddeurs, cl; Jim Williams, tu; Joe Walker, Buddy Curry, "Bow Legs," d. Fred Landry sometimes played trombone or piano for concerts where needed.

Schilling's Brass Band (1910–1917). Largely composed of members of Happy Schilling's dance orchestra.

The Reliance Brass Band (1910)
Seated is leader Papa Laine, who sometimes played drums. The others are Manuel Mello, Yellow Nunez, Leonce Mello, Pantsy Laine, Chink Martin, Tim Harris. The "Big Show" is Laine's Greater Majestic Minstrels. A hurricane that year blew down the tent, which had been erected behind the carbarn at Canal and White streets.

Terminal Brass Band (early 1900s–1908). Permanent nucleus: Harrison Barnes (usually a trombonist), c; Joseph Petit, tb, l; Willie Parker, cl; "Sheik-O," bh; Sleepy Robertson, bd.

Tuxedo Brass Band (1910–1925). Partial collective personnel: Papa Celestin, t, l; Manuel Perez, Mutt Carey, Louis Dumaine, Alcide Landry, Charlie Love, Joe Howard, Willie Pajeaud, Louis Armstrong, Peter Bocage, Dee Dee Pierce, Amos White, Maurice Durand, c; Tats Alexander, s; Bebé Ridgley, Buddy Johnson, Yank Johnson, Sunny Henry, Hamp Benson, Harrison Barnes, Eddie Atkins, Jim Robinson, Loochie Jackson, tb; Alphonse Picou, Sam Dutrey, Sr., Lorenzo Tio, Jr., Johnny Dodds, Jimmie Noone, cl; Isidore Barbarin, Louis Keppard, ah; George Hooker, Adolphe Alexander, Sr., bh; Joe Howard, tu; Chinee Foster, Zutty Singleton, Louis Cottrell, Sr., sn; Ninesse Trepagnier, Black Benny Williams, bd.

Williams, Abby, Happy Pals (late 1940s–early 1950s). Dee Dee Pierce, c; Kid Howard, Kid Clayton, t; Eddie Pierson, Jim Robinson, tb; Tats Alexander, cl; Noon Johnson, sou; Jesse Charles, s; Chester Jones, bd; Abby Williams, sn, l.

Williams, George, Brass Band (from late 1940s). Partial collective personnel: Albert Walters, Alvin Alcorn, Theodore Riley, Ernie Cagnolatti, t; Buster Moore, Showboy Thomas, tb; Steve Angrum, cl; Ernest Poree, as; Jesse Charles, ts; William Brown, tu; Son White Washington, sn; Cié Frazier, George Williams, bd, l.

Young Tuxedo Brass Band (1930s–1963). Partial collective personnel: Alvin Alcorn, Kid Howard, Thomas Jefferson, Kid Shots Madison, Edgar Joseph, Dee Dee Pierce, Vernon Gilbert, John Brunious, Andy Anderson, t; Sunny Henry, Kid Avery, Loochie Jackson, Albert Warner, Clement Tervalon, Homer Eugene, Wendell Eugene, tb; John Casimir, cl, mgr; Albert Burbank, cl; Tats Alexander, Andrew Morgan, John Handy, s; Eddie Jackson, Wilbert Tillman, tu; Ernest Rogers, Son White Washington, Emile Knox, Cié Frazier, Paul Barbarin, Alfred Williams, d.

The Henry Allen Brass Band
(Mardi Gras, 1926)
The snare drummer is Ramos Matthews.
In the rear is the leader on bass drum.
At right, face hidden by music, is
Louis Dumaine.

Fischer's Brass Band (1915)
Left to right are Freddie Williams, George Barth, Happy Schilling, Harry Shannon, Tony Shannon, Johnny Fischer.

Siegfried Christensen's New Orleans Brass Band (1912)

The picture was taken in Chattanooga, Tenn. George Peterson is seated on the white mule. Angelo Castigliola stands in front of the wagon with his trombone, next to the legendary Dave Perkins, holding the euphonium. Third from the right on the wagon is Joe Alexander. The leader stands, holding his cornet, on the front of the wagon behind the mule.

The Reliance Brass Band (1912)

The band was playing for the Firemen's Day parade in Biloxi, Miss. Kneeling, left to right, are Vincent De Corda, Manuel Mello, Papa Laine. Standing, Ragbaby Stephens, Chink Martin, Hans ———, Henny Brunies, Leonce Mello, Emile Christian, Merritt Brunies, Johnny Palisier, Alfred Laine. The men in the white-topped uniforms belong to another group.

The St. Francis de Sales Military Band (1910)

Courtesy Harry Shields

Members of this high school band later became jazzmen. Seated, left to right, are Jimmy Kendall, Father Hefferman (pastor and instructor), unknown. The small boy with the snare drum is Louis Burke. Middle row, Joe Barocco, Hugh Exerstein, unknown, Clem Camp (with eye patch), Larry Shields, next four unknown, Johnny Frisco. In the back row, Benny Deichman is at far right; next to him is Dominick Barocco.

Fischer's Ragtime Military Jazz Band (1909)

Courtesy Monk Hazel

The band members, kneeling in front, posed with the Big 50 Carnival Club in front of the new courthouse at Royal and Conti streets. The little boy seated in the center of the picture is Monk Hazel. Band members are, left to right, Charles Hazel, Henny Brunies, Manuel Mello, Emanuel Allesandro, Cack Riley, Johnny Fischer, Happy Schilling, Richie Brunies, Angelo De Corda, and "Sox" ———.

Clarinetist (1916)
Camelia Brass Band member Israel Gorman.

Bandsmen (1911)
Gus Zimmerman (left), leader of one of the Reliance units, and Martin Kirsch take time for a studio photograph.

The Reliance Band (about 1911)
Left to right are Ragbaby Stephens, unknown, Chink Martin, Henny Brunies, Emile Christian, Martin Kirsch, unknown, Ray Lopez, Gus Zimmerman, Manuel Mello.

Jefferson City Buzzards (1925)
This carnival club always used top bands. Wooden Joe Nicholas' Camelia Brass Band, which reorganized for several parades through 1932, was the choice this year.

Kid Rena's Band (1937)
Band members who can be identified on this parade through Storyville are Kid Sheik Colar, trumpet; Eddie Summers, trombone; George Lewis, clarinet; Edgar Mosley, bass drum.

Tuxedo Brass Band (1920s)
These members are taking a break. George Hooker kneels in front of, left to right, Yank Johnson, Manuel Perez, Papa Celestin Ninesse Trepagnier, Willie Pajeaud.

Eureka Brass Band (1958)
Traditional Mother's Day parade in Hahnville, La. Left to right are leader Percy Humphrey, trumpet; Alfred Williams, snare drum; Willie Pajeaud and Emanuel Paul, partially hidden; Albert Warner, trombone; Son Fewclothes Lewis, bass drum; Eddie Summers, trombone; Harold Dejan, saxophone; Red Clark, sousaphone.

Lafon School Band (about 1932)
Thomas Jefferson is the second trumpet player from the top on the left. Sport Young is second sax from the top on the right. The band is playing for a funeral.

The Young Tuxedo Brass Band (1959)
Left to right are Clement Tervalon, Wilbert Tillman, Alfred Williams, Edgar Joseph, Oscar Rouzon, Andy Anderson, Andrew Morgan. Drummer Emile Knox is almost hidden.

Courtesy Abby Williams

Abby Williams Happy Pals Brass Band (1949)
Left to right are Eddie Pierson, trombone; Noon Johnson, sousaphone; Jim Robinson, trombone; Tats Alexander, Jesse Charles, saxophone; Dee Dee Pierce, cornet; Kid Howard, Kid Clayton, trumpet; leader Abby Williams, snare drum; Chester Jones, bass drum.

George Williams Brass Band (1961)
Ernie Cagnolatti is kneeling in front. The rest, left to right, are Showboy Thomas, Buster Moore, Jesse Charles, Ernest Poree, William Brown, Albert Walters, Son White Washington, George Williams, Steve Angrum.
Courtesy Carey Tate

The Gibson Brass Band (1961)
Left to right are Louis Keppard, A. B. Spears, David Bailey, Eddie Richardson, Johnny Wimberly, Leon Bajeon, George Sterling, Carroll Blunt, Fred Thompson.
Courtesy Carey Tate

The Eureka Brass Band (1961)
At upper left, not in uniform, are some fans: Kid Thomas, Alec Bigard, Creole George Guesnon, and Emanuel Sayles. Band members are, left to right, Chicken Henry, Willie Humphrey, Emanuel Paul, Albert Warner, Happy Goldston, Son Fewclothes Lewis, Peter Bocage, Kid Sheik Colar, Percy Humphrey. In front, holding his hat, is Grand Marshal of the Second Line Slow Drag Pavageau.

The Onward Brass Band (about 1913)

Left to right are Manuel Perez, Andrew Kimball, Peter Bocage, Lorenzo Tio, Jr., Adolphe Alexander, Sr., Bebé Matthews, Dandy Lewis, Isidore Barbarin, Buddy Johnson, Vic Gaspard, Eddie Atkins, Eddie Jackson.

The Algiers Naval Station Band (1942)

The band was recruited in New Orleans. Front row, left to right, are Tats Alexander, James Davis, John Jones, Henry Russ, Harold Dejan. In the second row are Gilbert Jones, Bertrand Adams, —— Brooks, William Spencer, bandmaster Vernon B. Cooper. Third row, Polo Barnes, Herbert Trisch, Robert Anthony, Sidney Dufachard. Back row, Booker T. Washington, Ruben Roddy, Alexander, Leon Harris, William Casimir, Frank Fields.

Mathews Band of Lockport, La. (1904)
A true brass band—no reeds—this is the earliest known brass band photograph showing a slide trombone, along with the valve trombones customary at the time.

Marching Band (1900)
This early marching group includes Dave Perkins, trombone.

The Waifs' Home Band and Louis Armstrong's Orchestra (1931)
Louis, seated at center, returns to visit his alma mater. Other Orleanians in the band are John Lindsay, far left; Tubby Hall, on Louis' right; Preston Jackson, second from right. Above Jackson, leaning against the pillar, is Peter Davis, Louis' first music teacher.

Happy Schilling's Brass Band
The group was hired to advertise the movie *The Music Goes 'Round* at the Orpheum Theater in New Orleans. Left to right are Happy Schilling, Monk Hazel, Howard Reed, George Schilling, Jr.
Courtesy Howard Reed

Young Olympia Brass Band (mid-1960s)
The band was still marching, continuing the tradition under the leadership of Harold Dejan. In this photo are Paul Crawford, trombone; Emanuel Paul, saxophone; Andy Anderson, trumpet; Allen Jaffe, sousaphone; Louis Nelson, trombone.

The Reliance Brass Band (1914)
This was the first film ever made of Mardi Gras, a French (Gaumont) newsreel.

The New Young Tuxedo Brass Band (1974)
Left to right, standing, are Frank Naundorf, Jerry Greene, Lawrence Trotter, Daniel Farrow, Emile Knox, Herman Sherman (leader), John Simmons, Reginald Koeller, Theodore Riley, and Darrell Johnson, the grand marshal. In front are Greg Stafford and Joseph Torregano.

Bunk's Band
Left to right are Bunk Johnson, Isidore Barbarin, Lawrence Marrero, Kid Shots Madison, Jim Robinson, Tats Alexander, Baby Dodds, George Lewis, Red Clark.

Johnny Fischer's Band (1910)
Here, the band marches on North Rampart Street. The trombone on the extreme right is Happy Schilling; cymbal player in the center is Dave Perkins; tuba player in front is Joe Alexander.

212

The Onward Brass Band (1962)
Rear, left to right: Louis Nelson, William Brown, Chris Clifton, unknown. Left side: Louis Barbarin (with snare drum), Albert Walters, Kid Howard. Right side: Ernie Cagnolatti and Louis Cottrell, Jr. Center: Paul Barbarin. In the white sweater is British trombonist Mike Casimir. At extreme right is Dick Allen.

The Holmes Band of Lutcher, La. (1910)
Left to right are David Jones, Floyd Jackson, Nub Jacobs, Henry Sawyer (said to be the first jazz band slide trombonist), Professor Anthony Holmes (leader), Dennis Harris, John Porter, Joe Porter.

Eureka Brass Band (1956)
Left to right are Willie Pajeaud (at rear, almost hidden), Emanuel Paul, John Casimir, Alphonse Picou, Albert Warner, Ruben Roddy (almost hidden), and Sunny Henry.

WHERE'S WHERE
IN NEW ORLEANS JAZZ

Someday a book devoted entirely to a description of jazz landmarks will be published. It will have to be a thick volume indeed to do justice to a subject of historical importance and architectural fascination. The city seems to have spawned its characteristic sound on every corner, in every house. Here, we cannot pretend to fill the need for a detailed study of places associated with New Orleans jazz. But we hope to point the way by broadly outlining the relationship between the music and some of the town's real estate.

By now, jazz enthusiasts everywhere know, though they've never visited the city, that New Orleans has an "uptown" and a "downtown." Uptown is generally westward from Canal Street. The "canebrake" style generated in this area flowered into the likes of Buddy Bolden and King Oliver. The downtown area, below Canal Street and including both the French Quarter and Storyville, gave rise to the so-called Creole style, mainly associated with Armand J. Piron, John Robichaux, and Alphonse Picou.

Both of these areas produced neighborhood music for dancing, for weddings, for wakes, for picnics and burials, and just for fun. Innumerable church and lodge halls were available for nightly rental. The style of music played depended largely on the section of town in which it was heard.

All styles blended, though, in the city's celebrated resort areas along the Lake Pontchartrain shore, where much of the population betook itself on weekends for fun, fishing, boating, and assorted games. Hallowed now in jazz history are the stretches known as Milneburg, Old Spanish Fort, Little Woods, Bucktown, and West End. Commemorated in such evergreen jazz titles as "Milne-

burg Joys" and "West End Blues," these festive meccas remain only as nostalgic memories. But the names of such bands as the Bucktown Five sprinkled through our discographies help us to remember.

To a limited and lesser extent, Storyville, the legal red-light district that operated from 1897 to 1917, served as a forge in which some of the pure gold of jazz was smelted. It, too, has been celebrated in song. "Mahogany Hall Stomp" recalls its most famous brothel, and "Basin Street Blues" and "Franklin Street Blues" bring to mind its most hectic streets. However, the role played by Storyville in jazz development has been much exaggerated and deliberately misrepresented by self-elected "historians." Television, magazines, motion pictures, and other media have perpetuated the myth that jazz was a product of the red-light district. This is not only untrue but offensive and insulting to the vast majority of New Orleans jazzmen, including some of its brightest stars, who never played in Storyville—indeed, never even *saw* it. The district never employed more than two score musicians on any given night, not even on Mardi Gras! By the time Storyville came into existence there were hundreds of musicians who had already been playing jazz music for more than a decade.

Surrounding the district was the Tango Belt, an almost unbroken line of cabarets, dance halls, and honky-tonks where top dixieland stars spent their early careers. Here Armand Hug, Sharkey, Wingy Manone, and Raymond Burke, to name a few, learned about the jazzman's life.

The downtown hotels, especially the Grunewald (subsequently the Roosevelt and now the Fairmont) and the Jung, presented bands for dancing. These employed future dixieland stars, as did the pit bands of the leading theaters. Tony Parenti, Johnny Wiggs, Leon Prima, and Santo Pecora are among their best known alumni.

Cafes were scattered all over town, bearing names that still set melodies singing in many a jazz fan's heart—the Tin Roof, the Red Onion, the Halfway House. Ball parks, fair grounds, boxing arenas, all supplied backdrops against which the stars of New Orleans jazz improvised their music.

And consider the streets and alleys whose names are known to the ends of the earth through the music that was brewed in them! "Canal Street Blues," "South Rampart Street Parade," "Burgundy Street Blues," "Bourbon Street Parade," "Perdido Street Blues"—the list seems endless.

There is a tree-shaded park, now called Beauregard Square, in front of the Municipal Auditorium. In an earlier era it was a recreation area for slaves, known informally as Congo Square. There the African rhythms and vocalizing that many assert were the source of jazz were first heard in the New World.

Almost everywhere you look, you want to install a bronze plaque.

As for the little places over the river in Algiers, Gretna, Westwego, across the lake in Covington and Mandeville, along the Gulf Coast to Biloxi—not to mention such itinerant sites of jazz importance as the riverboats, the tailgate wagons every fan knows about, Smoky Mary, the train that hauled revelers to the lake—well, it becomes more obvious that the book we mentioned is a critical cultural need.

But in these pages we beg you to settle for a sample. Where the Big 25 stood, there is now a parking lot. Nothing on the blank wall of Krauss's Department Store tells us that here once rose Mahogany Hall in all its vulgar splendor. Such places live now only in our memories and in these pictures. Insofar as it has been practicable, we've listed locations, many important but obscure. We hope the ones selected to show in the photos are the ones the reader would most want to see.

Abadie's (1906–1917). Downtown lake corner, Marais and Bienville streets. Richard M. Jones's Four Hot Hounds—sometimes along with King Oliver, Wooden Joe Nicholas, and Sugar Johnny Smith—played here.

Alamo Dance Hall (1930s). Taxi dance hall. 113 Burgundy Street.

Alamo Theater. 1027 Canal Street.

Alhambra Gym Club. 535 Sequin Street, Algiers, La.

Alley Cabaret (1920s). Claiborne and St. Bernard avenues. Big Eye Louis Nelson.

Altmyer's. Corner of Annunciation and Robin Streets. Tom Brown's Band from Dixieland rehearsed in this saloon almost nightly before making its pioneer journey to Chicago in 1915.

Anderson's, Tom. 125 North Rampart Street. A restaurant with a bandstand where many great jazzmen—Louis Armstrong, Albert Nicholas, Paul Barbarin, Willie Santiago—performed.

Anderson's Arlington Annex (1901–1925). Basin and Iberville Streets. Early period (to 1905), string trio with Tom Brown on mandolin and Bill Johnson on bass. Middle period (to 1915), assorted jazz groups. Late period (World War I), Luis Russell band. End (1924–1925), Amos White.

Ann's Pleasure Club. 3436 Magazine Street.

Arlington Annex. See Anderson's Arlington Annex.

Armstrong, Louis. Was born in a house in Jane Alley, between Gravier and Perdido Streets. Torn down in 1964.

Armstrong, Louis, Park (dedicated June 15, 1980). Rampart Street. During the fifties, a huge demolition program obliterated some sixteen acres in the center of New Orleans. To the indignation of a host of preservationists, many jazz landmarks succumbed to the persuasion of the bulldozer, including San Jacinto Hall, the Gypsy Tea Room, Economy Hall, Hopes Hall, the Frolic, and Globe Hall. Through almost three city administrations, the stripped acreage lay while plans for its use proliferated. At last, the proposal to establish a park named for Louis Armstrong was approved by Mayor Moon Landrieu and his advisory committee. The park has great potential for a variety of jazz uses and at the very least provides an impressive and deserved memorial to the city's all-time favorite son.

Artesan Hall (1930s). 1460 N. Derbigny. Usually mispronounced "ar-tee-sian."

Associated Artists' Studio. 732 St. Peter Street. Informal jam sessions were begun by Larry Borenstein, art entrepreneur, during the forties. Their continued success enabled him to create Preservation Hall, next door to the old gallery, in which the revival of traditional jazz took place in the sixties.

A Corner of Haymarket Cabaret
Members of the Original Dixieland Jazz Band went on from here.

Astoria Hotel and Ballroom (1895–1963). South Rampart Street. Peak in late 1920s and early 1930s with the Jones-Collins Astoria Hot Eight.

Beauregard Square. See Congo Square.

Beverly Gardens Restaurant (from mid-1920s). Jefferson Highway. Duck Ernest Johnson frequently led the band. Joe Capraro's orchestra in the 1930s. Earlier known as **Suburban Gardens**; later, **Embassy Club**.

Bienville Roof (1920s–1930s). Lee Circle. Monk Hazel's orchestra. Sharkey.

Big 25 (1902–late 1950s). Franklin Street (earlier, Crozat Street) near Iberville (Customhouse). Musicians' hangout.

Blackstone's, Oren, Record Shop. During the late forties and early fifties, his shop not only provided the only decent catalogue of jazz discs in town but also served as a hangout and meeting place for jazzmen and their followers. His *Index to Jazz*, a four-volume discography, is of inestimable research value.

Blue Room. See Roosevelt Hotel.

Blum's Cafe (1900–1916). 114 Exchange Alley. A meeting hall where musicians formed bands.

Bolden, Buddy. At one time lived at 2527 First Street. The house has been torn down.

Advertising the Dance
This is the earliest known photo of an advertising "tailgate" wagon. The wagon was out publicizing a dance at Jackson Hall, a regular dance spot at the turn of the century. No one in this 1900 photograph has been reliably identified.

Boudio's Garden. Was a Milneburg resort at the end of the main street, before the piers. White jazzmen were always featured here, notably Harry Shields.

The Brown Derby. Villere and St. Ann Streets. This spot, under various names—Gypsy Tea Room, Japanese Gardens—was a stronghold for Kid Rena's bands through the twenties and thirties.

Brown's Ice Cream Parlor (1920s). Spanish Fort. Steve Lewis, p; New Orleans Willie Jackson, entertainer.

Bruning's Pavilion. On Shell Road in West End featured gambling and great music in the twenties and thirties. Merritt Brunies favored the place, but all the dixielanders played there.

Bucktown. Jefferson Parish, just across the Seventeenth Street bridge from West End. A rough, tough resort area on the lakefront, inhabited by commercial fishermen. Its Bucktown Tavern was the chief point of jazz interest.

Bucktown Tavern. Sometimes known as Martin's Cafe. First building on Bucktown side of bridge connecting Bucktown to West End. All Dixieland musicians played there regularly during the twenties, especially the Brunies and the New Orleans Rhythm Kings.

The Budweiser. Musicians have always called the premises at 1017 Iberville Street by this name because of the beer sign that always hung over the banquette there. See the Pup Cafe, Fern Cafe and Dance Hall No. 2.

Birthplace of Louis Armstrong

Bulls Club. A fraternal group that centered in a series of locations, first at Chippewa and Philip Streets; in 1966 on Harmony between Seventh and Eighth streets. Among the many trumpeter-leaders who performed under its sponsorship: Manuel Calier, Chris Kelly, King Oliver, George McCullum, Sr.

The Bungalow (1920s–1930s). Pontchartrain Boulevard near the lakefront. It was also known as **Chez Paree**; now **Masson's Beach House Restaurant**. Dixieland bands exclusively.

The Cadillac (*ca.* 1912–1925). 342 North Rampart Street. Before 1917, Willie Hightower was the house leader. About 1918–1923, Luis Russell was usually in charge. Later a dixieland stronghold.

Casino Cabaret (1907–1913). 1400 Iberville Street, in Storyville.

The Cave (1912–1926). A room in the Grunewald Hotel with a bizarre decor that featured stalagmites and stalactites. Tony Parenti, Johnny Bayersdorffer, and Johnny DeDroit were frequently on the podium. The room remains as part of the laundry room in the Fairmont Hotel basement, beneath the Blue Room.

The Champagne Room. Later the **Paddock**.

Cheapskate Hall. See Economy Hall.

Cherry Pickers Hall. Third and Magazine streets.

Chez Paree. See The Bungalow.

The Big 25
The club was demolished in 1956.

Club Forrest. A smart supper club of the prohibition era in Jefferson Parish. Featured the top-name attractions in larger bands. A. J. Piron, Louis Armstrong, the New Orleans Owls, Papa Celestin, John Robichaux, the Prima-Sharkey Orchestra, all had their turns.

Cobweb Club (1920s). 815 Iberville Street.

Cole's Lawn, Betsy. Josephine and Willow streets. Early jazz patron who frequently gave lawn parties and hired jazz bands. Made a historic spot of her front yard.

The Coliseum (1920s). Boxing arena. Conti and Derbigny streets. Dixieland bands on wagons roamed the streets advertising prize fights and later entertained in the arena. Pay? The musicians got to see the match free.

Columbia Park. On Bayou St. John opposite Southern Park had a few poorly kept rides, but mainly it was a picnic ground. Families came there for recreation and sometimes brought their own bands with them.

Come Clean Hall. Gretna, La. Frequently featured the Buddy Bolden band about the turn of the century.

Congo Square (now Beauregard Square). North Rampart and Orleans streets. Recreation area for the slaves where tribal dancing, African rhythms, and musical instruments were perpetuated. These activities forbidden here by city decree in 1843. Considered by many to be the real birthplace of jazz.

Co-operators Hall. Also called **Hopes Hall** by musicians. 922 North Liberty Street.

Crescent Dance Hall. Washington and Prytania streets.

Crescent Park. Algiers, La. Sometimes ball games were played here, but otherwise it was for general recreational use. Henry Allen, Sr., often played there with his band.

Crescent Park. Gretna, La. Frequently Emmett Hardy and Sidney Arodin played for picnics here.

Crescent Theater. In the Tulane-Crescent Arcade off Baronne Street. Minstrel shows, banjo bands.

Crystal Club (1930s). 1000 Tulane Avenue.

Danger Bar (late 1920s). Bienville Street. Amos Riley.

The Astoria Hotel and Ballroom
The building, on South Rampart Street, was demolished in 1972.

DeSoto Hotel. 420 Baronne Street. In the twenties and thirties, this was a favorite spot for fraternity and high school dances, using top local jazz bands.

Dixie Park. Bienville Street between Murat and Olympia streets. Outdoor amusement area.

Dixieland Hall (opened 1962). Bourbon Street. A small concert hall featuring authentic jazz artists, playing in a commercial dixieland style. "Uncle Tom" type dancers regularly featured.

The Dream Room (closed 1964). 426 Bourbon Street. Mainly rock-and-roll bands with occasional dixieland-style group. Formerly the **Silver Slipper**.

Dream World Theater (1920s). 632 Canal Street. Outstanding ragtime pianists accompanied silent movies. Tom Zimmerman, Irwin Leclere.

Druids Hall. 843 Camp Street.

Eagle Eye Hall (1900s). Algiers, La. The phrase Eagle Eye is a corruption of the hall's true name, *Égalité* (French, meaning "equality"). Torn down to make room for bridge approach.

Eagle Saloon. South Rampart and Perdido streets. Headquarters of the Eagle Band, from which the band's name is derived.

Early's, Frank, Saloon (1900–1913). Franklin and Bienville streets. Featured Tony Jackson in 1910, 1911, 1912.

East End Park (1900s). Jefferson Parish at the lakefront. Happy Schilling's band frequently seen at picnics. Also Fischer's Brass Band.

Old Dauphine Theater.
Lu Rose presented Sophie Tucker here in 1910 for her New Orleans debut. Tom Brown's, Happy Schilling's, and Johnny Fischer's bands all played here.

Bucktown (about 1920)

222

The Halfway House (about 1920)
This is the only known photo of the interior.

Eastman Park (through early 1900s). Off Metairie Road, past cemetery. Picnic and amusement grounds where Happy Schilling and Johnny Fischer frequently played for dancing in a wooden pavilion.

Economy Hall (1885–1940s). 1422 Ursuline Street. Buddy Petit, Earl Humphrey, Pinchback Touro, and King Oliver were frequent leaders. Among musicians, this place was nicknamed **Cheapskate Hall**.

Elite (mid-1920s). Nightclub on Iberville between Rampart and Burgundy streets.

The Elks Club. 1125 Dauphine Street. Regular dances and frequent parades.

Elmira Pleasure Grounds. Belleville and Evalina streets, Algiers, La. Grounds were kept up by several lodges and burial societies. Brass bands like Henry Allen's rehearsed there.

Embassy Club (1936). See Beverly Gardens; Suburban Gardens.

The Entertainers (1902–early 1930s). Franklin Street near Customhouse. Same premises were previously known as **101 Ranch, 102 Ranch, Phillips Cafe**. Some of the great jazzmen played here.

Esperance Hall. See Hopes Hall (1).

Eureka Hall. Bienville and Pelican streets.

Exchange Alley. Between Chartres and Royal streets, running from Canal to Conti. At **Martin's Saloon**, the nonunion musicians would hang around waiting for a phone call from Jack Laine. Union headquarters was upstairs over the saloon.

Fabacher's Rathskellar, 410–418 St. Charles Avenue. Music was supplied with the celebrated food in the first decades of the century. Jazzmen were frequently employed here—but the music they played was mainly waltzes.

Fairgrounds. Near City Park. The famed race track hired bands, too. Buddy Bolden and John Robichaux both were employed before 1910. Site of the New Orleans Jazz and Heritage Festival.

The Piron-Williams Publishing Company
By the time this photograph was taken, the site at 1337 Tulane Avenue was being occupied by a photographer.

Fairmont Hotel. See Grunewald Hotel, Roosevelt Hotel.

Fairplay Hall. 3053 Rampart Street.

The Famous Door (1940s—present). Bourbon and Conti streets. Favorite tourist spot featuring commercial dixieland-style music as demanded by the management. Some of top names that have played long engagements: Sharkey, Santo Pecora, Dukes of Dixieland, George Girard.

Fernandez', Butzie. 1024 Iberville Street. Active between 1905 and the 1920s. Amos White's orchestra.

Fern Cafe and Dance Hall No. 2. 1017 Iberville Street. In the middle and late twenties this was a popular "jitney dance" palace. Many dixielanders got their early schooling here. Among them, Armand Hug, Irving Fazola, Digger Laine.

Fewclothes Cabaret (early 1900s—1917). Basin Street between Canal and Customhouse. Some of its long-term performers: Alcide Frank's Golden Rule Orchestra, 1905; Freddie Keppard, 1913; Walter Decou, 1915; King Oliver, 1915—1916.

Fireman's Hall (1940s—1950s). Westwego, La. For many years a regular Saturday night dance with the Kid Thomas Band.

500 Club (1940s—1950s). Bourbon and St. Louis streets. Long operated by Leon Prima, featuring his own band.

Fountain Lounge. See Roosevelt Hotel.

Francs Amis Hall. 1820 North Robertson Street.

The Frenchman's (1900—1915). Downtown lake corner, Villere and Bienville streets. Traditional meeting ground for the "professors" of Storyville. Jelly Roll Morton, Tony Jackson, Buddy Carter, Alfred Wilson, Albert Carroll, Clarence Williams all played here after hours.

French Union Hall. See Perfect Union Hall.

The Frolic. St. Ann and Dorgenois streets. Later known as the **Top Hat**. Sharkey's band frequently at this location.

Funky Butt Hall (1900s). Perdido Street between Library and Franklin. Buddy Bolden's early base of operations. Its name was **Kenna's Hall**, but hardly anyone knew it by that name. Earlier it had been called **Union Sons Hall**.

Altmyer's Saloon

Globe Hall. St. Claude and St. Peter Streets.

Golden Pumpkin (1920s–1930s). Pontchartrain Boulevard. Featured dixieland-style bands exclusively.

Greenwald Theater. Dauphine Street.

Groshell's Dance Hall (1905–1913). Downtown lake corner, Customhouse and Liberty Street. A district hot spot.

Grunewald Hotel. Later the **Roosevelt**, now the **Fairmont**. Various bands played in the Cave and the Fountain Lounge.

Gypsy Tea Room. See The Brown Derby.

Halfway House (1914–1930). City Park Avenue at Pontchartrain Boulevard. Abbie Brunies led bands that included Stalebread Lacoume, Leon Roppolo, Leo Adde, Charlie Cordilla, and other dixieland luminaries.

Happy Landing (1940s–1950s). On the road to Little Woods. Some of the leaders: Lawrence Toca, Kid Clayton,

Albert Jiles, Charlie Love, Kid Avery, Louis Keppard, Israel Gorman.

Harmony Inn (1920s–1940s). Claiborne and Piety streets. Emile Barnes, leader through many early years. During World War II, George Lewis usually had a trio on the stand.

Haymarket Cabaret (to about 1917). Iberville between Burgundy and North Rampart Streets. Downtown spot that spawned the Original Dixieland Jazz Band.

Heineman Park. Baseball park at Carrollton and Tulane avenues. Happy Schilling's band. Later known as **Pelican Stadium**.

Herman's, Pete. See Ringside Cafe.

Hill's, Butchy. Protection levee at Oak Street.

Holy Ghost Hall. Toledano Street near Saratoga.

Hopes Hall (1). Burgundy and Spain streets. Active with jazz bands from about 1900. Also called **Esperance Hall**, **Jackson Hall**.

The Orpheum Theater Lobby (1932)
This house band played inside for the show, then in the lobby to attract customers. Left to right are Jac Assunto, Howard Reed, Alfred Gallodoro, Howard Tift, Henry Raymond, Charles Rittner.

Hopes Hall (2). 922 North Liberty Street. Headquarters of the Society of Friends of Hope. Also known as **Co-operators Hall**, and **Jackson Hall**.

The Humming Bird Lounge. 1501 Bienville Street.

Irish Hall. Gravier and Derbigny streets.

Italian Hall. Rampart and Esplanade streets.

Jackson Hall. See Hopes Hall (1) and (2).

Japanese Gardens. See The Brown Derby.

Jefferson City Buzzards Hall. Near the carbarn at Magazine and Arabella streets. Headquarters of this active marching group that has made jazz part of its life since the early 1900s.

Jung Hotel Roof (late 1920s–early 1930s). Ellis Stratakos Orchestra.

Kenna's Hall. See Funky Butt Hall.

Kingfish. See The Pig Pen.

Kolb's Restaurant (1900s–present). St. Charles Avenue. Johnny DeDroit Orchestra.

Lafon, Thomy, Hall. See Société des Jeunes Amis.

Lakeview Park. Terminal, West End, on the electric railroad. Private clubs maintained headquarters around here during the Gay Nineties, mainly featuring traveling attractions. Ben Harney, the "Creator of Ragtime" played here at the **Magenta Club** in 1897.

Lala's, Pete (1906–1917). Customhouse and Marais streets. Freddie Keppard, Kid Ory, King Oliver.

La Louisiane Restaurant. Iberville Street. For many years John Robichaux led an orchestra here.

Lavida Ballroom. St. Charles Avenue and Canal Street. Many early jazzmen, including Tony Parenti and Stalebread Lacoume, played in dance bands here. Most groups led by violinists.

Liberty Theater (1920s). 420 St. Charles Avenue. Tony Parenti's Liberty Syncopators. Steve Loyacano's orchestra.

Lincoln Park. Uptown, on Carrollton, between Forshey and Oleander. Buddy Bolden was often the standout attraction in support of a regularly performed balloon ascent stunt.

The Cave, Grunewald Hotel

Papa Laine's Home (1903–1909)
The house is located at 2405 Chartres
Street.

227

St. Katherine's Hall

Preservation Hall
Allen and Sandra Jaffe welcome jazz fans of the sixties.

Mama Lou's
Courtesy Carey Tate

Luthjen's
Destroyed by fire, Jan. 30, 1960.

229

Economy Hall

Associated Artists Studio (1950s)
Larry Borenstein was host to Noon Johnson, Sam Rankins, Harrison Verrett.

The Halfway House

Washington Artillery Hall

Little Club No. 1. Rampart, near Common Street. Featured dixieland.

Little Club No. 2. 205 Dryades. Featured dixieland.

Little Woods. Resort area on Lake Pontchartrain.

Loew's State. 1108 Canal Street. Dixieland in the pit band.

Longshoreman's Hall. 2059 Jackson Avenue.

Love and Charity Hall. Corner of Eagle and Poplar Streets.

Lucien Pavilion. At Old Spanish Fort. Dance pavilion.

Luthjen's (1940s–1950s). Marais at Almonaster Street. Popular weekend dance place. Big Eye Louis Nelson, Billie and Dee Dee Pierce were associated with the place for many years.

Lyric Theater. 201 Burgundy Street. The house pit band was led by John Robichaux. Burned in 1927.

Magnolia Plantation. Owned by Governor Henry Clay Warmouth, it was in the sugarcane business. The children of its hundreds of field hands were taught music once a week by Professor Jim Humphrey during the early 1900s. Among those who became prominent jazzmen were Chris Kelly, Jim Robinson and his brother, Sam.

Mahogany Hall (1903–1949). Lulu White's notorious bordello. Kid Ross played the piano from 1903 to 1912.

Majestic Hall. Seventh and Magazine streets. An uptown spot favored by Tom Brown and his coterie.

Mama Lou's (1940s–1950s). On Lake Pontchartrain toward Little Woods. A pier restaurant–dance hall open on weekends with dancing to bands led by Peter Bocage, Kid Shots Madison, and others.

Heineman Park (1936)
Here, the Pelicans played baseball and Happy Schilling's band played dixieland. Shown are Happy Schilling, guitar; Bob Aquilera, trombone; Henry Knecht, trumpet.

Fern Cafe and Dance Hall No. 2
Courtesy Scoop Kennedy

232

Mandeville Swells Social Club (1903–1909). 2403 Chartres Street. Papa Laine bands.

Manny's Tavern (1940s). Benefit and St. Roch streets. George Lewis.

The Maple Leaf Club. Oak Street in Carrollton. Society Jazz Band played here in the seventies and eighties; later, the Louisiana Repertory Jazz Ensemble.

Mardi Gras Lounge (1940s–present). Bourbon Street. Owner-clarinetist Sid Davilla frequently sat in with the house bands when jazz was played there. Some of the leaders: George Lewis, Papa Celestin, Percy Humphrey, Sharkey, Freddie Kohlman. Lizzie Miles was regularly featured.

Martin's Cafe. See Bucktown.

Martin's Saloon. See Exchange Alley.

Masonic Hall. See Oddfellows Hall.

Milneburg. Sometimes called **Old Lake**. Busy lakefront resort area. Each of the hundreds of camps had its own music. All jazz musicians worked at Milneburg frequently. The seawall put in by the WPA in the mid-thirties was the end of the camps.

Moulin Rouge (from 1918). Bourbon Street. This is now a strip joint, but in 1919 it offered the Silver Leaf Orchestra, and for many years after was the home base of Sharkey's Kings of Dixieland.

The Music Box (1920s). Canal and Prieur Streets. Willie Pajeaud.

Nancy Hanks Saloon (*ca.* 1900). Later, **Rice's Cafe**.

National Park. Ball park at Third and Willow streets. Customarily, bands were employed by sports entrepreneurs.

New Dixie Park. Bienville and Olympia streets. The big feature was a wading pool, but there were picnics with music, too.

New Orleans Country Club. Pontchartrain Boulevard. All of the top bands played here, but the A. J. Piron Orchestra was most steadily employed.

New Orleans Jazz Museum (1961–present). Museum operated by the New Orleans Jazz Club. Sold to the Louisiana State Museum in 1979.

New Slipper Night Club (1933). 426 Bourbon Street. Merritt Brunies orchestra.

No-Name Theater. 1025 Canal Street. Minstrels, blues singers, prior to World War I.

Oasis Cabaret (early 1920s). Iberville Street.

Oddfellows Hall. 1116 Perdido Street. Scene of the notorious French Balls given by the "Two Well-Known Gentlemen" every carnival for the madams and girls of Storyville. Also known as **Masonic Hall**.

The Old Absinthe House. On the corner of Bourbon and Bienville streets. Dates from 1801. During the twenties and thirties it featured outstanding pianists. Among those who worked there for long periods were Steve Lewis, Frank Froeba, Burnell Santiago, and Walter "Fats" Pichon.

Old Lake. See Milneburg.

Old Spanish Fort. An amusement park on the site of the original military installation. The ruins of the fort exist at the end of Wisner Blvd. "Tokyo Gardens" and "The Frolics," both cabarets, were regularly hosts to great Dixieland bands like Johnny Bayersdorffer's Orchestra and Johnny Miller's "Frolickers." Brown's Ice Cream Parlor also offered jazz entertainment.

Olympia Hall. Carrollton Avenue and Oak Street.

101 Ranch. See The Entertainers.

102 Ranch. See The Entertainers.

The Orchard. 942 Conti Street. Later, **Pete Herman's Ringside Cafe**.

Orpheum Theater. 125 University Place. Emile Tosso was leader of pit band, but some jazzmen were frequently employed.

Paddock Lounge (1940s–1960s). Bourbon Street. Papa Celestin, Alphonse Picou, Lee Collins, Albert Burbank, Octave Crosby, and Paul Barbarin, among others, have been bandleaders here. Management has always demanded a commercial product. Earlier known as the **Champagne Room**.

Congo Square

Anderson's Arlington Annex
The Annex was at the hub of Storyville.

The Happy Landing

Palace Theater. 201 Dauphine Street.

Palm Gardens. Algiers, La.

The Parisian Room (late 1940s–1950s). 112 Royal Street. Tony Almerico's base, from which his frequent coast-to-coast broadcasts emanated and where the New Orleans Jazz Club had its first session.

Patterson Hotel. Rampart near Julia Street. George Lewis and Kid Punch Miller were frequent performers.

Pecan Grove. Near Harvey's Canal, Gretna. Beer and dancing under the stars to the music of Elton Theodore or even Chris Kelly.

Pelican Hall. Royal and Bienville streets.

Pelican Stadium. Tulane and Carrollton avenues. Baseball park formerly known as **Heineman Park**. Happy Schilling, Tom Brown, Johnny Fischer, Punch Miller.

Penny-Wonderland (*ca.* 1915). Canal Street. J. Russell Robinson on piano and his brother on drums made a regular vaudeville act out of accompanying Original Dixieland Jazz Band records.

Perfect Union Hall. Also called **French Union Hall**. North Rampart and Dumaine streets.

Perseverance Hall. 1642 North Villere Street.

Perseverance Hall No. 4. Dumaine and St. Claude streets. Once the site of Masonic dances with music by the likes of Kid Rena or even the Tonic Triad Banc. It still stands in the middle of Louis Armstrong Park.

Frank Early's Saloon

Phillips Cafe. See The Entertainers.

Picou's Bar. Claiborne Avenue and St. Philip Street. Owned by Alphonse Picou from early 1950s until his death in 1961. The place had a stage and usually a band, often featuring Walter Blue and Lionel Tapo.

Pig Ankle Cabaret (early 1900s). Iberville and Franklin streets.

The Pig Pen. Decatur and Ursuline streets. Dee Dee and Billie Pierce played here. It was also known as the **Kingfish**.

Piron-Williams Publishing Company. 1337 Tulane Avenue.

Poodle Dog Cabaret (*ca.* 1908–1917). Liberty and Bienville streets.

Preservation Hall (1961–present). 726 St. Peter Street.

Princess Theater (1920s). 1828 Felicity Street.

Pup Cafe. 1017 Iberville Street. Until Prohibition, this was a leading jazz cabaret. In 1920 the premises became a taxi dance hall, **Fern Cafe and Dance Hall No. 2**.

Pythian Hall. Bermuda Street, Algiers, La. Favorite spot for weddings and dances. Manuel Perez, Bunk Johnson, Edouard Clem played here.

Pythian Roof. South Saratoga and Gravier streets. In the post–World War I era, Manuel Perez played here.

Quarella's. Milneburg. This popular lakefront spot was a stronghold for early dixieland stars. The Christian brothers, the Brunies family, and most of Papa Laine's gang played here on weekends. Sharkey, a nephew of the owner, got his start here as a teenager playing clarinet.

The Red Onion. Julia and South Rampart streets. Louis Armstrong, Johnny Dodds.

Rice's Cafe (1904–1913). Marais and Iberville streets. Earlier, **Nancy Hanks Saloon**. Manuel Perez.

Ringside Cafe. Dauphine and Bienville streets. Broadcasts of the Melon Pickers with Raymond Burke emanated from here. Later, George Hartman led a group for many years. Since the 1930s this has been known as **Pete Herman's Ringside Cafe**.

Mahogany Hall

Riverside Park. Dauphine and Andry streets. Tent shows, traveling carnivals, midway gambling games. Local jazzmen hired to play pit jobs for minstrel shows. Eli Green shows played here.

Roosevelt Hotel (1930s–1970s). University Place. Formerly the **Grunewald**, now the **Fairmont Hotel**. Many rooms where bands play—Blue Room, Fountain Lounge.

Saenger Theater (1930s). Canal and North Rampart streets. Louis Prima frequently featured here. Famed pit band with many dixieland stars.

St. Cere Hall. North Claiborne Avenue, between Columbus and Kerlerec streets. Early stomping ground for the New Orleans Rhythm Kings.

St. Charles Hotel Mezzanine. A. J. Piron.

Old Spanish Fort

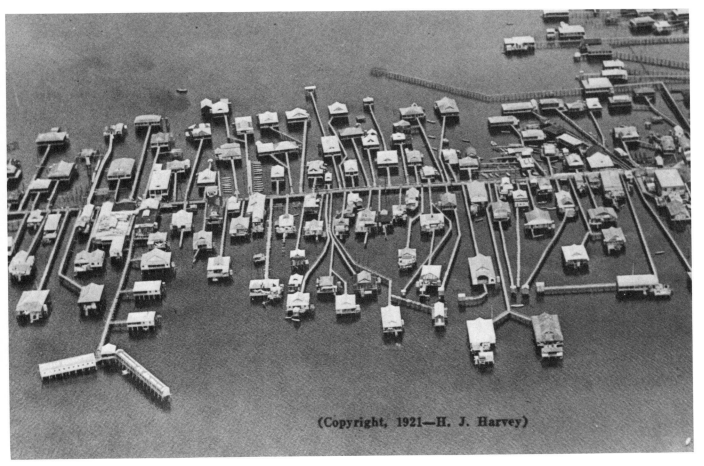

(Copyright, 1921—H. J. Harvey)

Milneburg (1921)

239

Pete Lala's

St. Katherine's Hall. 1509 Tulane Avenue. A major dance hall where Kid Ory, Bunk Johnson, King Oliver, John Robichaux, and the Crescent Orchestra frequently appeared.

San Jacinto Hall (to 1966). 1422 Dumaine Street, between Villere and Robertson streets. Historic spot where Bunk Johnson's band made celebrated American Music discs. Top traditional stars worked here. Used as late as 1965 for recording.

Sans Souci Hall. 2832 Howard Street. Bunk Johnson played here.

Shim Sham Club (mid-1930s). 229 Bourbon Street.

Shoto Cabaret (early 1900s). Iberville and Franklin streets.

The Silver Slipper. 426 Bourbon Street. Premises became the Dream Room. Tony Parenti, Jules Bauduc led groups here in the 1920s.

Sixth Ward Athletic Club. Boxing arena. Tom Brown, Happy Schilling, Johnny Fischer.

Société Des Jeunes Amis. 1477 North Villere Street. Also known as **Thomy Lafton Hall**.

Southern Park. Bayou St. John via Esplanade cars. Known before the Civil War as **Tivoli Gardens**. Built on the old Allard Plantation.

Southern Rifle Club Hall. Claiborne Avenue near Marigny Street. A dirty old saloon of the barrelhouse variety where some good piano players could be heard—notably, in the 1930s, Burnell Santiago.

Spano's (ca. 1900). Franklin and Perdido streets. Bunk Johnson, Jelly Roll Morton.

Spec's Moulin Rouge (1940s–1950s). Marrero, La. Kid Thomas.

Sportsman's Park. Gretna, La.

Stand-by Hall (ca. 1910). Frenchmen and Decatur streets. Frequently featured Frank Christian's Ragtime Band.

Stoltz's Union Hall. 132–34 Exchange Place. This was an old fashioned barroom where idle white musicians would gather and drink.

Storyville (1897–1917). Bounded by Basin Street, North, Robertson Street, St. Louis Street, and Iberville Street. New Orleans' legally constituted red-light district. Some jazzmen worked in its cabarets, and many pianists in its brothels.

240

The Bandstand at Tom Anderson's (1921)
At work, left to right, are Paul Barbarin, Arnold Metoyer, Luis Russell, Willie Santiago, Albert Nicholas.

Strand Theater (1920s). Baronne and Gravier streets. Music frequently supplied by the New Orleans Owls.

Suburban Gardens (*ca.* 1915–mid-1920s). Jefferson Parish, La. Papa Celestin held this job down in early years. During the 1920s the New Orleans Owls were often the house band, and in the early Depression years, Louis Armstrong opened here on his triumphal return to his hometown. Later known as **Beverly Gardens**, **Embassy Club**.

Tammany Social and Athletic Club (early 1900s). 334 South Liberty Street.

Thoman's Hall. Dauphine, near Elmira Street. Some dancing, but also boxing matches. Pre–World War I.

Thom's Roadhouse (1918–1938). Pontchartrain Boulevard, almost to West End.

Three Oaks Playground. Little Woods. Popular picnic spot with open dance pavilion where many dixieland musicians performed.

Tin Roof Cafe. Washington Street and Claiborne Avenue. Immortalized in song, the Tin Roof became a vinegar factory before 1910.

Tip Top Club (–1950s). West bank. Stomping ground for Kid Thomas band.

Tivoli Gardens. See Southern Park.

Tokyo Gardens (1920s). Spanish Fort. Longtime stronghold of Johnny Bayersdorffer's orchestra.

Tonti Social Club (1920s). 823 North Tonti St.

Top Hat. See The Frolic.

Tranchina's Restaurant (1920s). Spanish Fort. Longtime post of the A. J. Piron Orchestra.

Artesan Hall
The high bandstand protected the musicians.

Triangle Theater (1918–1920s). 814 Canal Street. Irwin Leclere accompanied silent movies on the piano.

Tulane Athletic Club. A boxing arena on Howard Street, between Canal and Gasquet streets. Tom Brown, Happy Schilling.

Tuxedo Dance Hall (1909–1913). Franklin Street, near Bienville Street. This is where the Original Tuxedo Orchestra began. Oscar Celestin, Peter Bocage were leaders here. A shooting brawl shuttered it.

The Twenty-eight (1895–1920). Franklin Street, between Canal and Iberville streets. Buddy Bolden's orchestra.

Tyler's Beer Garden (1930s–1940s). 119 Walnut Street. Tillman-Avery Band in the 1940s.

Union Sons Hall. See Funky Butt Hall.

Venice Inn. Same as **Bucktown Tavern**.

Vieux Carre Inn. Bourbon and St. Ann streets. Pete Fountain's place, it usually features his group.

Villa Cabaret (1906–1917). Franklin Street, between Bienville and Iberville streets.

Waif's Home. Canal Boulevard and City Park Avenue. Careers of Louis Armstrong, Kid Shots Madison, Kid Rena began here.

Washington Artillery Hall. 729–37 St. Charles Avenue.

Washington Garden. Milneburg. Not on the piers. Much like a German beer garden. Dixieland jazz and barbershop quartets.

West End. At the end of Pontchartrain Boulevard, on the lake. Resort area in the northwest corner of the city.

West End Bandstand
Seating was free at the sides and the tables, where refreshments could be ordered. The white-painted seats in the center were reserved. Note Mannessier's Ice Cream Parlor and the entrance to the scenic railway.

West End Roof Garden (1920s). West End. Some of the leaders: Kid Ory, Papa Celestin. Also the New Orleans Owls, the Silver Leaf Orchestra, many others.

White City (1900s). Carrollton and Tulane Avenues. An amusement park where many bands played for concerts and dancing. Later became **New Orleans Ball Park**.

Winter Garden (to 1915). Boxing arena. Baronne Street near Poydras Street. Tom Brown's band, Fischer's band, Happy Schilling's band, Papa Laine.

Wow Hall. 2501 Urquhart Street. Frequently hired for dances. The famed Johnny Wiggs record session that produced "King Zulu Parade" and "If Ever I Cease to Love" was made here in 1954.

YMGC (Young Men's Gymnastic Club) Rowing Club. Bayou St. John. The Invincibles, Six and 7/8 String Band.

The Champagne Room (1937)
Featured are Willie Joseph, Alton Purnell, and Alvin Woods. Later, this became the Paddock.

243

Storyville (1906)

Buddy Bolden's Home

Magnolia Plantation
Professor Jim Humphrey organized and taught a band of youngsters here, among them, Jim Robinson and Chris Kelly.

At the Lavida Ballroom in the Vieux Carré (about 1922)

Left to right are Eddie Faye, Harold Peterson, Buzzy Williams, Charlie Fishbein, Florenzo Ramos, Joe Kinneman, Stalebread Lacoume.

Thom's Roadhouse

The Elks Club
This was the scene of much musical activity in the 1930s. The Masonic Brass Band is shown. Identifiable are Albert Jones, leader, clarinet; Ophelia Grigsby, saxophone. To her right is A. B. Spears. Fourth from right is Red Clark, trombone.

The Shim Sham Club
(mid-1930s)
The band featured was led by saxman Harold Jordy. Others, left to right, are Emile Guerin, Dave Winstein, Von Gammon, Bob Wiley, Chink Martin, Tony Almerico.

Druid's Hall (1922)
Lodge official Dominick Barocco used his own band here. Left to right are Ferdinand Knecht, Gus Zimmerman, Martin Kirsch, Joe Barocco, Dominick Barocco, Leonce Mello.

Ringside Cafe (1927)
The New Orleans Harmony Kings are on the stand. Left to right are Chink Martin, Freddie Neumann, Joe Capraro, Sidney Arodin, Sharkey, Augie Schellang.

Old Spanish Fort (1924)
This picture shows the Frolic at lower left.

Courtesy Joe Mares

The Eagle Saloon

249

Pete Herman's Ringside Cafe

The Harmony Inn

The Alley

Interior of the Old Absinthe House (about 1926)
Frank Froeba is at the piano.

Home of Johnny and Baby Dodds (1901)
The house, located at 2123 Philip Street, is a duplex. The Dodds brothers lived in the left half.

Picou's Bar (1961)

Photo by Bill Russell

252

Bucktown (1910)

Photo by Bill Russell

Funky Butt Hall
By the time this photo was taken in the
1930s, the building had become a church.

253

The Pig Pen
This location is Decatur and
Ursulines streets.

Elks Hall (1962)
Earlier this was known as Bulls Hall.

Photo by Bill Russell

254

The Waifs' Home
Pictured are the home and its administrator, Captain Joseph Jones, during the period of Louis Armstrong's residency.

The Alhambra Club
Harrison Barnes and his NOLA Band and Charlie Love's Band played here, on Olivier Street.

NEW ORLEANS JAZZ AFLOAT

Part of the legend of jazz is the role played by steamboats in its history. Some of these side- and stern-wheelers plied Lake Pontchartrain as excursion boats. Others, more famous, carried passengers and musicians up the river to such romantic ports of call as Memphis and St. Louis. The roster of the jazzmen who supplied music for these cruises reads like a who's who of jazz.

More affluent members of the community who owned yachts and other seaborne equipment felt that homegrown jazz was just the thing to enliven a nautical party. People like the late Blaise D'Antoni, scion of the family that owned the Standard Fruit Company, frequently cruised to South and Central America with their friends, never failing to carry a complement of dixielanders on board. On one occasion, in a burst of enthusiasm, D'Antoni threw Sharkey overboard, but he made amends later by giving his favorite trumpeter a gold left-handed French Selmer horn (worth five hundred dollars in the 1940s), which Sharkey used for the rest of his life. Rear Admiral Ernest Lee Jahncke was a jazz fan, too. He owned various yachts and frequently threw musical parties on them featuring bands like the Six and 7/8 String Band and the Tuxedo Orchestra.

Since New Orleans, bordered by Lake Pontchartrain and the Mississippi, is surrounded by water, its no wonder that jazz found its way to the water too. Many older jazzmen cherish their recollections of jazz cruises among their fondest memories.

SS *Camelia*. Pre–World War I vessel featuring string trios and quintets.

SS *Capitol* (demolished in 1942). Famed as host to the Fate Marable Orchestra, that included Louis Armstrong and the Dodds brothers in 1919. In later years A. J. Piron's, Sidney Desvigne's, and Fats Pichon's orchestras all worked at various times on the *Capitol*.

SS *Dixie* (1920s–1930s). This ship ran an ocean run between New Orleans and New York and featured jazz by New Orleans bands.

SS *Greater New Orleans*. Desvigne Orchestra was the major musical attraction on this river steamer in the 1930s.

SS *Island Queen* (1920s–1930s). Clarence Desdunes, Dan Desdunes, and Sidney Desvigne all had their turns as bandleaders on this river steamer.

SS *J.S.* Fate Marable was often the leader in the twenties and thirties on a river run that often included Pops Foster and Lonnie Johnson.

SS *Madison*. A Lake Pontchartrain excursion boat. Band, sometimes led by Pete Pecoppia or Benny Deichmann in the twenties.

SS *Mandeville* (1915–1928). This lake steamer made excursions from West End to Mandeville. It carried horses and buggies, later small cars, so that passengers could use them on the other side of the lake. It then proceeded up the Tchefuncte River and docked near Three Rivers, making the return trip the same evening—and jazz music all the way.

SS *New Camelia*. A lake excursion steamer with a huge dance floor. Dominick Barroco usually led the band.

SS *President* (1942–present). Saturday dance cruises featured the Crawford-Ferguson Night Owls, the Dutch Andrus Orchestra, Johnny Wiggs, and other outstanding jazz bands.

SS *St. Paul*. One of the first to offer jazz on the river, it had Fate Marable at times, as well as Sidney Desvigne.

SS *Susquehanna*. This lake steamer's music was supplied by the band of Dominick and Joe Barocco, 1923–1925.

The SS *Dixie*
On deck are Harold Dejan, seated; Lester Santiago, standing behind the life preserver; and Casimir Paul, with the guitar.

The SS *Capitol*
During the steamer's last years Fats Pichon brought his band aboard. He's standing fourth from the left. To his left, wearing four-in-hands, are Irving Douroux, Sam Casimir, Al ———, Clarence "Perch" Thornton, Jack Lamont, Harry Lang, Manuel Crusto, Willie Casimir, and Ray Brown.

The NOJC
In 1958 the New Orleans Jazz Club celebrated its tenth birthday on the *President*. The event was telecast on Dave Garroway's *Wide Wide World* (NBC). Standing next to the ship's calliope are Raymond and Katherine Burke and Bill Russell.

Fate Marable's Orchestra
The SS *Capitol*, largest of the Streckfus line boats, always offered superb music. Leader Fate Marable, here at the piano, was probably the best-known bandmaster on the river. His group on this trip, about 1920: Henry Kimball, Boyd Atkins, Johnny St. Cyr, David Jones, Norman Mason, Louis Armstrong, George Brashear, and Baby Dodds.

The SS *J.S.*

Courtesy Frederick Way, Jr.

Somewhere on the Mississippi (1931)
Aboard the *J.S.*, clarinetist Meyer Weinberg
(Gene Meyer) and pianist Emile Guerin try
the calliope.

Lake Steamer
The SS *Madison* plied the lake during the
1930s with a quorum of jazzmen aboard.
Here are Louis Barbarin, Emanuel Sayles,
and Eddie Pierson.

Jahncke's *Aunt Dinah*
The Six and 7/8 String Band pose on the *Aunt Dinah*, a houseboat belonging to Admiral Ernest Jahncke, about 1921. Left to right, kneeling, are Howard McCaleb, Charles Hardy, Hilton "Midget" Harrison, Edmond Souchon, Bill Gibbons. Standing are Bob Reynolds, Admiral Jahncke, Shields O'Reardon.

Another Great Marable Band on the SS *Sidney* (1918)
Left to right are Baby Dodds, Bebé Ridgley, Joe Howard, Louis Armstrong, Fate Marable, David Jones, Johnny Dodds, Johnny St. Cyr, Pops Foster.

The SS _Capitol_ Band (early 1920s)
Among the players were many future jazz stars. Left to right are Harvey Lankford, Sidney Desvigne, Floyd Casey (standing), Ed Allen, Johnny St. Cyr, Ike Jefferson, Walter Thomas, Norman Mason, Gene Sedric, Pops Foster.

Yacht Party (1923)
Members of the Tuxedo Orchestra and the Young Tuxedo Orchestra aboard Admiral Jahncke's yacht. Left to right, seated: Henry Julian, Bush Hall, Willard Thoumy, Lawrence Marrero, John Marrero. Standing: Chinee Foster, Milford Dolliole, Bebé Ridgley, Bob Thomas, Duck Ernest Johnson, Eddie Marrero.

Courtesy Milford Dolliole

The Old Lake Steamer *Mandeville*

Desvigne's Bandsmen Take a Break
On the SS *Island Queen*, about 1929, are, left to right, Louis Nelson, Percy Servier, Fats Pichon, Henry Julian, Gene Ware, Ransom Knowling.

263

SS _Susquehanna_
Pictured on Lake Pontchartrain about 1915.

THERE'S NO BUSINESS LIKE SHOW BUSINESS

Since the turn of the century, jazz has been exported via tent shows, medicine shows, revivals, minstrel shows, and carnivals. By the twenties there was a plethora of Orleanians on the boards in vaudeville. People like Al Bernard, Esther Bigeou, Spo-dee-o-dee (Sam Theard) and Lizzie Miles, besides composers Joe Verges and Irwin Leclere, were headline attractions all over America. Since the forties, jazz has been finding an erratic but effective place in TV. What began as a neighborhood music, basically functional in character, has often had to warp its form and style to meet the superficial tastes of an ever growing audience. Indeed, in the earliest days the jazzman faced his public as a clown or buffoon, playing to people insufficiently responsive to the music as the art form it was. He learned to wear grotesque hats, "rube" outfits, blackface, striped blazers, and convict costumes. He might perform standing on his head or tooting two or three horns at once. He practiced dismantling his instrument as he played it, finally coaxing a blues out of his mouthpiece alone.

Other audiences permitted themselves to be awed by the musician's ability to sustain a single note through three whole choruses. They marveled at the facility with which he might play octaves above the intended range of his instrument. Our pioneer jazzmen cultivated these freakish skills because they put meat on the table and coins in their pockets. More people were prepared to pay to listen to animal imitations on horns than to the beauty of euphonic sounds.

As a result, out-of-town audiences of the twenties and thirties rarely got to hear the *true* sound of New Orleans jazz. Entrepreneurs applied pressure to pander to a public to whom music was not a part of daily living but an occasional exotic thrill.

Our musicians never thought of themselves as artists in the early years, or of their music as an art. As long as the pay was attractive the musician permitted himself to be exhibited rather than presented. It became a cliché among performers that you couldn't work out of town unless you were prepared to play "loud, fast and wrong."

Mainly through phonograph records, a hard-core, serious listening audience developed, which eventually provided concert platforms for great New Orleans jazzmen. By the last of the thirties, they could appear before the public wearing business suits, street clothes, or tuxedos and, without the need to make funny faces, hold audiences enraptured for hours. In the declining years of the twentieth century, New Orleans jazz was being performed with dignity at least once or twice a year on most college campuses. It is, though rarely, seen on TV and in Hollywood films.

In these photos you can see how these musicians looked in the strange and varied environments provided by show business. Some are superficially amusing if you don't consider the circumstances that forced such superior artists into such strange costumes and settings. At times it was like Toscanini conducting a pit band for a flea circus. This sometimes depressing portfolio of the jazzman away from home was difficult to accumulate. Many of the musicians don't look as contented as they sometimes do in their hometown photos—and we don't wonder.

The Tulanians (1925)
During the roaring twenties, jazz wasn't limited to the lower economic classes. On stage at the Strand Theater are, left to right, insurance broker Harry S. Kaufman, Jr.; investment broker Herman Kohlmeyer; attorney John M. "Buddy" Gehl; architect William Follansbee; sugar and rice tycoon Albert Broussard; Gerald "Skinny" Andrus (Rex, 1963), former head of New Orleans Public Service and chairman of the board of Mid-South Industries; dentist Fred Fridge. Another Tulanian, not shown, Isidore "Dede" Newman II, president of City Stores, Inc.

Courtesy Ernest Smith Collection, John Steiner

Rhapsody in Black and Blue (1931)
This Paramount short subject starred Louis Armstrong and his orchestra.

Jules Bauduc Orchestra (1928)
At the Silver Slipper are, left to right, Mike Lala, Luther Lamar, Roland Leach, Monk Hazel, Paul Peque, Jules Bauduc, Horace Diaz, Eddie Powers, Oscar Marcour.

Welcome to Disneyland (1960)
Two resident bands greet arriving New Orleans All-Stars. On the left is Johnny St. Cyr's Hot Five. St. Cyr is almost hidden, second from left. Clarinetist Polo Barnes and trumpeter Mike Delay are native Orleanians. On the plane steps, arriving from the Crescent City are Thomas Jefferson, trumpet; Paul Barbarin, drums; Frog Joseph, trombone; Raymond Burke, clarinet. Next to Burke is Stanley Mendelson, piano. The uniformed dixieland band on the right is the Straw Hat Six.

Connee Boswell (1955)
This member of the famed Crescent City singing trio was a guest on the Tony Almerico Show.

Courtesy Mrs. John Menville

Courtesy Rene Gelpi

The Original New Orleans Owls (1924)
At the Old Sazerac Ballroom, are, left to right, Dick Mackie, Monk Smith, Red Mackie, Benjy White, Eblen Rau, standing behind Rene Gelpi, and leader Earl Crumb.

Sharkey Auditions Mickey Rooney
(1940s)

Courtesy Ray Bauduc

The Bobcats (1939)
Four of them were New Orleans kids: Ray Bauduc, drums; Eddie Miller, saxophone; Nappy Lamare, guitar; Irving Fazola, clarinet. The others are Bob Haggart, string bass; Jess Stacy, piano; Billy Butterfield, trumpet; Warren Smith, trombone. Bob Crosby sits in the foreground, studying the live bobcat.

Remnant of Fame (1961)
Johnny Bayersdorffer stands in front of his old band banner at the New Orleans Jazz Museum.

Courtesy Duncan Schiedt

Louis Prima's Orchestra in Films (1930)
Band members are Gene Meyer, Godfrey Hirsch, Prima, Frank Pinero, Frank Federico, Louis Masinter.

Sharkey Tours the Orient (1940s)
On the runningboard is pianist Roy Zimmerman. It's Joe Rotis with the trombone and Sharkey in the derby. The photo was taken in Tokyo.

Jazz Tricks
Manuel Manetta played piano and any string, brass, or reed instrument. He taught music at his home in Algiers. He was well known for this stunt.

Publicity Hollywood Style
Dorothy Lamour takes a paradiddle lesson from Ray Bauduc in Hollywood as Eddie Miller stands by.

Courtesy Ray Bauduc

Benny Payton's Orchestra in Paris
(1920s)
Henry Saparo, New Orleans banjoist,
and Sidney Bechet, far right, go oriental.

Courtesy Duncan Schiedt

Original Dixieland Jazz Band at the Texas Centennial (1928)
Sharkey has replaced Nick La Rocca on trumpet. Larry Shields is on clarinet. Daddy Edwards plays trombone and Tony Sbarbaro holds the drumsticks. The other musicians are an unidentified piano player and Harry Barth on bass.

273

Sharkey in New York (1930s)
The group includes Johnny Castaign, drums, and Bill Bourgeois, clarinet.

Buckley's New Orleans Serenaders (1858)
This minstrel show wasn't from the Crescent City, but the use of the name shows the prestige already attained by New Orleans for its music.

The Legendary Tony Jackson (about 1918)
Here he is on stage with a trio of "Pretty Babies," including the celebrated Florence Mills.

275

A Royal Welcome Chicago Style

Courtesy Agnes Brown

King of vaudeville comics, Joe Frisco, greets Tom Brown's Band from Dixieland at the station. Billy Lambert is the drummer behind Frisco's right hand. Brown, in straw hat, stands behind Frisco, playing the trombone. Next to him, left to right, are Ray Lopez, Larry Shields, and Deacon Loyacano. Upper left, wearing cap, is musical comedy star Joe Cook.

The Five Rubes on Tour in Vaudeville
Tom Brown's Band from Dixieland dressed up to accompany entertainer Joe Frisco. Left to right are Al Williams, Tom Brown, Ray Lopez, Larry Shields, Deacon Loyacano.

Los Angeles (1924)
Papa Mutt Carey (seated, holding his trumpet) led this group, including, left to right, Leo Davis, Bud Scott, Ram Hall, and L. S. Cooper.

Opera vs. Jazz (1925)
Johnny Bayersdorffer's Red Devils represented jazz in this duel, which took place at the Metropolitan (Paramount) Theater in Los Angeles.

Clint Bush's Band (1919)
Two Orleanians, Tom Brown on trombone and Tony Giardina on clarinet, made this Chicago group into a jazz band. Leader Bush plays the banjo.

Zue Robertson
Zue, standing second from left, brought a Crescent City sound to the Kit Carson Wild West Show before 1920.

PROF. TONEY JACKSON

The above cut is a good likeness of Prof. Toney
Jackson, Pianist at Russell and Dago.

Mr. Jackson is one of the best entertainers in the
city, and is well liked.   He is a good card.

Early Advertisement
Professor Tony Jackson is featured on an advertising throwaway from a Chicago cabaret in 1912.

Bandsman (1909)
Barnum and Bailey's Circus band was enlivened by the horn of George McCullum, Sr.

Courtesy Charlotte Boutney

281

The Blair-Saenger Harmony Hoboes (1933)
Posing by the railroad tracks on Basin Street across from the Saenger Theater: front, left to right, Ellis Stratakos, Jake Gensberger, Johnny Miller, George Brunies, George Schilling, Jr., Joe Capraro; rear, Jimmy Rush, Mike Ryan, two unidentified band members, Luther Lamar, Marion Suter.

Making the Vaudeville Circuit (1917)
Left to right are Roy Palmer, Sugar Johnny Smith, Lawrence Duhé, Mamie Lane, Herb Lindsay, Louis Keppard, Montudie Garland.

François and His Louisianians
Francis Mosley, a New Orleans drummer, led this group in Chicago. Kid Punch Miller is in the center and guitarist Charles Ducasting, right.

The Band That Never Was (1914)
In rehearsal for an Orpheum Circuit vaudeville tour that never materialized, this band of superstars includes, left to right, standing, Clarence Williams, John Lindsay, Jimmie Noone, Bebé Ridgley; seated, Papa Clestin, Tom Benton, Johnny St. Cyr. The snare drummer is Ninesse Trepagnier; the violinist, Armand J. Piron.

The New Orleans Rhythm Masters (1926)
The group never played in New Orleans but was mostly made up of Crescent City natives. In the front row, left to right, are Jack Teagarden, Red Bolman, Sidney Arodin, Charlie Cordilla, Amos Ayala. The others, not "from home," are Terry Shand, piano; George Shaw, vocals; Jerry Fresno, banjo (standing at right).

The Oliver Band in Vaudeville (1922)
Here, appearing in California, are Ram Hall, Honore Dutrey, King Oliver, Lil Armstrong, David Jones, Johnny Dodds, James A. Palao, Montudie Garland.

In California (1921–1922)
Here, the Kid Ory Original Creole Jazz Band held forth for a while. Left to right are Baby Dodds, Ory, Mutt Carey, Montudie Garland, Wade Whaley.

Richard M. Jones's Jazz Wizards (1920s)
Here are Jones, Johnny St. Cyr, and Albert Nicholas.

The Brass Section of Joe Robichaux's Big Swing Band (late 1930s)
Seated are Kildee Holloway, John "Turk" Girard, Gene Ware. Standing are Frog Joseph, Clement Tervalon.

The Argentine Dons (1930s)
These were all Orleanians under the direction of Slim Lamar. Left to right are Tony Almerico, Irwin Kurz, unknown, Jimmy Rush, unknown, Slim Lamar, Jack Cohen, Von Gammon, George Schilling, Jr., Steve Massicot, Ellis Stratakos. The central figure framed by the stairway is the master of ceremonies. The picture was taken at the Peabody Hotel in Memphis, Tenn.

King Zulu (1949)
The king was Louis Armstrong, who also brought his All-Stars for a concert.

New Orleans Police Department Minstrels (1920)
Seated are Major Fennerty (left) and Dominick Barocco. Standing, left to right, are Freddie Williams, Joe Vitari, Manny Blessing, Yellow Nunez, Alex Coulon.

288

On the Road (1930)
Posed on the runningboard of this 1925 Studebaker is Charlie Cordilla in fashionable plus fours and argyle socks. Behind him is trumpeter Bill Gillen. Opposite, in the dark coat, is Joe Capraro and, behind him, Leo Adde.

Catskills or Bust (1930)
This jalopy carried a whole band plus instruments from New Orleans. Charlie Cordilla, Chink Martin, Bill Gillen, Leo Adde, Sidney Arodin, and Red Jessup were all aboard, along with the driver, Joe Capraro, seen seated on the front fender.

Police Convention (1960)
Sal Magiotta, clarinet, with Governor Jimmie Davis at the convention in Shreveport.

Gene Austin's Accompanists (1934)
Monk Hazel is flanked by Coco Himel
(right) and the replacement for the original
Candy Candido.

Chicago (1923)
An unidentified lady welcomes Chink Martin.

Arcadian Serenaders
Wingy Manone organized an all-new Arcadian Serenaders for this 1924 Okeh record date. They cut eight sides in eight hours. Wingy is the only Orleanian in the group.

On Tour in Texas (about 1925)
Left to right are Arthur Joseph, Annie ———, Freddie "Boo Boo" Miller, Octave Crosby, Henry Julian, emcee Sherman Cook, Lee Collins, Percy Darensburg.

Photo by Jack Hurley

Selling Their Candidate (1963)
Left to right are Placide Adams, Frog Joseph, Kid Howard, Louis Cottrell, Jr., Paul Barbarin.

Another LP
Eddie Miller and Al Rose recording another album for the State of Louisiana.

Radio Was Still Big in the 1950s
Here, left to right, are Raymond Burke, Al Rose, Blue Lu Barker, Harry Shields, Sherwood Mangiapane, and Chink Martin. The group recorded on Southland Records.

Recording Session (1974)

Photo by Mary Tunis

Raymond Burke records a harmonica solo in a session with Johnny Wiggs (cornet) and Jack Delaney (trombone) for Warner Brothers in Baton Rouge.

Chicago (1940s)
Barbara Reid (Edmiston), well-known jazz promoter, welcomes Sidney Bechet to Chicago.

First Live Musical Broadcast from New Orleans
Broadcasting for station WOWL are, left to right, Frank Mutz, Ed McCarthy, Pinky Gerbrecht, Eddie Powers, Ellis Stratakos, Ray Bauduc.

A NEW ORLEANS JAZZ
FAMILY ALBUM

New Orleans jazzmen at home are far different from the kinds of individuals jazz musicians are considered to be by much of the general public. The marijuana-smoking, gin-guzzling, hip-talking "cat" who turns night into day whether he's working or not belongs to a different place, a different time, a different music. The Crescent City jazz performer is usually a family man. In most cases he has more children than the average parent. Usually he has a full-time occupation outside the music business. Few have ever been in trouble with the law. Instances of alcoholism, narcotic addiction, wife beating, and other unattractive habits are rare in this fraternity.

New Orleans jazz at home was played by blacksmiths and judges, cigar makers and postmen, painters, carpenters, plasterers, tinsmiths, banking executives, shoeshine boys, and surgeons. Considering the size and diversity of our family, it's obvious that there's a reason for a certain pride as we introduce them to you at home and at play in these informal photographs.

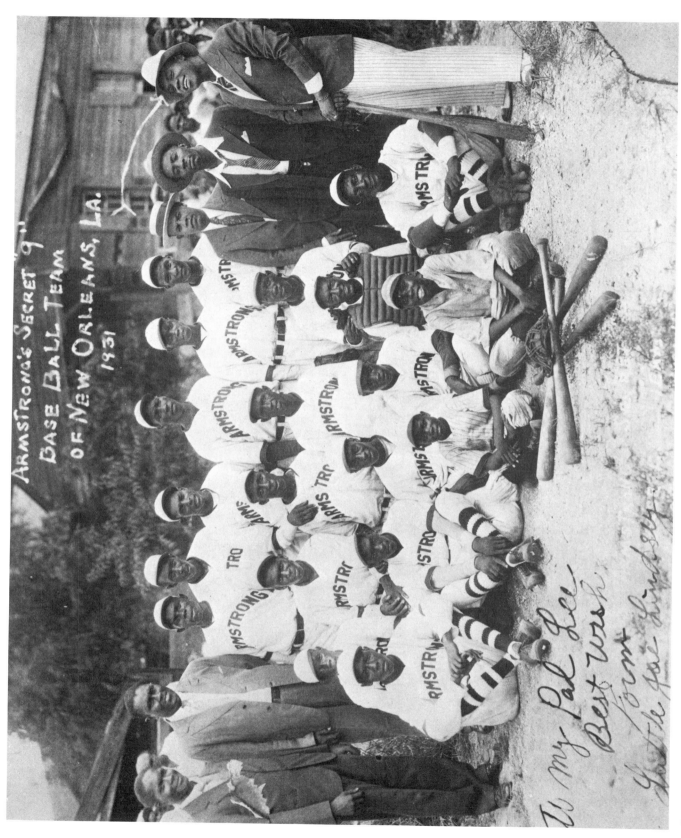

Armstrong's "Secret Nine" (1931)
Louis sponsored this baseball team. He's at the right. Next to him are Sherman Cook, a radio personality, and Little Joe Lindsey.

Mardi Gras (1946)
Bunk Johnson, Jim Robinson, George Lewis help celebrate.

Mardi Gras (1966)
The Rex bandwagon featured the Crawford-Ferguson Night Owls. Visible are Jack Bachman on trumpet and Paul Crawford on trombone. Al Rose (dark glasses) is bandmaster.

Jazz Little Leaguers of 1910
All three of these little boys went on to the jazz big leagues. The snare drummer is Buck Rogers; Abbie Brunies holds a cornet, and his brother George, an alto horn. The youngsters played for tips on the streetcars, and this picture was taken at the carbarn, Arabella and Magazine streets.

City Slickers (about 1918)
Freddie Keppard (seated) and Sidney Bechet.

Some of the Founding Fathers of Jazz (1944)
Left to right are Big Eye Louis Nelson, Pops Foster, Willie Santiago, Sidney Bechet, Albert Glenny, and Alphonse Picou. They posed in front of Dr. Leonard V. Bechet's office.

Bunk Johnson on the Steps of Mahogany Hall (1949)

Photo by Myra Menville

301

Courtesy Dave Stuart

Frankie Duson at Home (about 1922)
Duson is at right.

Courtesy Lee Tilton

Concert in the Parisian Room (1948)
Left to right are Roy Zimmerman, Joe Loyacano, Frank Federico, Sharkey, Monk Hazel, Irving Fazola, Digger Laine, Buglin' Sam Dekemel.

Clarinet Trust (1955)
Left to right are Raymond Burke, Tony Parenti, Harry Shields.

Congo Square Festival (1951)
Alphonse Picou (left) and Papa Celestin posed with Myra Menville at the New Orleans Jazz Club festival.

Record Session (1949)
The meeting featured rarely photographed or recorded Kid Avery on trombone and Wooden Joe Nicholas on trumpet. In the rear, left, Danny Barker looks on.

Fun in the Parlor (1950s)
The parlor belongs to trumpet man Albert Artigues, who is joined here by Raymond Burke, clarinet; Johnny McGee, piano; Henry Waelde, string bass; and Katz Maestri, drums.

Dr. Leonard V. Bechet (1946)

Photo by Myra Menville

Milneburg Joys (1920s)
Raymond Burke (left) and his uncle, Dooky
Cassard, enjoy the lakefront.

305

Future Jazz Greats (1912)
The group was rehearsing in front of a brewery on Jackson Avenue. The kid in the front with the alto horn is ten-year-old George Brunies. Holding instruments, left to right, are Happy Schilling, Abbie Brunies, Harry Shannon, Richie Brunies, Bud Loyacano.

Storyville Alumni (1944)
In front are Big Eye Louis Nelson (left) and Sidney Bechet. At the back are Alphonse Picou, Manuel Perez, Willie Santiago.

Watchin' All the Girls Go By (1956)
Eddie Pierson, Jim Robinson, Kid Howard, Chester Jones, Louis Gallaud, Sidney Brown.

Courtesy Duncan Schiedt

Jelly Roll Morton (1917)
Morton (right) was doing a "single" in vaudeville in Los Angeles.

Burnell Santiago (1930s)
The legendary pianist is shown with Sidney Pflueger on guitar and Ollie Papa on string bass.

Two Jazzmen
Professor Manuel Manetta (top) and Oscar Celestin, who in 1924 was still known as Sonny. Only later would he come to be called Papa.

Ready to Parade (about 1912)
Left to right are Honoré Dutrey, Louis Warnick, George McCullum, Sr.

Courtesy Charlotte Boutney

Kid Rena's Gang at the Gypsy Tea Room (about 1931)
The men in the front row are Harold Dejan, Rena, Burke Stevenson. Behind Rena is his brother Joe. Third from right is Clarence Tisdale. Behind Dejan is Smilin' Joe Joseph.

309

Manuel Perez in His Last Days (1944)

Photo by Scoop Kennedy

Jelly Roll Morton (about 1938)

Photo by Danny Barker, courtesy Duncan Schiedt

310

Don Juans of the High Seas (1919)
Tony Sbarbaro (left) and suave Emile Christian pose with two friends on shipboard en route to England. With bandmates Nick La Rocca and Larry Shields, they were about to introduce dixieland to the British Isles.

Lakefront Loungers (about 1920)
Abbie Brunies, Charlie Cordilla, and Stalebread Lacoume at West End.

A Pair of "Cake Eaters" (1915)
Tom Brown, in the skimmer, posed with
Larry Shields.

Courtesy Harry Shields

**Pantsy Laine in His Western Union
Uniform**

312

Nick La Rocca on His Papa's Knee (about 1891)

Courtesy Mrs. Dominick Palmisano and the New Orleans Times-Picayune

Long's Blacksmith Shop (1898)
Frank Christian stands at left next to Jack Laine, at the anvil. John Cazzeaux holds the maul. Laine was already organizing his bands.

313

Two Sheiks from New Orleans (1918)
Eddie Shields (left) and Emile Christian.

Louis Prima's First Band (about 1922)
Left to right are Prima, Ewell Lamar, unknown, Irving Fazola, Johnny Viviano, unknown.

Smoky Mary
This train carried weekend merrymakers to Milneburg via Elysian Fields Avenue for fifteen cents.

Members of Tom Brown's Band from Dixieland (1915)
Standing behind Billy Lambert are, left to right, Deacon Loyacano, Ray Lopez, Gussie Mueller. The boys sent this home from their historic date at Lamb's Cafe in Chicago.

315

Courtesy Jack Laine

Jack Laine (1919)
Laine brings his band to an open-air theater in Alexandria, La. He's at the drums. The piano player is Jules Reiner. Herman Ragas is on bass. Seated on the piano, left to right, are Baby Laine, George Brunies, Charlie Cordilla.

Mardi Gras (1949)
Louis Armstrong was King of the Zulus.

Four New Orleans Kids Record Together (late 1930s)
Sidney Bechet (left) and Albert Nicholas play clarinet; the drummer is Zutty Singleton; and Jelly Roll Morton plays piano in this Victor session. The outlander on trumpet is Sidney De Paris.

Kid Moliere (about 1937)
Moliere (clarinet) leads the band at this uptown bistro. David Bailey plays the drums.

Buglin' Sam's Famous Waffle Wagon (1921)
Sam used his valveless horn to sell waffles (four for a nickel) from this wagon. The senior Dekemel made the waffles. The lady in black is Sam's mother.

Chester Zardis and Sousaphone
He began thinking like a bass player when he was only fifteen.

Jelly Roll Morton in Vaudeville (1917)
He's third from the left. The lady in front of him is Bricktop, who years later would become Paris' celebrated café owner and hostess. This photo was taken in Los Angeles.

One of the First Amateur Pilots (1925)
With his plane for a background, Norman Brownlee shakes hands with Joe Loyacano.

On Tour (about 1918)
Big Eye Louis Nelson and Freddie Keppard pose for a studio shot to send home from Chicago. They were on tour with the Original Creole Orchestra.

**Armand Hug Makes His First Commu-
nion** (1923)

**Wingy Manone's Mishap Makes the
Papers**

Freddie Keppard After His First Communion

Louis Armstrong Joins King Oliver in Chicago

322

Just Married
Louis and Lil Armstrong in the 1920s.

Courtesy Joe Mares

The Gang's All Here
An army of dixieland stars turned out for Little Abbie Brunies' wedding reception on May 2, 1954. Standing, left to right, are Sharkey, Paul Edwards, Jack Delaney, Harry Shields, Stanley Mendelson, Raymond Burke, Tony Parenti, Sherwood Mangiapane, Santo Pecora. Kneeling are the host, Joe Mares, and Chink Martin. Behind Martin is young Billy Huntington, and Little Abbie sits at the drums.

Fisherman (1961)
Raymond Burke brings in a big one in Key Largo, Fla.

A Couple of Hot Piano Men
(1970)
Sing Miller and Li'l Papa Moliere.

Photo by Leonard Ferguson

324

Johnny Wiggs with Teenage Pete Fountain

Live Broadcast
Red Allen with George Lewis, broadcasting
over WDSU in New Orleans.

A New Orleans Jazz Band in Chicago (1947)
Left to right are Little Brother Montgomery, Lonnie Johnson, Bill Johnson, Oliver Alcorn, Pork Chop Smith, Lee Collins, and Preston Jackson.

Pee Wee Spitlera and Al Hirt

Part of Wingy Manone's Band (1930)
Left to right are Sidney Arodin, Wingy, George Brunies, Bobby Laine.

Chicago (1922)
Paul Mares (top) and George Brunies arrive
in the Windy City.

Lee Collins

328

George Blanchin and Frank Bonansinga

Getting Together
Barbara Reid Edmiston and two favorite trumpet stars, Lee Collins (left) and Louis Armstrong. Jazz historian Bill Russell looks on.

329

THE ENDURING ALLURE OF
AUTHENTIC JAZZ

By the beginning of the 1980s, jazz had reached that stage in its development at which preservation of its music and its history became the primary concern of its supporters. Through books, periodicals, radio, television, motion pictures, road shows, and a traveling exhibition, fans throughout the country and throughout the world are exposed to the delights of authentic New Orleans jazz and its fascinating history. Here in the city, institutions like Preservation Hall and, to a lesser extent, the New Orleans Jazz and Heritage Festival provide residents and visitors to the city a chance to sample the real thing in performance. In addition, the New Orleans Jazz Club, the New Orleans Jazz Museum, and the William Ransom Hogan Jazz Archive at Tulane University provide sources for serious students of the music to study this influential social and cultural phenomenon.

Jazz Books

Over the past half century, many significant books directly related to the world of authentic jazz have been published. Among the most valuable are the many biographies and autobiographies of New Orleans jazzmen. Of course, there are quite a few biographies of Louis Armstrong available. Fine ones on other jazz stars include: Sidney Bechet's autobiography, *Treat It Gentle* (New York, 1975); Tom Bethell, *George Lewis: A Jazzman from New Orleans* (Berkeley, 1977); George M. Foster, *Pops Foster: The Autobiography of a New Orleans Jazzman* as told to Tom Stoddard (Berkeley, 1971); G. E. Lambert, *Johnny Dodds* (Cranbury, N.J., 1961); Alan Lomax, *Mr. Jelly Roll: The Fortunes of Jelly Roll Morton, New Orleans Creole*

and 'Inventor' (Berkeley, 1973); Don Marquis, *In Search of Buddy Bolden* (Baton Rouge, 1978); and Martin Williams, *King Oliver* (New York, 1961).

Among the best books to consult on New Orleans jazz in general are: Frederic Ramsey and Charles E. Smith (eds.), *Jazzmen* (New York, 1977); Rudi Blesh, *Shining Trumpets: A History of Jazz* (New York, 1975); Rudi Blesh and Harriet Janis, *They All Played Ragtime* (New York, 1966); Al Rose, *Storyville, New Orleans: Being An Authentic Illustrated Account of the Notorious Red-Light District* (University, Ala., 1974); and Samuel B. Charters, Jr., *Jazz: New Orleans, 1885–1963* (Belleville, N.J., 1958).

Jazz Periodicals

Large numbers of magazines containing the word *jazz* in their titles continue to proliferate, though few of them contain anything of interest to followers of authentic jazz. Three of the publications that do *not* use the word have become our best sources of jazz information.

One of these, the *Second Line*, organ of the New Orleans Jazz Club, has had its fortunes guided by a series of competent editors since its beginnings in 1950. Edmond and Harry Souchon, Helen Arlt, Myra Menville, and Don Marquis have been mainly responsible for the publication's consistently high level of reportage and for its selectivity. Appearing quarterly for more than three decades, its files are a treasure house of valuable and accurate information, a prime research tool for jazz scholars.

Footnote, a small magazine published by Terry Dash in Cambridge, England, has built itself around affectionately detailed accounts of the careers of older, mainly black jazzmen. Exhaustive and sensitive interviewing and sometimes fanatical attention to minutiae at times give *Footnote* the character of an unabashed fan magazine. The publication has served an honest purpose, adding much useful knowledge to the lore and understanding of individuals of the jazz world past.

The *Mississippi Rag*, in tabloid format, is brilliantly edited by Leslie Carole Johnson. This monthly publication supplies endless photographic coverage of various jazz and ragtime festivals of interest primarily to the participants, but also thoughtful, competently edited theoretical articles and often perceptive reviews of jazz and ragtime books. Johnson and her staff and contributors demonstrate consistent good taste in record reviews and provide, thereby, a reliable guide to collectors.

Jazz Radio

Syndicated radio shows on jazz continue into the eighties. George H. Buck's jazz program originating in Atlanta continues to be heard on a number of southern stations, including WWNO in New Orleans on Wednesday nights. Al Rose's *Journeys into Jazz*, on the air since 1947, can be heard in this country and abroad. WWOZ carries it on Sunday nights in New Orleans. Although it's neither syndicated nor on a network, *Jazz from Congo Square*, the New Orleans Jazz Club program conducted by Rhoads Spidale, may have the largest listening audience. The Saturday night program, broadcast on fifty-thousand-watt, clear-channel New Orleans radio station WWL, can be heard by jazz fans across the nation.

Jazz Television, Movies, and Photography

Television, in recent years, has begun to focus on authentic jazz. In this regard European television is far ahead both in quality and quantity, thanks largely to the monumental achievement of the greatest of European TV directors, Jean Cristophe Averty. His 4 one-hour programs tracing the music and history of the Original Dixieland Jazz Band, which appeared on French channel 3 in 1973, have never been matched. Two hour-and-a-half specials he filmed in New Orleans, entitled *New Orleans, Bien Aimée*, maintain a standard of production quality and writing never approached in American jazz treatments. Unfortunately, none of these programs has ever been shown in the United States.

One documentary made in this country has, it is to be hoped, set a standard for future producers. This is Stevenson Palfi's *This Cat Can Play Anything*, a one-hour program reviewing the career of Emanuel Sayles, which won the Leigh Whipper Award for TV-jazz biographies.

Jules Cahn *Photo by Bernard Hermann*

The Public Broadcasting Service has done its share to present authentic jazz to the American public. Al Hirt and Pete Fountain appeared on its series *Live from Wolf Trap*. PBS also presented a program entitled *Mardi Gras and All That Jazz*, which featured the Olympia Brass Band. The highlight of the program was a sequence in which Bill Russell played an extended blues violin solo. John Byers' 1980 hour-long *Pete*, a documentary about the daily life of Pete Fountain, appeared several times on PBS, as well as cable television. The program, which included excellent old film of the Basin Street Six, proved to be a satisfying portrait of a lovable personality. Byers' television biography of Louis Prima was in production during 1982.

Even though programs devoted to serious authentic New Orleans jazz have been rare on American television, they have not been as rare as serious depictions on the movie screen. Authentic jazz has never had much of a life in the cinema. In 1980 Paramount released a film that claimed to avoid distortion of history, but unfortunately,

One Mo' Time (1979)

the film, *Pretty Baby*, fell far short of its claim. The movie did redeem itself, though, with a soundtrack full of beautiful Jelly Roll–style piano performed by Bob Greene, as well as jazz by such luminaries as Raymond Burke, Louis Cottrell, Jr., Kid Thomas, and the New Orleans Ragtime Orchestra. Its soundtrack LP was of more than ordinary interest.

Jules Cahn is known throughout the international jazz world for his highly valuable photographs and movie films on jazzmen, particularly in parades. During the 1970s the Historic New Orleans Collection presented a one-man show of his extraordinary photos.

One Mo' Time

Conceived by Vernel Bagneris of New Orleans, the unique stage production *One Mo' Time* made its debut in the Toulouse Theater in 1978. A rousing musical production reflecting the performances presented during the twenties at the old Lyric Theater at Burgundy and Iberville streets, *One Mo' Time* has supplied more work for jazzmen than any other phenomenon since the opening of Preservation Hall in 1961. Bagneris' show proved to be just the right combination of comedy, song, and dance to appeal to a national audience. It opened at the Village Gate in New York in 1979, maintaining a second company in New Orleans and a road company touring the United States and Europe.

Among the musicians regularly employed in one or another of the companies are Jabbo Smith, Lionel Ferbos, Orange Kellin, Pud Brown, Walter Payton, Jr., Stanley Stephens, John Robichaux, Morten Gunnar Larsen, Lars Edegran, Steve Pistorius, and Paul Crawford. With constantly changing personnel and occasional added material, the show remains fresh and continues to play to capacity audiences at each performance. Exhibitors say there seems to be no reason for it ever to close.

Larry Borenstein

Photo by Grauman Marks

Chris Botsford

Played with Immense Success

Among the benchmark achievements of the 1970s was the exhibit at the Louisiana State Museum entitled Played with Immense Success, a social history of Louisiana from 1840 to 1940 as seen in its published sheet music. The exhibit—conceived, created, and written by Al Rose, Vaughn Glasgow (senior curator of the Louisiana State Museum), and Diana Rose—presented over 350 items, including a great many very rare ragtime and jazz pieces. It ran in New Orleans during most of 1979 and then was solicited by the Smithsonian Institution for a tour of major American museums.

Played with Immense Success opened at the Kennedy Center in Washington, D.C., in January, 1980. Congresswoman Lindy Boggs threw a gala reception, and many government dignitaries and, of course, the press attended. Coverage in the Washington *Post*, the *Star*, and on television was extensive. After a successful tour, the exhibit returned to New Orleans at last at the end of 1981.

Preservation Hall

When Larry Borenstein, art dealer, collector, and real estate operator, arrived in New Orleans in 1943, there was very little jazz to be found in the city. He took an interest in the musicians and allowed them to play for tips in his art gallery on St. Peter Street. This was the origin of what soon became Preservation Hall, the bastion of traditional New Orleans jazz. Many musicians have played here. Among those are Peter Bocage, Kid Thomas, Sweet Emma Barrett, Percy Humphrey, George Lewis, Punch Miller, Jim Robinson, and Johnny Wiggs.

In addition to musicians, many dedicated people keep the hall operating smoothly and the musicians contented on the road. As proprietor of Preservation Hall, Allen Jaffe has given jobs to hundreds of musicians, many of whom, in advanced years, found themselves in prosperous careers with worldwide followings as a result of his efforts. Jaffe's wife, Sandra, shepherded the business end of Preservation Hall through its precarious early years and participated in the key decisions that determined its future and its role. She has managed the bands on the road, nursed the infirm, and tended to the needs not only of the elderly jazzmen but also of their not al-

Jane Botsford

Allen Jaffe

Sandra Jaffe   *Photo by Grauman Marks*

Resa and Alvin Lambert

335

Dorothea Simmons

ways prosperous families. Sandra's sister Resa and her husband, Alvin Lambert, joined the team in the sixties. Alvin manages the hall, and he and Resa often tour with the bands. Since the mid-seventies, Chris Botsford has managed the Preservation Hall bands on the road in both hemispheres with the help of his wife, Jane, the archivist of the valuable photographs and historical records in the extensive files of the hall.

New Orleans Jazz Club

In 1949 Johnny Wiggs had a brainstorm. It occurred to him that jazz musicians and their friends needed a place to gather to play, preserve, and listen to their own music. He began to meet with a group of friends, among them Gilbert Erskine, George Blanchin, Pete Miller, Don Perry, Al Diket, and Freddie King. The New Orleans Jazz Club had come into being.

By 1950 Edmond Souchon had instituted a club newspaper, which would soon become the *Second Line*. Memberships were coming in from all over the globe, and Myra Menville undertook to handle the enormous correspondence. A quiet but efficient gentleman, John Favolora, took over the club finances.

Almost before anyone knew what was happening, monthly meetings in the St. Charles Hotel (later in the

The New Orleans Jazz Club Is Born (1948)
Frank Federico (left) and Don Perry kneel at front. Behind them, left to right, are Boojie Centobie, Armand Hug, Freddie King, Al Diket, Gilbert Erskine, Digger Laine, Johnny Wiggs, and Chink Martin.

Pete Miller

Rita Morgan

Ed Morgan

Harry Souchon

Roosevelt) were offering the music of a cavalcade of jazz luminaries to hundreds of friends and fans. Throughout the fifties, personalities like Papa Celestin, Tom Brown, Johnny St. Cyr, Sharkey, Johnny Wiggs, the Basin Street Six with Pete Fountain and George Girard, and the original Dukes of Dixieland participated. Lee Collins, Santo Pecora, Raymond Burke, and Jack Delaney were all regulars. It was a jazz lover's paradise.

The club has done much to further the appreciation of jazz New Orleans style. Annually, it presents the concert series Jazz on Sunday Afternoon. It underwrites the weekly radio show *Jazz from Congo Square*. It started the New Orleans Jazz Museum and held it together for many

years at great cost before turning it over to the State of Louisiana.

Among the members who have made substantial contributions to the development of the NOJC are Pete Miller, Frank Bonansinga, Rita and Ed Morgan, Harry Souchon, Rhoads Spidale, Joe Mares, Gil Morris, and Ursula Bernard. Pete Miller, an original member of the club, served several times as its president. He was responsible for the preservation of many air shots of New Orleans musicians. Ed Morgan and his wife, Rita, both served as president at different times and were responsible for the success of the Jazz on Sunday Afternoon concert series at the Marriott Hotel. Harry Souchon, an

Don Perry

Duke Darnell

Helen Arlt   *Photo by Ed Lawless*

attorney and the younger brother of Edmond Souchon, also served as president. For years he hosted the "Wax Wing," a Sunday function at his home, where collectors met to play and discuss rare old records.

Don Perry, one of the founders of the club and a member of the advisory board of the William Ransom Hogan Jazz Archive at Tulane University, has documented much of the jazz of the fifties and sixties on film and has made a liaison between the world of jazz and the local television establishment. John Kuhlman, the official photographer of the NOJC, has documented club events for three decades, compiling a record of some of the greatest jazz musicians in their later days. Duke Darnell frequently serves as emcee for club functions and Jazz on Sunday Afternoon concerts. He has also hosted *Jazz from Congo Square*.

Almost since it began, Helen Arlt has been a force in the NOJC. She has served the club as president and secretary, and she has edited and contributed to the *Second Line*. A prime factor in the development of the New Orleans Jazz Museum, she also engineered its transfer to the Louisiana State Museum. Her courage helped to break down racial barriers among jazzmen during the sometimes tense fifties.

In this work she was joined by Myra Menville, for many years secretary of the club and, from 1968 to 1978, editor of the *Second Line*. She was able to find jobs for jazzmen

during even the leanest years. Working tirelessly, she turned up many a long-forgotten jazzman and thrust him back into the spotlight to hear once again the applause of appreciative audiences. In the earliest years of the NOJC, she began handling the correspondence that has kept alive communications with the world's far-flung jazz fans. She also maintained a steady correspondence with her good friend Louis Armstrong.

Myra Menville

At the Jazz Museum (1972)
Left to right are Al Rose, Johnny Wiggs, Joe Mares, Bill Russell.

Photo by Justin Winston

Don Marquis
The curator looks at a picture of Buddy Bolden.

New Orleans Jazz Museum

During the 1950s, under the leadership of Edmond Souchon, Myra Menville, and Helen Arlt, the New Orleans Jazz Club opened a jazz museum to house its accumulated treasures. Underfunded from the start, it managed to survive, first at 1017 Dumaine Street, then at Economy Hall in the Royal Sonesta Hotel, and finally at 333 Conti Street. At last, through Helen Arlt's initiative, the NOJC turned the museum over to the Louisiana State Museum. The transfer would, it was hoped, relieve the club of the heavy expenses it was struggling to meet and would made the exhibits permanently available to visitors. At this writing, the museum has not yet been opened to the public.

Among the permanent collection of the museum are such artifacts as Louis Armstrong's first horn, Larry Shields's clarinet, Tom Brown's trombone, Papa Laine's autographed drum head. There are countless documents and photographs, besides an extensive collection of New Orleans jazz records, tapes, and films.

Don Marquis, author of *In Search of Buddy Bolden* and editor since 1978 of the *Second Line*, became curator of the jazz collection in 1979.

New Orleans Jazz Archive

The William Ransom Hogan Jazz Archive was instituted in 1958 with a grant of $75,000 from the Ford Foundation to Tulane University. Supplementary grants later brought that total to $156,000. The archive adopted a policy of activism that challenged the casual way jazz had always been discussed. By the end of the seventies, it became apparent that its policies were working. Critics and commentators were slowly but surely being forced to higher levels of responsibility in matters of fact, definition, and theory.

The museum's first curator was William Russell, the respected researcher and archivist, author of definitive articles on jazz history, and producer of benchmark records that keynoted the revival of interest in authentic jazz during the 1940s and preserved the sound of many early jazz greats who had otherwise gone unrecorded. Russell was succeeded by Richard B. Allen, a writer and lecturer who settled in New Orleans in 1949. A masterful interviewer, he was able to obtain many wonderful oral histories of jazzmen. In 1980 Curt Jerde, the jazz musician, be-

Richard B. Allen

came the archive's third curator. Jerde conceived and organized the Hot Jazz Classic, Tulane's share of the 1982 New Orleans Jazz and Heritage Festival.

Among the holdings of the archive are bout 1500 reels of taped interviews with musicians and others in the jazz scene, of which 1200 have been transcribed verbatim and are scheduled for publication by the Microfilming Corporation of America.

The archive's holdings in music include about 800 tapes, 25,000 discs (78, 45, 33⅓ rpm), and a number of cylinders. The archive also houses over 20,000 musical arrangements for piano, orchestra, and band. There is a vast collection of sheet music, numbering over 15,000 pieces and including the rarest early rags and blues. Since 1980, Francis P. Squibb, editor and author of many articles on jazz theory, has been at work cataloguing this collection, which is already being used by a worldwide network of jazz musicians.

The collection of jazz photographs numbers nearly 8,000, including most of the ones in this volume, plus an international collection of jazz posters, new and old.

Also among the holdings are over 13,000 books and scholarly publications in the fields of jazz and popular music. There are also more than 12,000 issues of jazz-related periodicals in the files.

The archive is part of the Special Collections Division of the Howard-Tilton Memorial Library at Tulane. Researchers may visit during the week between one o'clock and five o'clock in the afternoon. Visits may be arranged at other times by appointment.

The New Orleans Jazz Archive is the only facility of its kind in existence—a boundless resource for study and research in the disciplines of jazz and related forms of American popular music.

TILL THE BUTCHER
CUT HIM DOWN

To pretend that New Orleans jazz as we have known it will go on forever is whistling in the dark. The jazz form cannot die as long as there are phonograph records, it is true—but very soon there won't be anybody around to play it. Through the seventeen years since *A Family Album* was originally published, several hundred of the titans of jazz departed from the scene, few replaced by the stars of a rising generation.

We considered omitting or expanding this section of the book. In the end we resolved to present it again the same way we did it originally because it illustrates some social and historical facts about New Orleans jazz that words can't. We note the fierce pride in their art that led some of our greatest stars to claim for themselves, in graven stone, the paternity of jazz. We still see the unmarked grave of Bunk Johnson near his home in New Iberia, La., clearly demonstrating how little conscious local folk are with the cultural importance of the great music, while Sidney Bechet's imposing black marble crypt gleams in oriental splendor near Paris as a testimonial to the idolatry in which jazz pioneers are held elsewhere in the world.

Funerals of fellow musicians seem a little sadder, the dirges a trace more lugubrious than other burials as the faces of the survivors in these pictures show. We see them here as pallbearers and mourners and we understand that very soon even these processions will cease.

But there are still a few great jazzmen left and if you hurry on down to the Crescent City, you may yet get a chance to hear them. The New Orleans jazzman keeps on playing until the butcher cuts him down. Until then, as the song reminds us, "He'll ramble."

World's First Man in Jazz
The inscription on Nick La Rocca's tomb.

Leon Roppolo's Resting Place

342

Tony Jackson's Death Certificate

Alphonse Picou's Funeral (1961)
The Eureka Brass Band is at graveside. Anderson Minor wears a black bow tie. Albert Francis is visible above sousaphone.

John Casimir's Last Parade

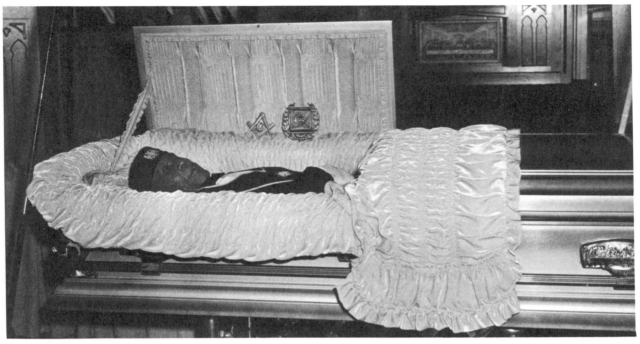

Papa Celestin Lies in State (1954)

Courtesy Floyd Levin

Jelly Roll Morton's Grave
The birth date on the grave, in Los Angeles, Cal., is obviously incorrect.

345

Bunk Johnson's Unmarked Grave
It's in the Negro Catholic Cemetery, New Iberia, La.

Kid Rena Is Laid to Rest (1949)
Ricard Alexis (left) and Alec Bigard are the pall bearers in the front.

Photo by Scoop Kennedy

346

Originator of Jazz Music
The claim on the headstone of Stalebread Lacoume.

Courtesy Charles Delauney

Sidney Bechet Reposes in Marble Splendor, Paris

The End Comes for Paul Barbarin (1969)
Dean Andrews (left), Barbarin's attorney, plays clarinet next to Pete Fountain and Louis Cottrell, Jr. Behind them are Freddie Kohlman on snare drum, Chester Jones on bass drum, and Alvin Alcorn (mostly hidden) on trumpet. Farther back is Jack Willis on trumpet.

INDEX

Baquet, Theogene V., 8, 12, 194
Barbarin, Isidore, 8, 9, 193, 194, 195, 197, 207, 212
Barbarin, Louis, 102, 138, 149, 153, 161, 182, 213, 260
Barbarin, Lucien, 195
Barbarin, Paul, 3, 7, 9, 15, 18, 21, 22, 31, 42, 58, 65, 86, 87, 94, 102, 111, 112, 120, 134, 153, 155, 197, 213, 216, 233, 241, 267, 292, 348
Barbarin Jazz Band, 134
Barker, Blue Lu, 9, 10, 294
Barker, Danny, 9, 10, 64, 111, 118, 127, 134, 194, 195, 304
Barnes, Emile, 10, 49, 58, 185, 225
Barnes, Harrison, 10, 57, 155, 193, 194, 197, 255
Barnes, Paul "Polo," 10, 11, 49, 60, 72, 105, 119, 121, 136, 161, 162, 207, 267
Barocco Brothers, 10, 34, 73, 85, 111, 131
Barocco, Dominick, 4, 10, 11, 61, 155, 159, 180, 189, 200, 258, 288
Barocco, Joe, 10, 11, 155, 159, 180, 200, 248
Barocco, Vincent, 10, 196, 197
Barrett, "Sweet Emma," 3, 5, 11, 12, 45, 50, 57, 58, 79, 121, 153, 155, 161, 172, 334
Bart, Willa, 11, 149
Barth, George, 11, 12, 134, 158, 194, 196, 198
Barth, Harry, 273
Barthels, Henry, 138
Basin Street, 62, 64, 74, 81, 99, 282
Basin Street Six, 39, 41, 45, 49, 64, 110, 131, 134, 332, 337
Batiste, Milton, 12
Bauddeurs, Ben, 196
Bauduc, Jules, 12, 37, 54, 71, 85, 148, 184, 240, 267
Bauduc, Ray, 12, 13, 72, 91, 134, 138, 142, 148, 161, 169, 269, 295
Bayard, Eddie, 12, 13
Bayersdorffer, Johnny, 2, 12, 13, 18, 27, 32, 54, 68, 72, 73, 78, 84, 85, 86, 97, 98, 113, 130, 134, 144, 146, 155, 158, 169, 233, 241, 270, 278
Bayersdorffer's Orchestra, Johnny, 68, 84, 134, 155, 169, 233
Bayersdorffer's Red Devils, 17, 278
Bazoon, Otis, 12, 143
Beaulieu, Paul, 12, 148, 155
Beaulieu, Rudolph, 12, 195
Bechet, Leonard V., 12, 14, 89, 301, 305
Bechet, Sidney, 12, 14, 43, 50, 70, 88, 128, 129, 143, 151, 162, 273, 295, 300, 301, 306, 317, 331, 341, 347
Behrenson, "Doc," 13
Behrenson, Sidney, 16
Beiderbecke, Bix, 54, 104, 115
Belas, Henry "Ants," 13, 119, 140
Belasco, Manuel, 13, 196, 197
Bell, John, 13, 148, 158
Ben, Paul, 13, 138, 162, 184
Benarby, Jim, 13
Beninate, Johnny, 13, 144
Beninate, Nick, 13
Benoit, John, 14
Benson, Hamilton "Hamp," 14, 15, 144, 153, 197
Benton, Tom, 14, 137, 284
Bergan, Stuart "Red Hott," 14, 15, 91

Bernard, Al, 265
Bernard, Ursula, 337
Berry, Mel, 14, 177
Bertrand, Buddy, 14
Bethell, Tom, 74, 331
Beverly Gardens, 62, 81, 104, 216, 223, 241
Bienville Roof, 217
Bienville Roof Orchestra, 134
Bigard, Albany "Barney," 9, 14, 15, 22, 31, 121, 149
Bigard, Alec, 14, 15, 50, 106, 147, 155, 206, 346
Bigard, Emile, 15, 147, 161
Bigeou, Clifford "Boy," 15, 134, 137
Bigeou, Esther, 15, 16, 265
Big Five, The, 85
Big 25, The, 99, 103, 216, 217, 220
Bisso, Louis, 15
Black and Tan Orchestra, Petit's, 134
Black Devils Jazz Band, 134
Black Diamond Orchestra, 34, 54, 78, 134
Black Diamond Orchestra, Dejan's, 78, 174
Black Eagles Jazz Band, 7, 52, 74, 84, 108, 120, 134
Black, Lew, 164
Blackstoe Record Shop, Oren, 217
Blair-Saenger Harmony Hoboes, 282
Blaise, Ed "Kid Totts," 15, 137, 181
Blake, Eubie, 29
Blanchard, Osceola, 176
Blanchin, George, 329, 336
Blesh, Rudi, 331
Blessing, Manny, 288
Blount, Jack, 16, 145
Blue Room, 217, 238
Blue, Walter, 237
Blum's Cafe, 217
Blunt, Carroll, 16, 195, 206
Bobcats, Bob Crosby's, 33, 268
Bocage, Charles, 16, 137, 153, 173, 175
Bocage, Henry, 16, 137, 153, 175
Bocage, Peter, 14, 15, 16, 17, 27, 34, 41, 54, 60, 84, 92, 121, 137, 139, 147, 153, 159, 173, 175, 186, 188, 193, 194, 195, 197, 206, 207, 231, 242, 334
Bodoyer, Rudolph, 16, 148, 162
Boggs, Congresswoman Lindy, 334
Boisseau, Edward, 194
Bolden, Charles "Buddy," 16, 21, 25, 27, 29, 30, 39, 46, 58, 62, 74, 78, 80, 81, 87, 91, 115, 118, 121, 125, 129, 131, 134, 164, 193, 215, 217, 220, 223, 224, 226, 242, 245, 331
Bolden's Marching Band, Buddy, 49, 54
Bolden's Ragtime Band, Buddy, 8, 62, 125, 129, 131, 134, 164
Bolman, "Red," 16, 149, 160, 284
Bolton, "Red Happy," 16, 17, 155
Bonano, Joseph. See Sharkey
Bonansinga, Frank, 17, 329, 337
Bontemps, Willie, 17, 147, 155, 161, 172
Borenstein, E. Lorenz "Larry," 334
Bose, Sterling, 17, 18, 134, 137
Boswell, Connee, 268
Botsford, Chris, 334
Botsford, Jane, 335
Bottley, Edmond, 136
Bouchon, Lester, 17, 18, 134, 142, 143, 161, 169, 176
Boudio's Gardens, 218

Boudreaux, Junius, 180
Bourbon Street Five, 12
Bourgeau, Joseph "Fan," 17
Bourgeois, Charlie, 37, 44, 46, 55
Bourgeois, Wilfred S. "Bill," 17, 274
"Bow Legs," 196
Boyd, George, 17, 137, 148
Brashear, Norman, 259
Braud, Wellman, 17, 18, 147
Braun, Billy, 18, 134, 144, 146, 158
Brazlee, Harrison, 18, 134, 185
Breaux, McNeil, 18
"Bricktop," 319
Brooks, Joe, 18, 143
Broussard, Albert, 266
Broussard, Theo, 18
Brown, Albert "Pud," 19, 333
Brown Derby, The, 89, 106, 125, 218
Brown, James, 19, 143, 144, 167
Brown, Johnny, 19, 27, 66, 88, 124, 193
Brown, Ray, 19, 137, 178, 258
Brown, Sidney, 6, 19, 75, 143, 148, 149, 153, 162, 307
Brown, Steve, 19, 151, 155, 164
Brown, Tom (mandolin), 14, 19, 50, 216
Brown, Tom (trombone), 5, 14, 19, 20, 43, 72, 76, 77, 83, 85, 90, 114, 116, 121, 134, 136, 142, 155, 161, 196, 216, 222, 231, 236, 240, 242, 243, 276, 277, 278, 312, 315, 337, 339
Brown's Band from Dixieland, Tom, 5, 43, 72, 76, 134, 137, 216, 276, 277, 315
Brown's Ice Cream Parlor, 58, 218
Brown, William, 19, 190, 197, 206
Brownlee, Norman, 2, 17, 18, 20, 32, 40, 45, 53, 81, 88, 98, 116, 127, 134, 153, 158, 320
Brownlee's Orchestra, Norman, 11, 53, 98, 134, 158
Brue, Steve, 20, 148, 160, 161
Brundy, Walter, 20, 37, 139, 147, 155, 159
Brunies, Albert "Abbie," 20, 54, 83, 87, 91, 109, 110, 125, 144, 163, 171, 225, 300, 306, 311
Brunies, Albert "Little Abbie," 20, 323
Brunies Brothers, 20, 21, 22, 30, 43, 46, 48, 104, 110, 111, 113, 218, 237
Brunies, George, 12, 20, 21, 22, 96, 103, 129, 151, 164, 196, 282, 300, 306, 316, 327, 328
Brunies, Henry "Henny," 20, 21, 195, 196, 199, 200, 202
Brunies, Merritt, 20, 21, 110, 129, 144, 153, 156, 194, 196, 199, 218, 233
Brunies New Orleans Jazz Band, 66, 137
Brunies, Richard "Richie," 20, 21, 155, 194, 196, 200, 306
Brunings' Pavilion, 218
Brunious, John "Picket," 134, 197
Bruno, Bartholomew, 195
Buck, George H., 332
Buckley's New Orleans Serenaders, 274
Bucktown, 20, 215, 218, 222, 233, 253
Bucktown Five, The, 215
Bucktown Tavern, 83, 218, 242
Budweiser, The, 218
"Buglin Sam." See Dekemel, Matthew
Bulls Club, 219, 254
Bulls Club Band, The, 119, 193
Bungalow, The, 219

ERA Orchestra, 32, 33, 39, 45, 50, 52, 53, 55, 89, 94, 102, 106, 119, 121, 123, 130, 143, 190
Erdman, Ernie, 143, 148, 154, 173
Erskine, Gilbert, 335
Esperance Hall, 223, 225
Esposito, Alex, 41
Eugene, Homer, 41, 186, 197
Eugene, Wendell, 41, 42, 197
Eureka Brass Band, 2, 3, 19, 27, 29, 30, 49, 54, 55, 56, 57, 58, 61, 63, 72, 74, 81, 90, 94, 96, 97, 98, 105, 106, 109, 115, 119, 121, 125, 128, 130, 194, 204, 206, 214, 344
Eureka Hall, 223
Evans' Band, Carlisle, 53
Evans, Roy, 42, 136, 148
Ever, John, 194
Ewell, Don, 111
Excelsior Brass Band, 3, 8, 14, 27, 35, 47, 48, 54, 56, 58, 61, 62, 79, 80, 85, 88, 95, 98, 101, 105, 109, 118, 119, 121, 124, 125, 129, 194
Excelsior Brass Band (Mobile, Ala.), 18
Excelsior Orchestra, The, 8
Exchange Alley, 223, 233
Exerstein, Hugh, 200
Extra Half Jazz Band, The, 106

Fabacher's Rathskeller, 223
Fairconnetue, Harry, 137, 178
Fairgrounds, The, 223
Fairplay Hall, 224
Fairview Baptist Church Band, 9, 118, 122, 127, 194, 195
"Family Haircut," 135
Famous Door, The, 23, 49, 63, 66, 71, 98, 107, 115, 224
Farrell, Bill, 159
Farrow, Daniel, 211
Favolora, John, 336
Faye, Eddie, 246
Fazola, Irving, 4, 14, 24, 27, 33, 42, 70, 77, 86, 97, 102, 103, 105, 114, 127, 144, 152, 159, 161, 162, 224, 269, 302, 314
Fazola Orchestra, Irving, 144
Federico, Frank, 42, 159, 162, 271, 302, 336
Fennerty, Major, 288
Ferbos, Lionel, 42, 136, 151, 187, 333
Ferguson, Leonard, 42, 91, 137, 141
Fernandez', Butzie, 224
Fern Cafe No. 2, pp. 42, 57, 124, 218, 224
Ferrer, "Mose," 42, 43, 144, 149, 156
Ferrer, Frank, 43, 144, 151, 172
Fewclothes Cabaret, 18, 19, 26, 45, 64, 120, 130, 224
Fields, Frank, 43, 149, 207
Fields, Mercedes, 43, 151, 153, 161
Filhe, George, 43, 48, 144, 153, 161, 166, 167, 185
Finola, George, 34, 43
Fireman's Hall (Westwego, La.), 224
Fischer, Johnny, 10, 18, 43, 66, 71, 100, 113, 115, 143, 153, 154, 155, 156, 173, 195, 196, 198, 200, 212, 221, 222, 223, 236, 240, 243
Fischer's Brass Band, 5, 10, 12, 21, 27, 85, 113, 115, 195, 198, 200, 212, 221, 223, 243
Fischer's Ragtime Military Jazz Band, 200

Fishbein's Orchestra, Charlie, 99, 128, 246
500 Club, The, 224
Five Rubes, The, 76, 116, 277
Five Southern Jazzers, 43, 70, 143, 173
Follansbee, William, 266
Footnote Magazine (England), 331
Ford, Clarence, 134
Ford, Henry, 43
Forrest, Club, 220
Fortinet's Banner Band, Gus, 53, 184
Fortmeier's Band, 81
Foster, Abbey "Chinee," 43, 50, 66, 134, 150, 161, 197, 262
Foster, "Dude," 44, 145
Foster, Earl, 44, 86, 106
Foster, George "Pops," 35, 108, 109, 110, 113, 114, 120, 137, 138, 143, 147, 161, 257, 261, 262, 301, 331
Foster, Willie, 44, 147
Fouché, Earl, 44, 148, 149, 161
Fougerat, Tony, 44, 51, 96, 114, 119, 127, 143, 159, 176, 189
Fountain, Pete, 4, 30, 31, 34, 41, 44, 45, 49, 64, 86, 87, 91, 128, 131, 134, 138, 193, 242, 325, 332, 337, 348
Fountain Lounge, The, 224, 238
Four Hot Hounds, 95, 117, 216
Francis, Albert, Jr., 194
Francis, Albert, Sr., 45, 87, 194, 344
Francis, Edna. See Mitchell, Edna
Francois' Louisianians, 86, 283
Francs Amis Hall, 224
Frank, Alcide, 19, 45, 134, 143, 224
Frank, Gilbert "Bab," 31, 45, 67, 80, 84, 124, 134, 166
Frank, Melvin, 153, 190, 194
Franklin, Henry "Careful," 45
Franks, "Bunny," 45, 134
Frazier, Josiah "Cié," 45, 137, 144, 153, 155, 162, 184, 185, 187, 190, 194, 197
Freeman, Albert, 152
French, Albert, 9, 43, 45, 46, 65, 67, 120, 130, 149, 153, 161
French, Behrman, 45, 134
Frenchman's, The, 224
French Market, The, 102, 111
French Market Gang, The, 6, 125
French Market Jazz Band, The, 12, 56, 87, 91, 143, 181
French, Maurice, 46, 145, 195
French Opera House, The, 77, 105
French Union Hall, 224
Frenchy's String Band, 33
Fresno, Jerry, 284
Friars Inn (Chicago), 21
Friars Society Orchestra, 143, 151
Fridge, Fred, 266
Frisco, Joe, 276, 277
Frisco, Johnny, 46, 135, 155, 200
Froeba, Frank, 46, 137, 174, 233, 251
Frolic Club, The, 216, 241
Frolickers, Johnny Miller's, 86, 233
Frolics, The (Spanish Fort), 224, 233
Fuller, Walter, 117
Funky Butt Hall, 224, 226, 242, 253
Fuzzy Wuzzy Twins, The, 73

Gable, Joe, 50, 148
Gable's Band, Joe, 92

Gabriel, Albert, 46, 134
Gabriel, Alberta, 148
Gabriel, Clarence, 46, 138, 148
Gabriel, "Dude," 196
Gabriel, Martin Manuel "Manny," Jr., 46, 72, 148
Gabriel, Martin Manuel, Sr., 46, 148
Gabriel, Percy, 148
Gagliardi, Nick, 46, 145, 179
Gallaty, Bill, Jr., 46
Gallaty, Bill, Sr., 15, 37, 46, 96, 130, 137, 196
Gallaud, Louis, 46, 47, 307
Galle, Jules, 46
Gallodoro, Alfred, 226
Galloway, Charlie, 27, 29, 47, 73, 78, 91, 125, 133, 134
Galloway's Orchestra, Charlie, 27, 29, 73, 125
Gammon, William A. "Von," 39, 46, 159, 161, 247, 287
Ganier, Albert, 190
Garland, Ed "Montudie," 47, 283, 285
Garroway, Dave, 259
Gaspard, Ed, 48, 49
Gaspard Brothers, The, 31, 49, 123
Gaspard, Octave "Oak," 14, 48, 147, 148, 153, 155, 180
Gaspard, Vic, 48, 85, 134, 147, 148, 153, 155, 194, 195, 207
Gautreaux, Alvin, 144
Gazebo, The, 102, 111
Gehl, Buddy, 143
Gehl, Buddy, and His Eight Winds, 143, 266
Gelpi, René, 143, 144, 156, 268
Genet, Malcom, 134
Gensberger, Jake, 282
Gerbrecht, "Pinky," 48, 78, 85, 103, 138, 148, 184, 295
Gerosa, Joe, 48
G.H.B. Records, 19, 31, 97
Giardina, Ernest, 48, 137
Giardina Orchestra, Ernest, 66, 111, 113
Giardina, Tony, 48, 103, 104, 137, 196, 278
Gibbons, Bill, 159, 261
Gibson Brass Band, The, 7, 16, 34, 45, 67, 88, 89, 106, 118, 122, 195, 206
Gibson, Jim, 48
Gibson, Marble, 196
Gilbert, "Blind." See Meistier, Gilbert
Gilbert, Vernon, 48, 197, 207
Gillen, Bill, 49, 289
Gillin, Mike, 49, 195
Gilmore, Eddie, 49, 145
Girard, George, 29, 30, 39, 41, 48, 49, 54, 64, 77, 114, 115, 118, 128, 134, 224, 337
Girard, Turk, 286
Glapion, Raymond, 49, 190
Glasgow, Vaughn, 334
Glass, Booker T., 49, 193
Glass, Nowell, 49
Glenne, Jim, 148
Glenny, Albert, 49, 134, 155, 185, 301
Globe Hall, 216, 225
Goby, Robert, 134
Goety, John, 135
Golden Leaf Band, The, 19, 29, 49, 94, 109, 111, 124, 143
Golden Pumpkin, The, 225
Golden Rule Orchestra, The, 3, 18, 19, 31, 45, 53, 124, 143, 144, 224